AUGUSTA

AUGUSTA

Home of the Masters Tournament

STEVE EUBANKS

Foreword by Frank Deford

BROADWAY BOOKS

New York

First Broadway Books trade paperback edition published 1998.

Page design by Bateman Design

Library of Congress Cataloging-in-Publication Data
Eubanks, Steve, 1962–
    Augusta : home of the Masters Tournament / Steve Eubanks ; foreward by Frank Deford. — 1st Broadway Books trade pbk. ed.
      p. cm.
    Originally published: Nashville, Tenn. : Rutledge Hill Press, c1997.
    Includes bibliographical references (p.   ) and index.
    ISBN 0-7679-0215-7 (pbk.)
    1. Augusta National Golf Club—History. 2. Masters Golf Tournament, Augusta, Ga.—History. I. Title.
GV969.A83E83   1998
796.352'06'075864—dc21   97-42348
                                                          CIP

98 99 00 01 02 10 9 8 7 6 5 4 3 2 1

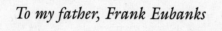

To my father, Frank Eubanks

CONTENTS

FOREWORD

To H. L. Mencken's mischievous observation: "If I had my way, no man guilty of golf would be eligible for any office of trust or profit in the United States," I would only add: "If I had my way, no journalist guilty of golf would be allowed to cover the Masters."

Certainly, no sporting event in America—if indeed, the whole world—has enjoyed such a sweetheart press. But, then, as one old golfing journalist advised me long ago: "Nobody who covers the World Series longs to play center field for the Dodgers. No theater critic expects to get a good role on Broadway himself. But trust me, kid, every guy who covers the Masters writes about it with the thought in mind that if he hues to the party line, someday he might get an invitation to play there."

Notwithstanding, even though the Masters benefits by such lapdog print coverage and absolutely controls television in a fashion that would make Nikita Khrushchev raise up in his grave with envy, the old rich men who rule the Masters still have a conniption fit anytime any observer dares get up on his hind legs and bark. The Augusta National Golf Club is often compared, in stuffiness, to the All-England Lawn Tennis and Croquet Club, which runs Wimbledon. Well, I have written about both institutions, and believe me, the All-England is a Greenwich Village block party compared to Augusta.

What a shame that the Masters has been disposed to arrogance and humorlessness. Bobby Jones wasn't himself at all like that. Besides, the Masters is, in so many respects, a truly precious sporting jewel. If you have never been there, listen: No matter how beautiful the breathless CBS shills make it out to be, the place is more gorgeous yet. The golf course provides for an intriguing athletic test, one that is invariably as dramatic as it is competitive. The tournament is wonderfully run, and has been inspired and progressive in its administration. By now, in fact, the Masters is an esteemed part of both the calendar and Americana.

I believe that Steve Eubanks's chapters that follow portray—accurately, with restraint and balance—the contradictions in this curious athletic organism. I am particularly delighted to learn from these pages that Augusta National actually deigns now to speak to the Fourth Estate—something that it would not lower itself to do as recently as two years ago, when I was doing a piece on the Masters for HBO.

The Masters is too fine a creation to need to be controlled. The more light and wit allowed to shine through the Georgia pines, the prettier it will be. This book, I think, is that first new ray.

—Frank Deford

ACKNOWLEDGMENTS

While this book is not officially sanctioned or approved by the Augusta National Golf Club or the Masters Tournament, anyone who says no one at the club will speak to you is just wrong. Glenn Greenspan, director of communications for Augusta National, never let the sun set without returning a phone call, and while he couldn't always answer my questions, he was always professional, fair, courteous, and a gentleman in every way.

This book would not have become a reality without some Herculean efforts. A world of thanks goes to the greatest research staff in the world: Elizabeth DeLaughter, Kathy Wagstaff, Ann Brinson, and Heather Fritz. If it was findable, this team of ladies found it. Also, special thanks go out to Whitney Crouse for first bringing this idea to me and to Mike Towle, executive editor at Rutledge Hill Press, for pressing this project through and for stepping forward with invaluable help and support throughout the process. Also, thanks to Larry Stone, publisher and friend, who believed in this idea and had enough confidence in all of us to see it through.

Special thanks go out to the following people and organizations who provided their time, memories, documents, and perspectives on Augusta, the Augusta National, and the Masters Tournament: Dr. Stephen Ambrose, Greg Asmond, Frank Beard, Jariah Beard, Robin Brendle, Jack Burke, Bob Burkett, Frank Chirkinian, Frank Christian Jr., Dr. Peter Cranford, Andy Dallos, Frank Deford, Kathie Edwards, Robert Eubanks, Sandy Farrell, Billy Fuller, Thomas Gilbert, Mark Godich, Robert Gray, Ken Green, HBO Sports, Steve Hale,

Frank Hannigan, Jim Herre, Richard Hill, Al Hodge, Rhonda Holliman, Christian Horsnell, Jim Huber, Bert Jacobs, Rusty Jarrett, the family of Robert T. Jones III, Marilyn Keough, Warren Lamar, David Lees, Al Ludwick, Gary McCord, Henry McGee, Steve Melnyk, Chris Millard, Mallory Millinder, Fred Moir, Patty Moran, Andy Mutch, Chris Nickelson, Jack Nicklaus, Tom Patania, Rob Pavey, Dan Quinn, Kristie Richards, Gerald Roisman, Tim Rosaforte, Jeff Rude, John Sands, Alan Schwartz, Larry Sconyers, Peaches Scribner, Beth Siciliano, Sam Snead, Phil Stambaugh, Gail Stebbins, Jackson Stephens, Nancy Stulack, Al Tays, Barry Terjeson, Sam Tweed, USGA, David Westin, Barry White, Dr. Wayne Wilson, and Jim Yancey.

And to everyone else who contributed in both small and big ways to this project, my sincerest thanks.

Most of all, to my wife, Debbie Eubanks, and our children, James, Jonathan, Andrew, Aaron, and Ben, I owe everything.

INTRODUCTION

Morning fog hangs thick in the east Georgia pines, and the sleepy town of Augusta has an almost moorish tint as it awakens to the slow, lapping currents of the Savannah River. It awakens as it has since 1798 in the days when Augusta was a shipping hub connecting inland mid-Atlantic with the coast, and mighty vessels carried indigo and cotton from plantation fields to the sea. Today the only thing rolling down the lazy Savannah is a sixty-foot Tierra bringing *Town and Country*-reading travelers to the one annual event that has shaped this city's personality for more than a half century. Numbering in the tens of thousands, they come not only by boat but by car, bus, and RV. They come by so many private jets that for a week each April a special control tower has to be installed and special instructions given to FAA employees as far away as Montgomery, Alabama. They come to Augusta, a little southern city 150 miles east of Atlanta that, in some ways, is 150 years behind much of the developed world.

A convoy of cars turns off the interstate onto Washington Road, where they enter a low-rise commercial area crowded with strip shopping centers and fast-food restaurants. Traffic grinds to a halt as vehicles from as far away as Idaho, Michigan, Kansas, and New York funnel down two lanes of highway. Up ahead a police officer stands beneath a traffic

Two lines of bumper-to-bumper traffic along Washington Road in Augusta means only one thing: It's Masters week. (*Augusta Chronicle* photo)

light. Ahead of him, another. Patiently and methodically, the cops direct the cars to turn, alternating from each direction. One by one they file past the thick hedges that line the street, past the green barricades, through the gates, off the pavement, and onto the hallowed grounds of Augusta National.

Welcome to Augusta National Golf Club, home of arguably the No. 1 golf course in the world and venerable site of the greatest of golf tournaments played on the same course in the history of the game: the Masters Tournament. It's the first Wednesday in April, and the world is watching Augusta as it does every spring during this unofficial launch of the golf season in America.

It's Masters week.

Jock Hutchison and Fred McLeod won't tee off as the ceremonial first group for another full day, but to a young golf enthusiast visiting Augusta National for the first time in 1973, this is game seven of the World Series, Green Bay in the Super Bowl, and fifteen dates with Christie Proctor from algebra class all rolled into one. This is golf's ultimate pilgrimage, the Mecca and Medina of purists and novices alike. It is golf's holy week.

"Anyone who can appreciate the roots of golf and its traditions and has feelings for where golf came from knows what Augusta and the Masters mean," golfer/television commentator Frank Beard says. "It's a myth, but by that I don't mean it's a bunch of falsehoods. It's a believable, lovable myth. It's like going into one of those old caves exploring and seeing the writings and drawings on the walls from ancient times. You don't know if it's all true, but it sure is fun to be there and see it."

A group of awestruck spectators stroll over to Magnolia Lane and gaze down the narrow driveway leading up to the clubhouse. The first-time pilgrims had imagined these stately and legendary trees marking golf's greatest entrance would be one hundred feet tall. Instead, the sixty-five magnolias turn out to be only thirty feet at their highest point, yet there is not an iota of disappointment. They stand beneath the canopy formed by interlacing branches and run their hands along the bark. Dew is like a layer of silk, and a few hands reach out and caress the cream magnolia blossoms just to make sure they're real.

At the end of the drive stands the most photographed clubhouse in all of golf. Freshly painted and glistening against the morning sun, the white structure, originally constructed in 1854 when the property was an indigo plantation (and later a commercial nursery), shouts of an era long gone but never forgotten in the South. The plantation-style building is situated less than two thousand feet from a Piggly Wiggly shopping center, but the distance is not measured in feet as much as it is in years. The gates at Augusta National are a time warp to a more stately period when names such as Jones, Hagen, Sarazen, and Armour were first spoken with deferential reverence.

An RV is parked on the grass next to the driving range that borders Magnolia Lane. A local bank is giving away Chick Fil-A sandwiches, Cokes, and Miller beer—at 7:55 in the morning. Balloons have been attached to the antenna to distinguish this camper from the convoy of RVs flowing into the lot like an army of ants. Closer inspection reveals a commotion in progress near the camper. A heavyset man employed by the advertising bank, his beer clutched firmly in hand, is having a heated discussion with a distinguished-looking grayhaired gentleman adorned in a kelly green sport coat. On the breast pocket is a logo that identifies the gentleman as a member of Augusta National. The exchange is brief, brought to closure when the man in the green jacket points to the balloons adorning the RV's antenna and says, "Sir, you are creating a carnival-type atmosphere inconsistent with the policies of this club. Remove those balloons or we will have to rescind your invitation to this event."

The balloons come down.

And so it has been since the club first opened its doors in 1933: all things prim, proper, and in their place, with fine southern gentlemen—and all the members are gentle*men*—ruling their domain with less-than-subtle iron fists. Even players who have been bestowed that honor (as honorary members) by virtue of winning the Masters are not immune to Augusta's parochial ways. In 1989 past Masters winner Bernhard Langer arrived in Augusta a week early to practice. During one of his let's-get-reacquainted rounds, Langer, much to the chagrin of a group of members playing immediately behind him, hit several balls and practiced putting to different locations on each green. After the round, club chairman Hord Hardin, who just happened to be playing in the group, politely yet bluntly informed Mr. Langer that being a former winner did not guarantee future invitations and that all invitations to the Masters are at the discretion of the members.

Everything about the Masters and Augusta National is at the discretion and pleasure of the members: who gets tickets (and more appropriately, who does not); who sponsors the event; which holes are covered by television; and what the television commentators can and cannot say. CBS golf commentator Gary McCord, one of the most colorful figures in golf, added descriptive—and scripted—levity to the 1993 event by using such metaphors as bikini wax and body bags, to make some shrewd observations regarding the Augusta course. While not incredibly offensive—nor particularly funny—the comments cost McCord his place in the announcing lineup at future Masters telecasts. A similar fate in the mid-1960s had befallen esteemed television sports essayist Jack Whitaker, who had referred offhandedly to a group of Augusta spectators as a mob. Augusta banished Whitaker for what turned out to be five years. While CBS executive golf producer Frank Chirkinian handled the chore of meting out the bad news in both cases, CBS had nothing to do with the sentences given Whitaker and McCord; the decrees came down from on high, from behind the closed doors of Augusta National.

Just exactly who *are* these guys in their green jackets; and why do golfers, spectators, sponsors, and networks bow and cater to their provincial whims? Augusta National's membership is made up of some of the most powerful and influential men from around the world. A roll call of its three hundred members includes Roger Milliken of Milliken Industries, Warren Buffett of Berkshire Hathaway, Hugh McCall Jr. of Nationsbank, Robert Allen of AT&T, and former secretary of state George Schultz. The National, as it's familiarly called, probably has more CEO members than any other club its size. Winged Foot, Pine Valley, Los Angeles Country Club, and Burning Tree all have powerful and influential members, but none is in a position to dictate policy to CBS or any other media entity. Augusta National's membership is clannish and secretive, but can't the same be said for golf clubs all over the country? Perhaps not. Sam Snead, a Masters veteran of six decades, says the National members have always kept a low profile, at least when it comes to their Augusta connections.

"I couldn't name you five members at Augusta," Snead says. "They aren't at the [champions'] dinner and they don't come to the clubhouse when the tournament is going on."

There is history and tradition at the National, but it's not the oldest club in America or even in Georgia. As classic golf clubs go, it's younger than Pinehurst No. 2, Philadelphia Country Club, Merion, and a host of others. Even so, when golfers think of tradition and all things pure in the game, two courses instantly come to mind: the Old Course of St. Andrews, Scotland, which is five-hundred-odd years old; and Augusta National, just over sixty years old. So, what is it about Augusta National that makes this 365-acre tract of land surpass all other golf clubs, reaching beyond special and approaching the realm of magical? Much of the answer rests in the legacy of one man: Bobby Jones. All golfers, even those hackers who play a couple of times a year at corporate outings, know that Jones is the only man to win golf's Grand Slam, which in 1930 consisted of the U.S. and British Opens and

The grounds outside the Augusta National clubhouse offer a nice setting for those lucky enough to gain access to the most prestigious golf club in America.

the U.S. and British Amateur Championships. Jones then abruptly announced his retirement from tournament golf. He was twenty-eight. By then Jones had carved out his niche as golf's first worldwide ambassador, embodying the qualities of character, intellect, talent, drive, and humility that Americans long for in their heroes but rarely find. As golf writer Herbert Warren Wind put it, Jones was "that rare sort of hero, in sports or any other field, whose actual stature exceeds the mythological figure he has been made into."

Jones also founded and is president in perpetuity of Augusta National Golf Club, although he passed away more than a quarter century ago. The personality of the club was shaped by golf's most legendary figure, and everything about the club and the Masters is still done in keeping with the Jones legacy. What would Bob think? is the unasked question that drives the decisions, shapes the personality, and perpetuates the mystique at Augusta National.

The club is unlike anything else. Even for those folks with the means to play golf and who belong to numerous clubs, Augusta is a curious departure from the ordinary. As writer Dan Jenkins once pointed out, "It is not a country club as most golfers think of country clubs. There is no swimming pool. There are no tennis courts. There are no Saturday-night dances, no Sunday buffets, no spring fashion shows, no debutante galas, no teenage party rooms. There isn't even a club championship, and thus no club champion."

If there were an Augusta National club champion, it probably would be classified information, anyway, not to be discussed outside the gates. Augusta members guard information about the club in a draconian way that separates the National from the other clubs of the world. How much does it cost to join the Augusta National? The club won't say, and, to use the words of the late Clifford Roberts, "If you have to ask, you have no business being a member." The amount is twenty-five thousand dollars, with dues of about three thousand dollars a year, but no current members will confirm or deny that figure. What about prize money at the Masters? Again, unpublished and unspoken until after each year's event. The 1997 purse totaled $2.7 million, and Tiger Wood's first-place check was $486,000.

Why the green jackets? That information *is* published. Ohio-based Globe Corporation makes the much-coveted and conspicuously colored green sport coats, but representatives of the company will not comment on any aspect of their arrangement with the National. How many coats have been made over the last thirty years? No comment. How many do they send down each year for the tournament? Again, no comment. How and where are they constructed? None of your business, and if you want any more answers call Augusta National. A little bit of digging finally reveals that the green jackets were first manufactured by the Brooks Company of New York in 1937 and were given out to members so that spectators at the Masters would know whom to approach for "reliable information." Today, however, most visitors know better than to walk up to Jack Stephens or someone like Warren Buffett and ask directions to the pimiento cheese sandwich stand. Sixty years later, members still wear the jackets and locals fondly refer to Augusta National members as "greencoats." In the grand pooh-bah fashion that is Augusta National, however, members are not allowed to wear their jackets anywhere but on club grounds. To do so means instant expulsion.

Other sins, from the egregious to the sublime, can cause a member's bill to stop coming—that's when you know you've been thrown out. According to a former member, "It's as easy to be kicked out as it is difficult to get in." Even members who have belonged for years live with the nagging uncertainty that any slipup, no matter how minor, could carry the National's equivalent of the death penalty. As three-time Masters winner Gary Player put it, "They don't put up with any nonsense. Things are done a certain way and that's it." That's it indeed. No appeals, no mediation, no political representation. In the words of veteran journalist Frank Deford, spoken during an HBO *Real Sports* segment, Augusta National is "the American Singapore: small and rich, efficient and successful, spotless and humorless, and totally unforgiving."

Then there is the golf course itself. No clubhouse or golf enthusiast's den is really complete without at least one oil or watercolor of Augusta National hanging from a wall. The course is art, and even those who have never seen it in person speak of it like a Rembrandt painting. Amateur sculptors have been known to tinker by recreating bits and pieces of Augusta in a basement or garage, although golfer Bert Yancey's National handiwork involved much more than mere tinkering. A manic depressive whose legendary obsession with golf's traditions included an encyclopedic knowledge of Augusta's every nook, cranny, and quirk, Yancey crafted clay models of the course's eighteen greens. Each year he would bring them with him for study during Masters week.

"Bert always got pumped up for the majors because that's where he knew golfers could put their names in the history books, particularly at Augusta," says Beard, who was one of Yancey's few close friends in professional golf.

Every spring, dozens of golf writers from around the world poetically opine on the beauty, majesty, and serenity of Augusta National as if milk and honey somehow flow from its soil. What most spectators don't know is that the course has undergone no fewer than thirty-one major renovations with as many as sixteen different architects and players dabbling in the original Jones/Mackenzie design. "They're doing something to the golf course every year," Snead says. "Every year at the champions' dinner we would discuss different things about the course. They've never been satisfied."

Greg Asmond, who served as an assistant superintendent at the National, put the renovations into perspective: "This isn't even close to the same golf course Alister Mackenzie designed. If you talk about history here, you need to talk about the golf tournament. The golf *course* has a new history each time something gets changed."

Augusta's nines have been reversed twice, once before the club officially opened and again before the 1935 tournament. The 170-yard par-three sixteenth that has been the site of innumerable Masters dramas was originally 110 yards long with a completely different green design. The tenth was a much-shorter, much-straighter par-four; and number eleven, the long par-four that has been the deciding hole in four sudden-death playoffs, was originally a much shorter dogleg right, with no water. The bunker on the right of the fifteenth green was Ben Hogan's idea, added in 1957. And the fairway bunker on number two was moved from the left to the right side in 1966 at Gene Sarazen's insistence.

Number twelve, the par-three in the heart of Amen Corner that has been called the toughest tournament hole in golf by an expert no less qualified than Jack Nicklaus, undergoes almost yearly renovations, not all of which see the light of day. Underground piping was added in 1981 so that hot and cold water could regulate the ground temperature and keep the newly installed bent-grass green alive. By today's golf real estate development standards, the twelfth hole probably wouldn't even exist. Its green, nestled behind Rae's Creek on the edge of the property that borders Augusta Country Club, rests on the site of a Native-American burial ground, which, in the nineties, would be enough to put a stop to construction.

There have been dramatic changes at the Masters as well, starting with the name. In 1934 the event was called the First Annual Invitational Tournament at Augusta National. Although Cliff Roberts wanted to call it the Masters from day one, Jones considered that name to be pretentious and vetoed the idea.

Horton Smith, the first winner, was awarded fifteen hundred dollars in prize money (green jackets weren't awarded to Masters winners until 1949). The total purse that year was five thousand dollars, the same amount the USGA paid out in the U.S. Open. Because the National's event was an invitational with no organizational backing, club members had to make up the shortfall when expenses and prize money exceeded revenues.

In 1946 the total purse doubled from five thousand dollars to ten thousand dollars, and the Augusta membership decided to charge three dollars for weekday passes and five dollars for weekend passes, making the Masters the first golf tournament ever to charge five dollars for a ticket. It wasn't a good move, either for marketing or for public relations. Augusta's 1947 galleries averaged only five thousand a day compared to the more than eighteen thousand a day showing up for the U.S. Open.

The early fifties were golden years for the Masters, with Snead and Hogan, especially, regularly doing battle. The chilly reality of part of that era, however, was that ticket sales sagged. CBS, which televised the Masters for the first time in 1956, had to black out stations within two hundred miles of Augusta to help boost gate receipts. Citizens in Augusta were solicited to support the event. They were told it was their civic duty to support this golf tournament since it was the one and only event that brought national attention to their little town.

"In the beginning, you could get all the tickets you wanted," Augusta resident W. A. Herman said. "They were begging people to buy them. They would give them to corporations to sell."

The National even ran promotional ads at local movie houses before each show. The marketing blitz worked. Many locals bought Masters tickets even though they had little interest in golf. But that soon changed, almost overnight, thanks in part to the classic 1954 tournament and mainly because of a charismatic Pennsylvanian with the forearms of a lumberjack and the smirk of a movie star.

Arnold Palmer attacked golf more than he played it, and his swashbuckling ways performed to the hilt at Augusta. Because of Arnie, the Masters, and with it televised golf, became much more than just a viewing curiosity. His outgoing demeanor and nonclassic, roundhouse, swing-from-the-heels persona endeared him to the eye of the camera and to the hearts of millions. Palmer's thespian instincts were preordained for Augusta's theatrical setting. It was a partnership that put sports and entertainment together in a special way every bit as memorable as Ali and Cosell a decade later.

First came Palmer, then Player, then Jack Nicklaus, and finally a whole slew of new talent with names such as Weiskopf, Watson, and Miller. Like no other golf setting–event in the world, Augusta and the Masters became an annual event as eagerly anticipated as the Kentucky Derby, the Indy 500, the World Series, and the Rose Bowl.

By 1978 the National had stopped putting people on a waiting list for tickets, as the average waiting time exceeded most applicants' life expectancy. Just like Grandma's Persian rug or Great-grandpa's watch, Masters tickets are passed from generation to generation, much like heirlooms. For those fortunate enough to get their hands on them, Masters tickets remain the best bargain in sports, at one hundred dollars for all four days, although scalpers have garnered as much as five thousand dollars per day. Not only do members frown on such practices, they go to great lengths (including the hiring of undercover agents to pose as purchasers of scalped tickets) to catch and prosecute the ticket hawks, who are then removed from future consideration for tickets.

The tournament has a generous policy of allowing all card-carrying PGA golf professionals and GCSAA superintendents into the event at no charge; but when a PGA pro "lent" his card to a buddy, the iron fist came down quick and hard. That professional is no longer welcome on club grounds. The club also generously gives two free tournament series badges to each full-time club employee—provided the employee signs a document promising that the badges will be used by family or friends and won't be sold. In 1996 three employees were fired for allegedly breaking that policy and selling their tickets. Even the practice rounds, which for years were open

The most reasonably priced ticket in sports also happens to be the hardest to come by, as evidenced by these folks alongside Washington Road in Augusta, not far from the gates to Augusta National. (*Augusta Chronicle* photo)

to anyone who showed up and paid admission, now have lotteries to determine who gets inside the gates and who gets shut out.

Those who do get in see the most immaculate golf course on the planet. The greenest greens, the whitest sand, and the brightest azaleas and dogwoods combine to send a definitive message: There's nothing like this anywhere else in the world. As with all things at Augusta, what goes on behind the scenes to maintain that heaven-sent look is not for public consumption. Course maintenance personnel are sworn to secrecy about everything from mowing height to green speed to what it takes to keep the flowering plants alive. Any questions? Don't bother. The mantra from course superintendent Marsh Benson and his staff is, "Mr. Jack Stephens is the chairman of Augusta National and he will address all issues relating to the club."

This tight, some might say obsessive, rein has fueled the fires of speculation. Augusta rumors have run rampant for decades. It has been reported, and many people believe, that the sixteen hundred azaleas behind the thirteenth green are packed in ice prior to Masters week to regulate their blooming time. They are not (well, Clifford Roberts did it once), and most horticulturists agree that it wouldn't do much good if they were. It also has been rumored that the grass is painted for television. Also false. However, the water in Rae's Creek *is* dyed for effect. The white bunker sand is not from Australia, Bora Bora, or even Pensacola; it's trucked in from North Carolina. What is also true is that Augusta National closes the course from late May until mid-October, the height of the golf season in most of the country. During this downtime, the maintenance staff gases the greens and rips up acres at a time. They also chain sixteen one-thousand-watt lightbulbs over the twelfth green every year to simulate sunlight. Also true: Course superintendent Marsh Benson carries a stop-watch when the crew mows the golf course. Start-to-finish mowing time? Exactly one hour, forty-five minutes.

As well-known and popular to the public as it is, Augusta National is somewhat of a bastard child among golf's establishment. On the record, other leaders in the golfing world will sing the usual praises of beautiful Augusta National and its glorious Masters, if they say anything at all. Off the record, those same folks will criticize the greencoats for their stuffy, pretentious, even arcane ways. When asked for an interview for this book, USGA executive director David Fay respectfully declined, saying only, "You would need to speak with them. We are not associated with the club."

Much has been written about the Masters and all the dramatic events that have taken place inside the gates at Augusta National. Yet comparatively little has been published about the club itself. The only official chronicle is the misleadingly titled book *The Story of the Augusta National Golf Club*, written in 1976 by Clifford Roberts, then Augusta National chairman. The book is as rich in historical detail as it is devoid of objective scrutiny. *All the President's Men* it is not. One year after having the book published, Roberts strolled down to Augusta's par-three course, sat on the grass near Ike's Pond, and shot himself in the head with a .38-caliber pistol. A financier who had survived the Great Depression, a man who discovered a kindred spirit in the greatest athlete of a generation, and an executive who managed the world's most prestigious golf club and tournament died at his own hand at the age of eighty-four.

Even in death the enigmatic Roberts has continued to live on at Augusta through word of mouth, starting with since-abandoned whispers among employees that someone other than Roberts pulled the trigger that night. Another story, which is apparently much more than fiction, concerns the whereabouts of the pistol itself and the great lengths the Augusta membership went to reacquire the gun after it had ended up in the hands of a collector.

After Roberts's death many of the overbearing policies he had established were relaxed, especially when it came to the Masters. Playoffs were shortened from eighteen holes on Monday to sudden death starting at the tenth hole immediately after the end of seventy-two-hole regulation play. Also, tour players finally were allowed to use their own caddies (a precedent that changed the complexion of the tournament in a number of ways); and limited television coverage was allowed for the first time on Augusta's front nine.

Not all of Augusta's idiosyncrasies were buried with Clifford Roberts. The Masters is still the only one of golf's four major championships that strictly limits television coverage and allows only two advertisers—Cadillac and Travelers. It remains the only major golf tournament and the only big-time sporting event with a one-year network contract. CBS renegotiates and renews the agreement every year (as of 1997 so far, so good). It is also the only sporting event that approves or rejects, occasionally even dictating, to the broadcasting network who the announcers will be, what the on-air talent can and cannot say, and exactly how many minutes per hour can be sold to the approved advertisers. The policy is four commercial minutes an hour, by far the lowest of any televised golf tournament. No logos or billboards can be found at the National—except, of course, those plastered on the clothing of the players themselves—and you will see no aerial coverage from the Goodyear, Met Life, Budweiser, or any other blimp. Likewise, on-site observers need not hold their breaths waiting for any corporate eighteen-wheelers to come rolling down Magnolia Lane anytime in the near future. The National will have none of that. Former club chairman Hord Hardin put the National's position on corporate sponsorships into perspective when he said for the record, "We don't intend to become the Pizza Hut Masters."

The Masters is the refreshing antithesis to today's commercially rich athletic event where swishes and Swatches relegate athletes and achievements to supporting roles. Even Coca-Cola, makers of the unofficially official soft drink at the Masters, hides its logo on cups and fountains. Everything, even the plastic wrappers used to cover the pimiento cheese sandwiches that have been served as a staple since 1941, is green. Make that PMS-560: Masters green.

The undeniable drama of the Masters Tournament itself seems to be a never-ending source of lore. All true golfers relive the memories of Jack Nicklaus's miraculous 1986 victory at the age of forty-six, and everyone who watched the 1996 tournament shared the pain of Greg Norman's slow-motion train wreck in the final round. Even President Bill Clinton felt the Shark's pain, invoking Norman's name in cautioning his followers not to be overconfident about a double-digit lead in the polls during the 1996 presidential campaign. (Clinton certainly had to do some fast talking shortly after his reelection when he found himself paired with Norman for a friendly round of golf.)

Perhaps a good portion of the Masters' long-term success and the fans' passionate loyalty resides in familiarity. It is the only major tournament held on the same course every year. Places such as Amen Corner, Ike's Tree, the Butler Cabin (one of ten such extravagant "cabins" on the grounds), and Rae's Creek have a homecoming feeling that activates the dormant golf gene in players from Detroit to Dublin. All true lovers of the game have watched. All have felt the emotions. And if honesty is anywhere in them, all will say they too have stood in the parking lot or in the living room or on the practice tee and dreamed the dream Bill Murray so hilariously portrayed in the movie *Caddyshack*: "an incredible Cinderella story . . . out of nowhere . . . tears in his eyes . . . a former greenskeeper about to become the Masters champion."

As the thirst for knowledge about Augusta National and the Masters grows, so does the disappointment when few of the answers to questions are found. For an inquisitive author visiting Augusta in 1996 for the twenty-third time, there comes the realization that, like so many things held sacred, the realities of life often tarnish polished dreams. Such is the case with the mythical view of Augusta. It is, without question, one of the most magnificent golf courses in the world, but the magic is not quite what it was twenty years ago, largely because of a more-inquisitive media's uncovering of warts, and Augusta, as we know by now, has them. Perhaps this is golf's equivalent to learning of Mickey Mantle's drinking problem, Pete Rose's gambling problem, or the royal Windsors' adultery problems. Like the boy in the "Shoeless" Joe Jackson legend, the man secretly begs for someone to "say it ain't so" about many things he's heard over the years.

The course is, as always, in magnificent condition, and the veteran pilgrims smile as they overhear this year's batch of newcomers making the same familiar comments:

"It can't be real."

"Do they paint the grass?"

"Television doesn't do this place justice."

"Look at all those hills!"

The first tee is a flurry of activity as another morning twosome is properly announced to polite applause. Sam Snead and Gene Sarazen? Not exactly. That ceremonial twosome teed off about an hour ago. Could it be the Bear? Arnie? Tom Watson or John Daly? None of the above, in this instance. The hordes of spectators have gathered and are abuzz in anxious anticipation, craning their necks to catch a glimpse of U.S. Amateur champion Tiger Woods, golf's reigning phenom and only the fourth African American to tee it up in this annual rite of spring.

An onlooker stands back in the vicinity of the clubhouse, attempting to steal some shade from the towering oaks. He watches in amazement as thousands of fans head off into the distance in pursuit of more Tiger sightings. Turning his head back to the left, the onlooker spots several members sipping drinks and chatting through charmingly formal club smiles while milling behind the gallery ropes that separate the clubhouse lawn from the course. They all wear the green jackets, and they all have distinguished countenances. Off to one side near the clubhouse, not far away from the rest of the members—but alone nonetheless—stands a single member. No one speaks to him. No one greets him. No one enjoins him in clubby camaraderie. He is Ronald Townsend, presi-

Masters statesman Gene Sarazen, circa 1980, stops to drink in the view from the second-floor veranda of the Augusta National clubhouse.

dent of Gannett Television Group and Augusta National's first black member, now one of only two.

Maybe it's nothing. Maybe Ron's been the life of the party inside the inner sanctum of the clubhouse and he just wants to get away and reflect for a few minutes. Or maybe the allegations of racial exclusion and a caste system are true. Maybe Augusta is, as a former member called it, "a walled city," polite, charming, and tasteful, but steeped in southern traditions, some good and some bad.

In all fairness, the members own the place. It is their club and their golf tournament. The Masters is an invitational put on and sponsored solely at the discretion of the members of Augusta National who will tell you, quite happily, that if the tournament ever becomes a bother, they will simply stop having it. As far-fetched as that sounds, former chairman Hord Hardin and current chairman Jack Stephens have both said as much. This is their party; if you like it, fine; if you don't like it, tough.

Clubs such as Muirfield in Scotland are equally, if not more, stuffy. But nowhere outside Augusta is perfection in golf so closely reached while the secrets of the club are so zealously protected. That is what makes Augusta National special. After sixty-three years, fans of the Annual Invitational at Augusta National are still amazed by the awesome beauty of springtime Augusta, but they still hunger for any morsel of knowledge, for any gleaning of new perspective on this tournament and this place. Those who watch, whether in person or on television, can't help but think some part of this event—some part of this club—belongs to them and to all the other hackers who dust off their clubs and polish their spikes during this week every year.

Any of the spectators at this Masters could walk right up to a "reliable source" in his green jacket and say, "Hey, why is the black member standing over there by himself while you guys talk and drink and do member stuff?" The response would be, "Mr. Jack Stephens is the chairman of Augusta National, and he will address all issues relating to the club."

Everything else, you must find out on your own.

CHAPTER 1

THE MAN

AND SO TO SUMMARIZE BOB JONES, WE FIND TALENT, PERSONALITY, MASTERY OF SELF, FOCUS, AND A DESIRE FOR SOMETHING MORE IN LIFE THAN PARTICIPATION IN THE SPORT HE HAD DOMINATED. THERE IS, HOWEVER, A SIXTH FACTOR THAT STANDS OUT, SILENT AND IMPRESSIVE. IT IS, IT SEEMS TO ME, THE COMPLETE ABSENCE OF ANY BESMIRCHING OR DEMEANING OR UNETHICAL ASPECT OF HIS LEGAL OR EXTRA-LEGAL CAREER.

—UNITED STATES SUPREME COURT
JUSTICE HARRY A. BLACKMAN, IN A
SPEECH AT THE EMORY UNIVERSITY
LAW SCHOOL.

Only two Americans have been made an Honorary Burgess of the Borough by the people of St. Andrews. They are Benjamin Franklin and Bobby Jones.

Jones wasn't supposed to live past his fifth birthday, but he became the greatest sports legend of the first half of the twentieth century. He was and is golf's consummate icon, the measuring stick against which all aspiring champions gauge their muster. In a sport where so many compete so regularly, no player has ever totally dominated the way Robert Tyre Jones Jr. did between 1920 and 1930. In that ten-year stretch, Jones competed in forty-five events, winning twenty-one and finishing second seven times. From the age of nineteen to the

1

age of twenty-eight, he won thirteen major championships and set records that have stood for more than sixty years. He also is the only man in history to win all four of his era's major golf championships in one year: the British Open, the British Amateur, the U.S. Open, and the U.S. Amateur. Given the fact that no amateur has won the U.S. Open since the 1930s, that version of golf's Grand Slam is likely to be the one sports record that remains intact as long as the game is played, thus ensuring Jones's status as an athlete without equal—in any sport.

When Jones won the Grand Slam, the Great Depression was one year old. Stocks were barely worth the paper on which they were printed, men of great social standing jumped from office windows, and mothers and children stood in line for potato soup. It was a time when people everywhere needed some source of inspiration. Many found it in the person of a handsome Atlanta man whose infectious smile, slicked-back hair, and penetrating stare radiated the depth of his intellect and intensity. Belying the choir boy looks, Robert T. Jones—Bob to his friends, Robert to his mother, and Bobby to the rest of the world—pummeled opponents on the golf course with the same flair he exhibited while riding in honorary parades.

Jones also was the paragon of virtuous sportsmanship. At one point during the 1925 U.S. Open, he penalized himself for a ball moving after address. No one else had witnessed the incident. Everyone, even United States Golf Association (USGA) officials, praised Jones for his honesty in the heat of competition. Bemused by all the attention, Jones retorted, "You might as well praise a man for not robbing a bank." Of course, today pros and amateurs penalize themselves regularly. Jones set the precedent, and golfers for seventy years have been trying to live up to the man's uncompromising standards.

Jones also drank profusely, chain-smoked, reeled off obscenities, and, as a young man, threw more golf clubs than

Tommy Bolt and Tom Weiskopf combined. He also kept on the tip of his tongue a vast repertoire of off-color jokes that he could reel off with dry comic timing, and he gambled on everything from boxing to billiards. On the other hand, he was, when the moment required, the perfect southern gentleman. Jones was so revered that when he attempted to play a leisurely round at the Old Course in St. Andrews on his

JONES ALSO DRANK PROFUSELY, CHAIN-SMOKED, REELED OFF OBSCENITIES, AND, AS A YOUNG MAN, THREW MORE GOLF CLUBS THAN TOMMY BOLT AND TOM WEISKOPF COMBINED.

way to the 1936 Olympics in Berlin, thousands of people showed up to watch and the other members of his group had to step aside. At that same course in 1921, he withdrew from the British Open by tearing up his scorecard and storming off the eleventh green in a fit of anger.

He was a lawyer, but he was far too congenial to engage in the combativeness of courtroom law. The star of sixteen short Hollywood features and the author of four books, Jones never grew particularly attached to his celebrityhood and would become visibly irritated when he felt people were making "too much of a fuss." An engaging conversationalist, he had a natural gift for making everyone he encountered feel comfortable and important, but he was also a disengaged father who would not allow his children to eat with the adults until age nine or at least until they demonstrated an ability to contribute to the dining experience.

Even more than a quarter century after his death, Jones remains an athletic legend about whom much has been written and whose name still strikes an emotional chord in golfers around the world. He was also a complicated intellectual

Bobby Jones still drew a crowd during a warm-up round prior to the 1937 Masters Tournament. (AP/Wide World Photos)

whose personal life was as full of pain and tragedy as his public life was rich with triumph and glory. Before Hank Aaron and Ted Turner were born, in an age when the South was still recovering from Reconstruction and Peachtree Street still had parking meters, Atlanta's most famous resident was a handsome, charming, humble, temperamental, and sometimes self-effacing lawyer named Bob Jones.

4

So what made Bob Jones so different from all the rest? Why was he so idolized? What was it about this golfer-lawyer from Georgia that made such an impact at a time when golf was still about as elitist an activity as owning a new car? The answer lies in both the personality of the man and in the times in which he lived. By 1930 Jones was considered the greatest golfer who had ever played the game, but he was also more than that: In Jones, the public saw the ideal American gentleman—strong and courteous, competitive and polite. Jones exuded charisma long before it was something Madison Avenue could bottle and market. A smile and a subtle glance and Jones would have galleries swooning while his commanding presence had many of his opponents beaten before they ever stepped up to the first tee. He was one of those athletes who defeated half the field just by showing up.

Scotsman Andrew Jamieson pulled an upset by beating Jones in the sixth round of the 1926 British Amateur, then he actually wrote a letter of apology in which he called himself an "imprudent fool" for winning! And in 1929 Horton Smith, who would later become the first Masters Tournament winner, said, "We've all tried to corner the elusive Mr. Jones but haven't succeeded. We certainly would like to beat him better than anything else in the world, but we haven't had any experience in doing it."

Professional Tommy Armour regularly received one-up a side when playing a casual match with Jones, even as late as 1929 when Armour was the reigning U.S. Open champion. When asked how he could accept a handicap, Armour said of Jones, "That's how —damn good he is." Jones was the odds-on favorite every time he teed it up. While most golfers insisted that they played their own game or that the golf course was their only true opponent, everybody knew that there really was one man to beat, and keeping up with this Jones was the necessity of knowing where one really stood.

Bobby Jones was a living enigma. In an age when gambling on golf was as common as today's fantasy football pools, Jones was usually given two-to-one odds over the rest of the field. During one particularly lucrative calcutta before the 1929 U.S. Open, Jones was auctioned off for twenty-three thousand dollars, the highest amount ever paid for a single golfer at that time.

Naturally, every detail of his persona became legendary. Jones never asked a caddie for advice. Had there been such a thing as a slow-play penalty in those days, Jones would never have had a problem. He moved from a preshot routine directly into his fluid swing with no hesitation or deliberation. His motion seemed effortless, yet his shots were long and dramatic. Years before Ben Hogan set forth the myth that there was actually a "secret" to golf, every aspect of Jones's game had been examined and reexamined as players searched fruitlessly for the one single factor that made him so dominant. Many said it was feel. Years before clubs were measured by swing-weight, Jones's feel was so precise that when weighted years later, his clubs all fell within a two-swing-weight range (roughly the weight of two paper dollars).

Many of those who knew him said that the single, special factor that set him apart was Jones's competitive drive, but the record doesn't support that assertion. Jones blew a fair number of leads; and long after his retirement, he considered complacency to be his greatest weakness in golf. He was intimidating, yet disarming. He had talent and intellect, but he wasn't particularly large or naturally athletic. He possessed a disciplined, methodical mind, but he would slip into lapses in concentration that, more than once, cost him matches and championships. At the end of it all, however, Jones had a command of his game like no other.

As a golfer, Jones displayed a presence so commanding and an amount of charisma so enveloping that it was difficult at times to fully comprehend that this was, indeed, a human being. But he was made of flesh and blood, and sometimes the latter ran hot. But with Jones the man and citizen, there was little mystery. You knew exactly where he stood. Sure he threw clubs. In the 1921 U.S. Open he threw a club that struck a woman in the leg, prompting then-USGA-president George Herbert Walker (of Walker Cup fame and grandfather of future president George Bush) to fire off a letter admonishing Jones and informing him that he would not play in another USGA event until he learned to control his temper. Jones eventually managed to refrain from further public outbursts.

In private Jones threw clubs and swore at errant shots right up to the day he played his last round of golf at East Lake Country Club. He also drank booze and smoked unfiltered cigarettes and fine Cuban cigars. While at Harvard his job as assistant golf team manager (he was ineligible to play for the Crimson) was to transport and protect the team's victory liquor. Victorious or not, the team usually went thirsty, because Jones never let good drink go to waste: On a road trip to one particularly cold early-season match, Jones actually drank the team's inventory of bourbon during the drive. As for his use of foul language, he reserved the harshest words for himself, and by today's rap music standards, Jones's tongue would be rated a mild PG-13. He was, however, consistent in his profanity, even around his children. At age four, Bob III is reported to have told someone looking for his father, "He's out back fixing the—damn lawn mower."

The world loved Mr. Jones, blemishes and all. Part of the admiration was for his monumental sports achievements. A generation later Ben Hogan would win sixty-three PGA tournaments, including three of the "big four" events of 1953: the Masters, the U.S. Open, and the British Open. Like Jones, Hogan received a ticker-tape parade and was called "the World's Greatest Golfer" by more than one noteworthy publication. While Jones received accolades from presidents, princes, novelists, and Supreme Court justices, both while he was playing and for many years after his retirement, Hogan's contemporaries said such things as, "He was an odd man" and "I knew him as well as anyone, but I didn't really know him." Everyone assumed he *knew* Jones and, with few exceptions, everyone loved him. Frank Chirkinian, CBS's longtime executive producer of golf coverage, says of him: "Bobby Jones was the warmest, kindest person I've ever met in my adult life. Everyone else is second." Golf writer Herbert Warren Wind added: "He is the only person I know, in or out of sports, who has the Churchillian quality of being larger than life and at the same time intensely human and intimate. I love his company."

Certainly, Jones's more colorful, albeit off-color, traits weren't hyped the way they would be in today's tabloid media, and he did have the advantage of having a good friend in O. B. Keeler, a well-respected writer and drinking buddy from Atlanta who traveled with Jones and ostensibly became the champion's personal scribe. Still, a good argument can be made that Jones didn't need the media or any other conduit or filter. He was what he was, and that was that.

Jones would have been a hero in any generation, particularly one in which athletes are paid millions to spit in the faces of umpiring officials, spew steady streams of verbal abuse in public, and even throw baseballs at the heads of unsuspecting photographers. In Jones's day there were no high-dollar agents or signing bonuses or lavish retirements to exclusive estates. He turned down millions in endorsements after his retirement. There was the law practice, although he took out very little in terms of disposable income. He owned a couple of Coca-Cola bottling franchises as well as stock in the Jones companies his grandfather had founded, but none of those ventures netted him what he potentially could have made at the time. Certainly, nothing he could have done would have approached the commercially rich deals offered to today's rookies. Even if Nike had been around to offer

Jones a forty-million-dollar contract, the idea of selling his name for endorsement's sake was as foreign to him as not taking that penalty in the U.S. Open. In fact, years later, he still despised the commercially extravagant aspects of sports. In a letter to Cliff Roberts, he wrote:

> The unfortunate part of the whole business is that the poor bone-headed public goes to fantastic extremes, first to glorify the players and second to maintain a paternalistic devotion to the golf pro. Insofar as the top players are concerned, we may as well reconcile ourselves to the fact that box-office appeal will always be paid for extravagant figures. As long as Nicklaus, Palmer, et al can pack 'em in at the gate, they are just as well entitled to high pay. All this can be applied to baseball players, automobile racers, and whatever. The trouble is we are living in an idiotic society; frankly, if I knew any more profitable ways of taking advantage of the idiots, I would exploit them. This is no time for idealism.

Jones did enter into an arrangement as vice president of the A. G. Spalding and Brothers company in which he approved the development of a Robt. T. Jones line of clubs. Then there were the sixteen Warner Brothers short features in which Jones was subjected to such laughably corny dialogue as, "Gee, Mr. Jones, do you always chip with your niblick?" Jones: "Most certainly not. I often choose to chip with other clubs from the niblick to the mashie niblick, or even the mashie . . ." Such classics netted Jones around two hundred thousand dollars and kept him in California for over six months (the longest period he would stay away from his native state). He also received several feature film offers while on the West Coast, which he rejected out of hand (again, "too much of a fuss").

He chose to stay at home in Atlanta, working in his law office and traveling between a house in Highlands, North Carolina (where he also founded the Highlands Country Club), and a cabin in Augusta. He wrote articles and books and had a weekly radio show, but beyond that, much of his golf instruction consisted of admonishing his law partner, Arthur Howell, by saying, "Stop trying to kill the damn ball, Arthur."

Jones was a down-to-earth sophisticate who carefully protected his name, his family, and his friendships, and that was the magic that made him so great. He was totally and completely unpretentious. "What the hell is there to be pretentious about?" he asked at the height of his career. And he meant it! Years later, once history had had a chance to measure the enormity of the Grand Slam, Jones wouldn't speak about it. That would have been bragging, and he would rather no one know about his championships than have anyone think him a braggart.

If anyone deserved a few boastful words, it would be the man who won the U.S. Amateur, the Southern Amateur twice, the Davis-Freeman Tournament, the Yates-Gode Tournament, and the Georgia Amateur, and tied for second in the U.S. Open—all before his twenty-first birthday. At the age of eleven Jones broke 80 on a course measuring sixty-five hundred yards. At fourteen he made it to the quarterfinals of the U.S. Amateur, an age record that still stands. By the age of twenty-five he had won the U.S. Open twice, the British Open twice, the U.S. Amateur three times, and the Southern Amateur three times. By age twenty-eight he had won almost everything he could possibly win.

Even before embarking on the greatest golf accomplishment in history, Jones had decided he would retire from competition and try to regain a little of the love for the game

With every crease and hair properly in place, gentlemanly Bobby Jones blasts out of an Augusta bunker while competing in the 1937 Masters Tournament. (AP/Wide World Photos)

that gets lost in the grueling pressures of championship play. He wanted to build his own golf club and spend time with his family. As we know all so well now, it was a club that would become the greatest in the world. His family was another story: Rich in Georgia tradition, the Joneses would become one of the great tragedies of their day.

The roots of Jones the man and, ultimately, Jones the legend can be found in the small northern Georgia town of Canton, forty miles north of Atlanta in what is now one of the nation's fastest-growing "burb" communities. Even today, when lawyers and bankers walk across the small town square, past the courthouse, and beyond the fire station to the town's only hoagie shop, they realize that things aren't much different in Canton than they were at the turn of the century. That's when there was one name in town more important than the rest, and it referred to the one man who could make things happen: Mr. Jones. Robert Tyre Jones Sr., commonly known as R. T., was Bobby Jones's granddad.

In 1879 R. T. Jones founded the Jones Mercantile Exchange, and in 1899 he formed Canton Textile Mills. By 1925 the company was earning more than $1.5 million a year, making Grandpa Jones the town's leading employer and by far the wealthiest man in the region. He was literally one of the biggest men in town. Standing six feet, five inches and weighing 235 pounds, R. T. had a large presence in every respect. When Mr. Jones spoke, whether it was praising the opportunities in the New South or preaching the gospel to his Sunday school class at Canton First Baptist Church, everyone listened. The 1930 book *Eminent Georgians* said of R. T., "In the annals of business and industry in Georgia, there is no career more remarkable and outstanding, and there is no citizen of the State more universally and sincerely respected."

Respected or not, R. T. was accustomed to getting his own way. When fellow north Georgia businessman Sam Tate discovered an enormous vein of marble on his property, R. T.

concluded that diversifying his professional interests to include marble refining made a lot of sense. Within a year he was in the marble business. When his textile operation lost 10 percent of its operating capital, he prophetically stated that he was "not used to running a business at a loss." Eighteen months later mill operations had netted four hundred thousand dollars.

The father of fourteen, R. T. had little time for the subtleties of fatherhood. He didn't drink, smoke, or curse, and he did not tolerate those who did. He was a serious man with serious ways who showed his disdain for what he perceived as wasted time and energy. When his son Robert P. (Bob's father) was offered a professional baseball contract with the Brooklyn Trolley Dodgers, R. T. said, "I didn't send you to college to become a professional baseball player." He never saw his son take an at-bat, and R. P. never took the field as a professional.

The elder Jones had vision and a hard-nosed, hard-edged approach to business that suited him well. He moved the mills into denim production reaping huge profits, and he kept the mills open and the economy alive during the Great Depression. During these hard times, he said he was "determined that his people should be provided for," to the extent, if necessary, of his entire fortune. It wasn't necessary; the fortune remained intact, as did the mill operations, long after R. T.'s death.

Today, however, Canton's mills are silent, their mammoth brick structures standing as monuments to a lost American industry. Lewis Jones, Bobby's cousin, still lives a few blocks from Main Street, but as of 1997 he was the only "direct" relative still residing and active in the town. The industrial base has shifted and the family has dispersed. Even so, the legacy of the Joneses can still be found in every corner of town. Patients who visit the R. T. Jones Memorial Hospital have no idea that the man whose name adorns the building was the grandfather of the greatest amateur golfer in history, nor do school children who visit the R. T. Jones Library know the legacy that goes with the name on the door. Members of Canton First Baptist Church don't know that R. T. Jones, founding deacon, used to admonish his grandson and namesake by saying, "Bob, if you must play on Sunday, play well." Most golfers who play the nine-hole Canton Golf Club have no idea that the course was designed by the immortal champion himself.

Robert T. Jones Jr. never lived a day in his grandfather's town, yet the Jones mystique can certainly be traced there. It was in Canton that the family laid deep southern roots and established a legacy of hard work, philanthropy, faith, leadership, and a respect for democratic order—all the attributes that Bobby carried with him to St. Andrews, Scotland; Hollywood, California; and ultimately back home to Atlanta and Augusta, Georgia.

A drive through downtown Canton recalls the familiar images of Bobby Jones. Small white cottages with oversized columns and inviting front porches sit behind specimen oak trees, similar in look to the ten cabins on the grounds at Augusta National. Although the nine-hole Canton Golf Club cannot compare to anything around Augusta, the trained architectural eye can see a relationship in thought and design. Large open fairways, inviting greens, a few bunkers—it is a course that requires thought to master, but it does not embarrass or overly punish the careless. Even after the Georgia Department of Transportation demolished three of the holes to clear the way for an interstate highway, the course still has the charm and character of the age and of the man.

Bob would probably have been born and raised in Canton near the family and the family business had his older brother, William Baily Jones, not died at the age of three months from pneumonia. Convinced her child died because Canton lacked adequate medical facilities, Bob's mother,

Clara, told R. P. to move to Atlanta and to set up his law practice there. Within a year Clara gave birth to another boy, Robert T. Jones Jr., a frail, gaunt child with a birth weight of just over five pounds, who was plagued throughout his childhood by digestive disorders. Doctors in Atlanta gave the young Jones little chance of living past age five. He did, of course, but not without doting from a nursemaid named Camilla and a mother who was not about to lose another child. For years young Bob was not allowed to play outside and, when he finally was given permission to roam, he played alone or with the dog and only in areas where he wouldn't get dirty.

Golf became the perfect compromise for an athletic father who wanted his son involved in sonlike activities and a protective mother who didn't want her little one exposed to anything. Golf was safe: no rough physical contact, no overexertion, no cuts, bumps, or bruises; yet it was involved, engaging, and active enough to satisfy the boy's needs and his father's wishes.

At the ripe age of five and a half, Bob Jones hit his first golf ball with a "cleek," the hickory-shafted version of a two-iron. It had been given to him by Atlanta neighbor Fulton Colville, who had spotted the skinny, sickly youth staring at him while he chipped some shots around his yard.

"Something inspired him to give me that club," Jones later told Atlanta sportswriter Furman Bisher. "I didn't have any interest in golf. . . . Dad took it [the two-iron] over to Jimmy Maiden, who was the pro at East Lake Country Club then, and Jimmy sawed it down and put a grip on it."

A little kid slapping a two-iron around a makeshift three-hole course wasn't exactly front-page news in 1908, but it was the inauspicious start to what would eventually be called the greatest career in sports history. R. P. and his son Bob became inseparably close, mostly because of a shared passion for golf, forging a relationship that R. P. had not had with

R. T. SR. LENT HIS GRANDSON THE FIFTY THOUSAND DOLLARS NEEDED FOR THE HOUSE. THE REPAYMENT TERMS WERE ONE DOLLAR A YEAR FOR FIFTY THOUSAND YEARS.

his own father. R. P. and Bob would play many rounds together at courses all over the world. Years before the green jacket presentation from the Butler Cabin, it was R. P. Jones who presented the check to the Masters winner.

Though R. T. Jones Sr. is often forgotten in the history of the Jones legacy, the entire Jones family owed a tremendous debt to the uncompromising gentleman who continued to rule over the Canton domain well into his eighties. Senior not only provided the moral compass and character model for the family, he provided them with access to things and people that otherwise would have been unavailable. When Bob needed a house and the members of East Lake gathered the funds to buy him one, the United States Golf Association (USGA) stepped in and squelched the project, informing Jones that such a gift would jeopardize his amateur status. R. T. Sr., well into his eighties by then, lent his grandson the fifty thousand dollars needed for the house. The repayment terms were one dollar a year for fifty thousand years.

The Joneses were well off. They weren't rich, but R. P. owned stock in Jones Mercantile and Canton Textile Mills, and the business connections developed from the family name enabled him to build a successful law practice. It also enabled him and his family to enjoy the amenities of country club living at a time when fewer than one hundred thousand people played golf, and most of them belonged to what could be described as American nobility. Bob Jones's skill, talent, dedication, and drive are the qualities most often credited when discussing his enormous success in golf, but a person doesn't win more than 40 percent of the U.S. and British Opens he enters and gain the adoration of people all over the world without strength of character. In the case of Bob Jones, that strength of character can be traced to his family bonds.

Tragically, what might have been a storybook life was, in the end, marred by one of the rarest nerve disorders known to modern medicine. In 1948, X rays showed an abnormal bone growth on three of Bob's vertebrae. Doctors attributed Jones's increased pain, back spasms, weakness, and atrophy to these growths. Eight years and two surgeries later, doctors at Columbia Medical Center in New York diagnosed Jones with syringomyelia, a congenital disorder which disconnects the motor nerves in the body from the brain. The condition does not by itself cause death, but the body wastes away until a side effect, such as heart failure or pneumonia, kills the patient. Jones lived from 1948 until 1971 as a slave to this debilitating disease, although the public believed he suffered from arthritis. He didn't try to hide his affliction and, as for the public's misunderstanding, he said, "Just let it go at that. [Arthritis] is easier to understand."

Although his condition made him totally dependent on others, Jones continued to display the strength of character that made him a champion. He attended the Masters as long as he could, well into the sixties. Even after he could no longer go out on the course, he would welcome guests into his cabin on the grounds, where he would engage visitors in warm and stimulating conversation. That is not to say that Jones accepted being crippled. In a letter to his doctor at Columbia Medical he wrote, "My life day and night is as nearly miserable as one could imagine." At one point he told his life-long friend Alexa Stirling: "I still can't accept this thing. I fight it every day. When it first happened I was pretty bitter and there were times when I didn't want to go on living. But I did go on living, so I had to face the problem of how I was going to live." Then in typical Jones style, he summarized his life both with and without the disease: "I decided I'd just do the very best I could."

Bob Jones, the greatest amateur golfer in the history of the world, died in December 1971. Two years later, his son Bob III died suddenly of a heart attack. Two years after that, his wife, Mary, died from a bleeding peptic ulcer. And almost exactly two years after that, Jones's youngest daughter, Mary Ellen, died of cancer.

Bobby Jones's legacy remains in places such as Highlands, North Carolina; St. Andrews, Scotland; Tuxedo Road in Atlanta; and, of course. Canton. But nowhere is there such a monument as is off Washington Road in West Augusta, behind the gates of the National.

CHAPTER 2

BROTHER,
CAN YOU SPARE
FIVE GRAND?

[AUGUSTA NATIONAL] IS LIKE PLAYING A SALVADOR DALI LAND-
SCAPE. I EXPECTED A CLOCK TO FALL OUT OF THE TREES AND HIT
ME IN THE FACE.

—DAVID FEHERTY

If Canton and the family business molded Jones the
man, Augusta and the family retreats were the genesis of Jones
the visionary. Throughout his golf career, even after his
celebrity kept him from playing a leisurely round without an
entourage of reporters and fans crooning over every shot,
Jones managed to travel with his dad and other companions
to Augusta for a little golf, rest, and relaxation.

Augusta straddles the Georgia–South Carolina border,
and other than being a halfway point on Interstate 20 between Atlanta and Columbia and the home of the Army Signal School at Fort Gordon, little entices the vacationing
traveler to visit the area. Of course, the Metro Augusta Chamber of Commerce would vehemently disagree, pointing with
pride to the River Walk, a downtown revitalization effort
along the banks of the Savannah that annually attracts

2.5 million out-of-towners to regattas, concerts, and street festivals where entrepreneurs sell folk art, quilts, and handmade crafts. In terms of being a tourist destination, however, Augusta doesn't make many travel agents' top-ten list. Such was not the case with the Augusta of 1930.

At the height of the industrial revolution, Augusta was "discovered" to be more than just a plantation and mill town. Even though the city had fewer than fifty thousand residents, most of whom were black mill workers and Chinese immigrants originally brought in to dig canals, northern industrialists who ventured south to inspect their Savannah River operations were pleasantly surprised by the warm climate and lovely flora of the region. Augusta also had the flavor of the Old South, with its many stately homes and even statelier homeowners who had survived the ravages of Sherman's romp through Georgia.

Old northern money met old southern money, and the end result was one of the more popular destination resorts of the late nineteenth century. Augusta, lying in a valley only 137 feet above sea level, provided a warm winter respite to northern men and women of leisure long before anyone had heard of Hilton Head Island and at a time when travel to Florida was tantamount to leaving the country. Even residents of Atlanta (elevation 1,100 feet) realized that the 150-mile jaunt east changed conditions dramatically. Augusta could be as much as thirty degrees warmer than Atlanta during the winter months. Those who could afford the trip made it.

Augusta was small, quaint, and delightful, with ample money and an enshrined caste society where everyone knew his or her station. No major train line ran through town and the airport was small and inconvenient. Neighboring Aiken, South Carolina, quickly and quietly became a world-class equestrian retreat. With the help of the Bon Air Vanderbilt Hotel and a few Donald Ross–designed golf courses, Augusta gained a reputation as a winter golf haven. Augusta Country

Club, a private thirty-six-hole club, and the Forest Hills Ricker course were considered by many (Jones included) to be demanding and challenging, yet fun tests of golf. Both measured over sixty-six hundred yards, and when the Southeastern Open, a winter stop on the tour at that time, picked Augusta as a host city, the tournament was divided between the ACC and Forest Hills Ricker courses.

One of those Atlantans who played in that Southeastern Open and who could afford to make regular trips east to Augusta was Bob Jones. It was only a day's trip by car and was home to two first-rate golf courses and one darned nice hotel, so Jones made Augusta a regular winter stop. However, despite the fact that Augusta Country Club No. 1 was one of Jones's favorite winter courses, the idea of building the National on property that butted up to the ninth hole of that course was something the great champion hadn't even considered. For his first club Jones had his heart set on building something in or close to Atlanta. He wanted it to be a winter retreat and he desired that it be a "national" club attracting members from all parts of the country. It would be his dream course, a place where he and a few friends could escape the pressures of work and other competitions and enjoy a leisurely four-ball wager without the crowds and the constant feeling of being on display.

The idea, although not fully formed, for what would become Augusta National had been ruminating in Jones's head since at least 1928. That was the year he began contemplating retirement. By then he had won the U.S. Open twice and finished second three times. He'd won four U.S. Amateur titles and two British Opens, all while playing in a limited number of events and balancing the demands of a family and a career. He never took a dime in prize money and would have it no other way. With few exceptions, professionals were seen as gypsy hustlers who didn't deserve the prefix "Mr." before their names. Mr. Jones, the consummate amateur, incurred all the expenses, all the worries, and all the pressures while living up to the highest expectations and for no money. He did so gladly, but with a wife and three children he had other considerations. Law and other interests awaited him, and retirement from competition began to seem appealing.

By 1929 Jones had not only decided that 1930 would be his last season of competitive golf, he had also determined that he would build a golf course where friends could gather, drink, laugh, play golf, and do so privately. He still hadn't spoken publicly of his plans, but he began to contemplate all the variables he would need to build a club: an architect, a site, and some cash.

As for an architect, Jones had expressed his views on design many times, and it was clear he wanted hands-on involvement in the design. He was, after all, the greatest player in the world, and this would be his dream club. He also knew he didn't know enough to take on the project alone. "No man learns to design a golf course simply by playing golf, no matter how well," he said.

First consideration was given Donald Ross, the world-renowned architect of Pinehurst No. 2, Augusta Country Club, and East Lake Country Club. Ross, a native of Scotland who had come to America and achieved great fanfare as one of the world's premier architects, was an independent thinker and artist with an ego that wouldn't give in, even to a living legend like Jones. Since a clash would be inevitable, Jones never even approached Ross with the concept. The private search for the architectural partner continued.

Then in 1929 Jones suffered a fortuitous defeat. A gritty nineteen-year-old from Omaha named Johnny Goodman beat him in the first match-play round of the 1929

U.S. Amateur at Pebble Beach. With Jones being the gentleman that he was and the Monterey Peninsula being the place that it is, he decided to stay in California, watch a few matches, play a little golf, and, as luck would have it, spend a little time with Cypress Point architect Dr. Alister Mackenzie.

THE FIRST TIME HE PLAYED ST. ANDREWS, HE HATED IT. IN LATER YEARS, THE OLD COURSE BECAME HIS ALL-TIME FAVORITE, AND HE BECAME ST. ANDREWS'S FAVORITE ADOPTED SON.

Cypress Point was brand-new. It hadn't officially opened when Jones got a special invitation to play. (When word leaked of this "informal" round, close to three hundred people showed up to watch.) Jones's reaction to Cypress Point was precise and unequivocal: "Perfect," he said at the time and continued to say it for years after. Pacific Ocean waves crashing against the cliffs of Monterey make it tough for anyone to say anything less, but what Jones found particularly appealing was Cypress Point's total lack of artificiality. Nothing in Mackenzie's design was contrived. He didn't design the golf course as much as he "found" it on the ground. Relatively short compared to its neighbor Pebble Beach, the club offered awesome vistas of the Pacific, but it had very little in the way of design-flair. That was classic Mackenzie, as Jones would discover during numerous conversations with the retired physician. A native of Birmingham, England, with a colorful and somewhat mysterious past, the good doctor would sip single malt scotch, tilt his head, smile a wry smile, and tell Jones, "A good golf course is like good music. It isn't necessarily a course which appeals the first time you play it." Jones found the statement prophetic. The first time he played St. Andrews, he hated it. In later years, the Old

Course became his all-time favorite, and he became St. Andrews's favorite adopted son.

Jones also respected Mackenzie for his principles. He wouldn't design a golf course on what he deemed "improper" land, meaning land that was "obviously unsuitable for golf." It's clear that Mackenzie would have had a difficult time making a living in today's development-driven golf environment, where the good land is usually reserved for homesites and the course architect is expected to meander eighteen or more golf holes through whatever is left. If Mackenzie felt he couldn't create a course where "excellence is more felt than fully realized," he would simply pass on the offer. He also felt that if a course cost more than $100,000, it was too "manufactured." That sort of frugality (although Augusta National would ultimately cost $101,000 to build) appealed to Jones's southern sensibilities. The fact that Mackenzie seemed affable and willing to work in tandem suited Jones's personality and fitted his desire to be intimately involved in the process.

When he left California and headed back to Atlanta, Jones had a vision of the perfect golf course and, in his estimation, the perfect architect. He also had one more year of competition ahead of him, a year in which he would break what his trusty scribe, O. B. Keeler, called the "impregnable quadrilateral," even though most people had no idea what that meant. People did understand what a Grand Slam was, though, and they knew a historic achievement when they saw one.

They saw one in 1930. By the time Jones won the U.S. Amateur at Merion Cricket Club near Philadelphia, men and women who wouldn't have known a golf ball from a goose egg celebrated a moment in history that would never be equaled. His slicked-back hair glistening and his trademark smile wider than ever, Jones stood outside the Merion clubhouse holding the last championship trophy he would ever win.

But a few other things had happened between that fateful week on the beautiful rocky shores of Monterey and that historic day in Philadelphia. The country's most eligible bachelor, Charles Lindbergh, broke the hearts of girls across America by marrying Anne Morrow; construction began on the Empire State Building; the New York Yankees lost the World Series when Babe Ruth was caught stealing to end game seven; and four months after the 1929 U.S. Amateur at Pebble Beach, a series of sell orders on Wall Street started a snowball that wouldn't end until the market had crashed, sending the economy into a tailspin and forcing unemployment rates over 40 percent for the first time in the nation's history.

Even with the economy in shambles, Jones the champion had no doubts about the country or his own ambitions. He began to speak openly about his dream club and he began, ever so subtly, to solicit advice from friends and potential members. One of those whom he bounced the idea off was a thin, dry midwesterner named Clifford Roberts, who was a Wall Street whiz kid connected in all the right financial circles. The two men had been introduced during Jones's playing career, and they shared a number of mutual friends.

One of those friends was a fine New York fellow named Walton Marshall. In addition to being a member of the Knollwood Country Club and the Two-Cent Bridge Club in New York, Marshall managed a chain of luxury hotels that included the Bon Air Vanderbilt in Augusta.

Along with all other American enterprises, the hotel business had taken a hit during the depression, and the largest blow was suffered by luxury resorts. Augusta was such a resort and the Bon Air Vanderbilt was a resort hotel that had shown a steady decline since the mid-twenties when Henry Ford's Model T and, later, airplanes as means of travel began enticing some vacationers to bypass inland retreats such as Augusta for more tropical, oceanfront destinations.

Walt's Augusta hotel needed a boost, Bob Jones was looking to build a club somewhere near his hometown of Atlanta, and Bob liked Augusta. Cliff Roberts knew Bob well enough to make a suggestion, and from having served a stint in the army and taken a few trips to the Bon Air Vanderbilt, Cliff knew Augusta. It was all starting to fall into place.

Another mutual friend of both Roberts and Jones was future Augusta mayor Tom Barrett. The timing for Barrett couldn't have been better. Augusta was grappling with the depression like every other town in America, with many of its textile mills laying off workers and selling off assets. As was the case in most parts of the nation, people latched on to any glimmer of economic opportunity. A club founded by the immortal Bob Jones would be seen as a windfall by any city he chose.

Barrett knew exactly what tract of land to recommend. It was a 365-acre abandoned nursery off Washington Road called the Fruitlands. The property was an old indigo plantation that had been bought by a Belgian baron in 1857. In 1858 the baron, an avid horticulturist, had opened the South's first commercial nursery, setting up his son, an agronomist and horticulturist, to run the business. The son died, leaving the property to his young second wife, and the nursery, for all practical purposes, shut down. The trees, plants, grasses, and manor house remained. Gently rolling and home to everything from pear trees to azaleas, the land seemed perfect for a golf course, especially because there already was one—Augusta Country Club—right next to it. As a rule, top-notch golf courses aren't situated adjacent to each other, but Barrett and Roberts didn't know that. This would be Bobby Jones's club, which could be next to a landfill and still be successful.

The Fruitlands had another interesting twist. In 1925 it was reported that a Miami hotelier named Commodore J. Perry Stoltz had acquired the property and was making plans for a second hotel in what would be a chain of Fleetwood Hotels spanning the nation. The Fleetwood was to sit behind the old manor house on the plantation, with construction scheduled to begin in early 1926. Ground was broken in February and excavation progressed nicely for about five months. Before the end of the year, however, Stoltz and the Fleetwood chain filed for bankruptcy after a hurricane, literally, blew through the Miami Fleetwood. While not openly reveling in the misfortune of others, Walt Marshall and the folks at the Bon Air were quietly relieved, as Augusta wasn't big enough for another luxury hotel. The best way to ensure that the Fruitlands didn't become a hotel was to make sure it became something else: a golf course. One featuring the greatest golfer in the world, would do nicely.

Jones had seen the Fruitlands through the trees while playing Augusta Country Club, but he'd never actually visited the site. After driving Jones and Cliff Roberts out to the land for the first time, Tom Barrett walked them around the large manor house to an area that is now the putting green. Jones looked out over the slopes of the nursery and said, "And to think this ground has been lying here all these years waiting for someone to come along and lay a golf course on it." Years later Jones would write of that first trip: "The long lane of magnolias through which we approached was beautiful. The old manor house with its cupola and wall of masonry two feet thick was charming. The rare trees and shrubs of the old nursery were enchanting. But when I walked out on the grass terrace under the big trees behind the house and looked down over the property, the experience was unforgettable."

Quickly and quietly, a group of five investors—Jones, who put in no money; Roberts, who put in a little money; Bob's good friend sportswriter Grantland Rice, who chipped in what he could; William Watt, chairman of United Drug Company and a Jones fanatic, who did his part for the till; and Alfred S. Bourne of New York, the mercurial, wealthy son of the Singer Sewing Machine Company founder—optioned the Fruitlands property for seventy thousand dollars under the shell name of Fruitland Manor Corporation. Jones named his course-to-be Augusta National, and he named Alister Mackenzie the official architect of the yet-undesigned project.

With a sportswriter, a politician, a couple of wealthy investors, and the most famous athlete in the world on board, any subterfuge they had hoped to put forth was short-lived. On July 15 the banner headline of the *Augusta Chronicle* read "Bobby Jones to Build His Ideal Golf Course on Berckmans's Place" (Berckmans was the baron who owned the Fruitlands nursery).

Jones, through trusty scribe Keeler, made an uncharacteristically rambling statement to the paper:

> I am joining with a group of friends as one of the organizers of a new club to be known as the Augusta National Golf Club. It is strictly a private undertaking and is in no sense a commercial project. Although my time now is largely devoted to the business of law, and I have retired forever from competitive golf, this great game will always be my hobby, and my ambition in connection with the Augusta enterprise is to help build a course which may possibly be recognized as one of the great golf courses of the world.
>
> Augusta is in my home state. It has a singularly fine climate, and my experience in this city, in the Southeastern Open Championship last spring, convinced me that nowhere in the hemisphere was there anything to surpass the golfing conditions in turf, greens, or climate offered by this immediate locality.

Of course I cannot deny that it is an idea very dear to my heart, to see in reality a golf course embodying the finest holes of all the great courses on which I have played. But I am not having this dream alone, or without the most expert collaboration. Dr. Mackenzie is the man who will actually design the course. His name needs no presentation to the American golfing public or the golfers of the world. I am happy to accompany him this morning on a tour of the property and to assume the role of consultant with him for this golf course. I know it is his ambition, and my earnest hope, to present a course that will find a place in North American golfing history as one of the layouts truly national in character and characteristics. English sportsmen and Canadians have been invited to join this club; and I am sure we shall have in Augusta a representative group of members from all over the world. This club, as I hope, is to be a truly national golf club.

The citizens of Atlanta heartily disagreed on several counts. To begin with, Jones was *their* native son, and while he referenced Georgia and his commitment to a truly "national" club in his statement, the people of Atlanta were hurt. There were plenty of great tracts of land a lot closer to home and just as suitable for golf (as everyone would later see when Jones developed Peachtree Golf Club just north of Atlanta). Atlantans were upset, not just by what they perceived as a personal shun, but by the fact that their town was passed up as a potential site for this economically prosperous venture. Jones's statement about this being a "private undertaking" and not a "commercial project" rang hollow in his hometown. Augusta still had money, even after the crash, and Bob's neighbors harbored unspoken feelings that he had somehow sold them out. As a result, only one man from Atlanta, Harry Atkinson, who in 1930 was too old and too rich to give a damn what anybody said about him, joined during the first membership offering.

The minimum commitment for membership was five thousand dollars. More was accepted from those willing to contribute, and there were some who gave upwards of twenty-five thousand dollars. Roberts, the kind of guy who would audit a restaurant bill down to the last penny, was put in charge of the money. Through Roberts's contacts in New York and the attention given Augusta National by the press, the club grew to eighty members. The early roster included such names as Lewis Maytag, B. B. Taggart, Chicago's Henry Crowell, and Beechnut Packing Company president Bart Arkell, who was instrumental in the renovation of the old Berckmans manor house. By Roberts's own admission, if any of them had known exactly how long and how devastating the depression would be, the project would have been abandoned. But eternally optimistic and unaccustomed to failure, Jones, Mackenzie, Roberts, and the high-powered first members of Augusta National broke ground before the end of 1931.

Mackenzie and Jones were complementary partners in every respect. A short hitter, Mackenzie hated rough. He regarded golf not in terms of par but in terms of "even-fours," whereby all the holes would work out to be played in four shots rather than in the traditional and obvious mix of par-fives, par-threes, and par-fours. There would, of course, be par-threes, -fours, and -fives in his design, but his thinking was

This 1933 aerial photo of the original golf course at Augusta National Golf Club represents three years of preparation, with Bobby Jones having helped noted architect Dr. Alister Mackenzie in the design. (AP/Wide World Photos)

in terms of fours. Jones liked that. He hated long par-fives where, in his words, "you don't start playing golf until the third shot." Augusta National would have reachable, strategically challenging par-fives.

Mackenzie also had several design "essentials" he would incorporate into his plans for Augusta National. First, he believed a great golf course must be pleasurable to the greatest possible number of people, a philosophy Jones passionately shared. Mackenzie also believed that a course must require strategy as well as skill for it to be enduringly interesting. It must also give average players a fair chance and at the same time require the utmost in skill and strategy from the expert. Since most of the Augusta National members were average players, these essentials appealed to Jones from the outset.

Mackenzie drafted what would in today's vernacular be called the routing plan, which included a strangely unconventional nineteen holes. The nineteenth, a par-three that was designed to play uphill between the ninth and eighteenth greens to what is now the putting green, was put on the drawing board in case any members wanted to play double or nothing, or to break any untidy deadlocks through eighteen holes. Of course, the Masters wasn't even an idea at that stage, so this unique tie-breaker hole was strictly something to help members settle their bets. And bet they would, although not on the double-or-nothing nineteenth. In the end, Jones was too much of a traditionalist and he vetoed the idea.

While not a big deal since the hole was never built, this was the first "who's in charge?" issue that arose between Jones and Mackenzie. Jones answered the question in short order. He was *the man,* and while Mackenzie's fingerprints are evident throughout, Augusta National screams of Jones's personality and philosophy of the game. Years after the course was built, Jones outlined his thoughts to *Sports Illustrated*:

> Our overall aim at Augusta National was to provide a golf course of considerable natural beauty, enjoyable for the average golfer and at the same time testing for the expert player striving to better par. We want to make the bogeys easy, if frankly sought, pars readily obtainable by standard good play, and birdies, except on par-fives, dearly bought. Obviously with a course as wide open as is needed to accommodate the average golfer, we can only tighten it up by increasing difficulty of play

around the hole. This we attempt to do by placing the flags in more difficult and exacting positions and by increasing the speed of the greens. Additionally, we try to maintain our greens at such firmness that they will not hold a misplayed shot.

The course was considered long at the time, although today many of the features in the original design are overpowered by three-hundred-yard-plus tee shots. Jones himself was long, and he was extremely adept at hitting long irons exactly where and how he needed. With that playing out in Jones's mind, Augusta National was designed to reward the smartly played, well-executed long shot. It was also built so as not to embarrass players, even if they were making a double bogey. Wide, inviting fairways with little or no rough and few bunkers (twenty-two in the original design and still only forty-five today) seduce players into believing that Augusta National is easy: Just put the brain in neutral and swing away. That hypnotic enticement is the course's secret and its curse. Jones was very clear about his intentions: "I have always said that this can be a very easy golf course or a very tough one. There isn't a hole out there that can't be birdied if you just think. But there isn't one that can't be double bogeyed if you stop thinking."

A lack of clear thinking was inexcusable to Jones, and when he was a player, it was his worst fear. "The shot carelessly played" was, to Jones, far worse than the carefully planned shot that was poorly executed. However, Jones refused to accept that anyone should be embarrassed on a golf course—penalized, yes; but embarrassed, never. His primary design philosophy, from the nine-hole Canton Golf Club to Peachtree Golf Club in Atlanta to Augusta National, was to make golf

JONES REFUSED TO ACCEPT
THAT ANYONE SHOULD BE
EMBARRASSED ON A GOLF
COURSE—PENALIZED, YES;
BUT EMBARRASSED, NEVER.

enjoyable. He said, "The primary purpose of a golf course is to give pleasure, and that to the greatest possible number of people without respect to their capabilities."

Not everyone immediately associated Augusta's beauty with golfing pleasure. Decades after Jones and Mackenzie had designed and birthed their golden child, which soon was being compared to Pebble Beach and, of course, Cypress Point for its sheer beauty, a golfing and design expert no less qualified than Tom Weiskopf in the late 1970s offered the notion that "Augusta National's reputation is built largely on brainwashing." Added Weiskopf: "For six months you're in the frozen North and chomping at the bit. . . . Then the Masters hits you. . . . Whatever the course has going for it is magnified in your eyes. Back in my hometown of Columbus, Ohio, alone there are four courses—Muirfield Village, the Golf Club, Scioto, and Ohio State—as good as Augusta. You can go elsewhere, too, and find other courses that play as challengingly without having to resort to putting the pins on slopes and knolls."

Tricky slopes and goofy knolls aside, the National has eighty acres of fairway; most courses have about thirty-five. While undulating, Augusta's greens are huge, a total of more than 101,000 square feet of putting surface. Most courses today have no more than 70,000 square feet of greens. Jones said of the putting surfaces at Augusta, "Generally speaking, the greens are quite large and rolling, with carefully contrived undulations, the effect of which is magnified as the speed of the surfaces is increased."

Big, inviting, open, and subtle, Augusta was, and is, the antithesis of what many feel is a "championship" golf course, whatever that means. But after sixty-four years, it is still the course golfers say they would most love to play, the club most people say they would join if they could. The Masters is, by far, one golf tournament many players say they would most like to win, and even though pundits every year say the golf course is too open and too easy, 63 remains the lowest score ever shot, even with no rough and big greens.

The debate over rough hasn't been only among "experts" in the media. In the 1950s Ben Hogan wanted Cliff Roberts to grow the roughs up to U.S. Open standards. One of the most accurate shotmakers in history, Hogan saw great wisdom in his request. Sam Snead, on the other hand, quipped to Roberts, "What do you want us to shoot, 300?"

As late as the 1960s Jones was still having to answer questions about the openness of Augusta National. He said to *Sports Illustrated*: "Our golf course was designed for the enjoyment of our members who do not delight in playing all day from sand and long grass. For this reason we expect to keep the course about as it is regardless of what the long hitters may do."

Jones was still *the* long hitter in 1931, and he hit thousands of shots from different locations during the construction of the course. It was "design by feel," much like Jones the player and Jones the man, and much to the delight of Mackenzie who believed Augusta National to be "the world's wonder inland course."

Help was cheap, fifty cents a day, and the job site was busy from "can to can't" (from the time you can see until the time you can't, first light to last). Under that

Bobby Jones follows through on a long-iron shot during Masters play at Augusta. Jones was considered the best long-iron golfer of his time, and that particular strength played a key role in his vision for helping Alister Mackenzie with the design of the course. During construction of the course, Jones spent many hours hitting shots with specific clubs at specific points on the course to test his blueprint designs. (AP/Wide World Photos)

schedule, the course opened to limited play in December 1932 and officially in January 1933.

Alister Mackenzie didn't make it to the grand opening. After a trip to Scotland in 1933, he became gravely ill and died in California in 1934, a full year after his masterpiece opened, but he never saw the finished product. Before he died, he said, "The Augusta National represented my best opportunity, and I believe my finest achievement." He also wrote a detailed guide to playing Augusta National in which he made continual comparisons to other holes at other courses, most notably, the Old Course at St. Andrews:

- Number four, par-three—"This is a very similar hole to the famous eleventh at St. Andrews"
- Number five, par-four—"This is a similar type hole to the famous seventeenth (Road Hole) at St. Andrews"
- Number seven, par-four—"This hole is similar in character to the eighteenth hole at St. Andrews"
- Number fourteen, par-four—"This hole embodies some of the features of the sixth at St. Andrews"
- Number seventeen, par-four—"The construction of the green is somewhat similar to that famous fourteenth at St. Andrews"

Mackenzie and Jones obviously agreed that St. Andrews was one heck of a good golf course. Before Augusta National opened, however, Jones did make one bad design decision: He reversed the nines from Mackenzie's original plan, making the back side the front and the front the back. His thinking was that the front nine was measurably harder than the back, so it would provide for more of a "down the stretch" challenge. He was wrong.

The club opened with what is now number ten being number one and vice versa. That made what we now know as Amen Corner numbers two, three, and four; and numbers fifteen and sixteen, arguably the most dramatic two back-to-back holes in tournament golf, were numbers six and seven. Seven, eight, and nine offered a reachable uphill par-five sandwiched between two very good but not overly dramatic holes and provided the finishing holes in year one. Fortunately, Jones quickly saw the error of his ways and—in large part, too, because of an early-morning frost that affected one nine much more than the other—reversed the nines back to their original design for the 1935 season.

The National also opened under a form of rule that would shape its existence for the next sixty years, thus making it an icon. During the initial membership meeting, sportswriter Grantland Rice, fair drinker and good friend of both Jones and Roberts, proposed that the only effective form of government in a club was autocratic rule. He made a motion that the members of Augusta National vote, right there, to make Bob Jones and Cliff Roberts official club dictators. All agreed.

Autocratic rule was not new to clubs. For many years Pine Valley had been ruled by Philadelphia lawyer John Arthur Brown, whose idea of rule-of-law would have shamed any Third World dictator. Brown, who lived just off one of the fairways, once saw a member hit a shot and then forget to replace his divot. That member's locker was cleaned out and his resignation letter was issued the next day. Other clubs around the country were run under similar authoritarian rule, but the National was different in a number of respects. Its members weren't influential businessmen from one particular city; they were influential tycoons from all over the United States. Most would be too absent and too busy to engage in the minutiae of running a club, so it seemed to make sense for Jones and Roberts, the two men who had put this thing together in the first place, to be co-dictators.

There was only one problem: Jones was incapable of being anything remotely approaching dictatorial. He would be president of the club and he would be the man most acclaimed for its ultimate success, and it was because of his personality that Augusta National would become a true dictatorship. His genteel persona and conciliatory nature made him an unsuitable autocrat. Thus into perpetuity the club's chairman would become the supreme ruler of all things at Augusta National: Clifford C. Roberts.

CHAPTER 3

YOU ARE CORDIALLY INVITED . . .

IT STARTED OUT AS AUGUSTA NATIONAL INVITATIONAL FROM A SMALL GROUP OF BOB'S FRIENDS. I DON'T THINK HE REALLY MEANT TO BRING IT INTO WHAT IT IS. IT HAPPENED BECAUSE OF JONES. . . . THEY DIDN'T KNOW THEY WERE GOING TO HAVE A CHAMPIONSHIP THERE. IF [JONES] THOUGHT HE WOULD HAVE THE EVENT THAT HE WAS GOING TO HAVE, I'LL GUARANTEE YOU THEY WOULD HAVE BUILT [THE CLUB] IN ATLANTA.

—JACK NICKLAUS

The first thought was to host the U.S. Open. It was one of Bob's favorite tournaments, and certainly he was the USGA's favorite champion. The USGA had never held its national championship south of the Mason-Dixon Line, and who better to bring the Open south than the great Atlanta native, Bobby Jones? (Jones would be posthumously credited with bringing the Open south when the USGA saw fit to hold it at Atlanta Athletic Club in 1976.)

Prior to the opening of the National, meetings were held with USGA officials who seemed amenable to the idea of the U.S. Open in Augusta as long as it fell in line with their regular June schedule. The USGA held the Open in June and that was that. Host clubs had nothing to say on the subject—at least nothing the USGA was interested in hearing.

Jones and Roberts had something to say: No. Augusta is brutally hot in June with temperatures approaching 100 degrees, humidity that climbs to over 90 percent, and no breeze. In fact, during course construction, temperatures along Rae's Creek reached upwards of 110 degrees and foremen had to regulate work to avoid killing any laborers from heat exhaustion. Jones had played under these kinds of grueling conditions and he didn't want his golf course to be a test of stamina in the sweltering Georgia heat. He also hadn't built Augusta National for the summer. It was a winter golf course, closed in the summer from its inception. The USGA would simply have to move the Open to March or April when conditions are ideal for golf in Augusta. The top brass at the USGA politely declined.

Snubbed by the organization he had helped bring into adulthood, Jones decided to host his own invitational in the spring when the flowers were in bloom and Augusta was rich with warm air and clean blue skies. Augusta temperatures in the spring average in the low seventies, ideal conditions for golf. The National was built for those ideal conditions and a spring invitational would be the club's one and only tournament.

That wasn't the only time a summer event for Augusta National has been considered. In 1992, when Billy Payne and the Atlanta Committee for the Olympic Games (ACOG) proposed bringing golf back into the Summer Olympics, there was only one course they considered: Georgia's finest—Augusta National. Though the idea received a cool reception from many players who felt the Ryder Cup was golf's play-for-God-and-country ritual, Payne and the ACOG pressed ahead, naming the National as the venue for the games. To the surprise of many, Jack Stephens and the National members jumped on board, agreeing to keep the club open into late July and early August for the Olympics. In October 1992 Payne and Stephens made the announcement at a press conference on the lawn near the tenth tee, at which time Stephens said, "We're trying to send a message that we're for both men and women's golf. We have no prohibition for any member or any type member and that's always been the policy of the club." However, when civil rights leaders, Atlanta

THE FIELD WOULD BE SO STRONG THAT EVEN BEFORE INVITATIONS WENT OUT, CLIFF ROBERTS SUGGESTED CALLING THE TOURNAMENT THE MASTERS. JONES WOULD HAVE NONE OF IT. "TOO PRESUMPTUOUS," HE SAID.

city councilmen, and other interested and/or involved parties spun their politically creative agendas into an "anti-Augusta National resolution" it became obvious to everyone that Augusta National, golf, and the Olympic games were not going to mix well in 1996. By 1994 the entire idea was dropped, and the National preserved its long-standing tradition as a spring golf course.

With the exception of an occasional regatta or regional golf event, Augusta's only big-time sports claim in the 1930s was hometown hero Ty Cobb, a man who once went into the stands and assaulted a quadriplegic fan for allegedly calling Cobb a half-nigger. Even native Augustans who might have shared Cobb's minority views weren't necessarily happy to consider him a neighbor. What the town really needed was a sporting *event* to call its own, and Bob's spring invitational fit the bill nicely. Locals, many of whom had never seen a golf course, diligently worked to support the National's efforts to bring respect to Augusta.

41

In spring 1934 the club hosted its first annual invitational tournament by inviting a group of Bob's friends, who happened to be the greatest players in the world. The field would be so strong that even before invitations went out, Cliff Roberts suggested calling the tournament the Masters. Jones would have none of it. "Too presumptuous," he said. But Roberts wouldn't let it die. Through his own blend of back-door maneuvering, Roberts was able to unofficially name the tournament the Masters and make the name change look like a totally spontaneous event. Old friend and member Tom Barrett got wind of the Masters name idea (wink, wink), and he made a few calls to the press (nod, nod), who thought the name entirely appropriate. Jones hated it, and referred to it as the "so-called Masters" as late as the 1960s even though the club officially adopted the name in 1938. The first event was officially called the First Annual Invitational Tournament, but the Masters was being used quite openly as a substitute.

Also, from the very beginning Jones hated the idea of anyone calling the tournament a *championship*. "Championship of what?" he snapped. It was his contention that the "so-called Masters" was an invitational tournament put on by the members of Augusta National; nothing more, nothing less. The winner hadn't gone through any preliminary qualifying and no ruling body of golf sanctioned the event. This was a member-owned club hosting a member-run invitational. The fact that the club president just happened to be Bobby Jones and the members were America's premier movers and shakers didn't make it a championship, and Jones denounced any motions to that effect.

"I remember a meeting with Bobby Jones early in my years of covering the Masters," says CBS's Frank Chirkinian. "He sat in his wheelchair and smoked . . . He said, 'It's not the championship of anything. It's not even a club championship.' That's why we [CBS] never refer to the winner as 'the

Masters champion.' He's 'the tournament winner' or 'the winner of the green coat.' "

In 1934 there was no green coat, but there would eventually be a winner, and everyone wondered if that winner would be the tournament's host, the officially retired Bobby Jones. Sixty years before Michael Jordan returned to the NBA after a year of chasing minor league curve balls, the press ran rampant with speculation on "the triumphant return of Emperor Jones."

Jones didn't especially want to play. He was satisfied being the club president and presiding over the event in an official capacity. Cliff Roberts, on the other hand, knew that the gate receipts were going to be tight in a town the size of Augusta, and he had already passed the hat among members to raise enough prize money to make the event worthwhile. Without Jones as a participant, the club ran the risk of hosting a financial disaster. U.S. Open receipts had dropped from $23,382 in 1930, when Jones won, to $12,700 in 1931, when Jones was a retired spectator. Being the savvy facilitator that he was, Roberts convinced Jones to play by appealing to his gentleman sensibilities: Cliff told Bob he couldn't invite all his friends down to Georgia and then *not play with them*. Jones agreed. He would play in the "so-called Masters."

Jones was also put in charge of invitations. That presented another problem: He was too much of a gentleman to say no to anyone. Roberts came to the rescue again. With Jones's approval, Roberts established a set of guidelines, which in 1935 became the official Qualifications for Invitation to the Masters. While these qualifications have undergone some strange revisions over the years (including an occasional invitation to the winners of the Scandinavian Masters, for instance), the original invitees were:

- present and past U.S. Open champions,
- present and past U.S. Amateur champions,
- present and past British Amateur champions,
- present and past British Open champions,
- present and past U.S. PGA champions,
- present members of the Ryder Cup team,
- present members of the Walker Cup team,

along with a few of Bob's old dear friends.

These guidelines produced a field that included such great golf names as Craig Wood, Gene Sarazen, Walter Hagen, and Horton Smith. Strong as the field might have been, though, the press had only one interest: Jones.

"I hope to be able to step four fast rounds," Jones said to interviewers in atypical doublespeak. "It looks like a wide-open tournament to me and I hope we will all have a good time."

It wasn't a major in those days. It wasn't, as Jones had vehemently pointed out, even a championship, but if the press coverage offered any indication, this invitational was the new dawn of golf in America.

"Jones to Tee Off at Augusta Today," blared the *New York Times* headline. Said the *Times*'s subhead, "Eyes of Golfdom on Southern Course as Ex-Champion Stages Comeback; Faces Brilliant Field." As sensational as those headlines were, the man who wrote them, William Richardson, wasn't even in Augusta to cover the event. Southeast Georgia just wasn't for him, so he opted to stay in New York, where he was to cover something of more significance that year—regional qualifying for the U.S. Open.

Although retired from full-time competitive golf at this point in his life, Augusta and Masters Tournament cofounder Bobby Jones gives it a go in Augusta National's First Annual Invitational Tournament, contested in 1934. (AP/Wide World Photos)

Jones's "comeback" was a reluctant one. He hadn't donned his spikes in anything but friendly four-balls in almost four years, and his primary golf interest for the previous two years had been designing and building the National. His rustiness showed. In a practice round Scotch foursome, Bob and his partner, Ross Sommerville, fired a best-ball 76, and Jones missed no fewer than nine short putts, prompting him to spend two hours on the practice green. His comeback might be futile, but he would not be embarrassed.

The next day, Thursday, March 22, 1934, Johnny Kinder stepped up to what was then the first and is now the tenth tee at a little before 10:00 A.M. At 10:02 he struck the first shot of what would become the Masters Tournament. At 10:36 Paul Runyan and his fellow competitor, Augusta National president Bob Jones, teed off in front of a gallery estimated in the thousands. A little over two hours later Jones stroked a five-foot eagle putt so badly that his second putt was longer than his first. He struck the second putt even more poorly, but the ball found its way into the hole. Then he three-putted number fourteen (now number five) from a distance where birdie would have been expected from Jones in his prime. He then three-putted seventeen (now eight), although at that time it was actually possible to have a blind putt on that green. The surrounding mounds were so huge that they blocked a player's view of the back of the green from the front. Golfers said the green called for "putts that hook." Discouraged but still the great champion, Jones pressed forward to eighteen (now nine) where he again three-putted to shoot an uninspiring 76.

He still made the lead headlines. The *Times*'s front page headline was, "Unsteady Putting Drops Jones to Tie for Thirty-fifth, Six Shots Behind Golf Leaders." Those golf leaders were Horton Smith and Jimmy Hines, who each shot an opening-round 70 only to find their names buried deep in the body of the story.

After the second round, when Jones shot an equally lackluster 74, the *Times*'s headline was, "Jones Trails by Eight at Halfway Mark in Augusta Golf Tourney." Horton Smith, who fired an even-par round on Friday, still had to comb the fine print to find his name.

It wasn't until after Smith fired another 70 in Saturday's round that he earned front-page billing: "Smith's 212 Leads Jones by Ten." Jones's putting got better—he finished the tournament with two straight even-par rounds—but the expectations were just too high. Monday's *Times* reported, "Augusta Golf Tourney Won by Horton Smith as Jones Finishes Thirteenth." Jones actually tied for thirteenth, but his performance had an enormous impact on the tournament, the town of Augusta, and the future of golf in America.

Smith's victory was no runaway. He won by only one shot over Craig Wood. Smith birdied the seventy-first hole and parred the seventy-second to secure that narrow margin. Regardless of that drama, the tournament coverage was devoted to Jones and the comeback that wasn't. Cliff Roberts had been right: Without Jones, nobody would have cared and the tournament would have been page-five news. With Jones, even though he played poorly, it was a national news event.

Another thing members of the club had going for them was the affection sportswriters had for the beautiful town of Augusta. The press corps from the Northeast and Midwest could justify a weeklong stop in the charming southern town because it was "on the way back home" from baseball spring training camps. Furthermore, the tournament was the one and only time the immortal Bobby Jones teed it up in competition. Reporters also loved the fact that Augusta during Masters week was a drinker's and gambler's paradise. Although nestled in the heart of the Bible Belt, law enforcement officials in the 1930s turned a blind eye to the highly publicized auctions, or calcuttas, that took place at the Bon Air and Forest Hills Ricker Hotels, as well as the bookmaking, drinking, and other activities that occurred nightly at places such as Spec Reds, a small establishment near the airport. The tournament was a gentlemen's stag party, and who were the cops to say anything? This was, after all, the Masters.

Roberts made sure there was no trouble. He manipulated the press and the locals to his and Augusta's benefits by extending invitations to some of them as members and by luring others with the prospect of such. Grantland Rice and O. B. Keeler were among the first to join. Tom Barrett, Jerome

THE TOURNAMENT WAS A GENTLEMEN'S STAG PARTY, AND WHO WERE THE COPS TO SAY ANYTHING? THIS WAS, AFTER ALL, THE MASTERS.

Franklin, and influential textile tycoon Fielding Wallace were among the locals who found themselves invited into charter membership. Local politicians and businessmen attended the tournament and offered all the assistance they could. You never knew when you might be asked to join, they assumed.

Roberts also hired a security force, the Pinkertons. Known around the nation as the lawmen who chased Jesse James from Texas to Tennessee, the uniformed Pinkertons were polite and professional, and they did *exactly* what Mr. Roberts said. No monkey business went on during tournament week. The Pinkertons checked badges, patrolled the grounds, and later monitored and squelched such egregious acts as spectators' trotting from one venue to another and cheering inappropriately. As for gambling, that sin was conveniently overlooked until 1949 when, to his credit, Roberts heeded the strong urging of the USGA to discontinue golf auctions. Members were discouraged from attending public calcuttas, and private auctions held at the club were canceled.

Gambling continued with or without club approval, and it is still a part of the Masters today. Local calcutta pools have risen as high as a quarter million dollars. One gentleman from neighboring South Carolina has won so much money on the tournament that he has displayed a sign in his window proclaiming himself "the Number One Money Winner at the Masters."

In 1949, the year the USGA put out its "strong urging" against calcuttas and gambling, many of the Masters

An ever-vigilant Pinkerton security guard holds down the fort at a grandstand overlooking the fifteenth green. Spectating patrons without proper tickets beware! (© Morgan Fitz Photographers, Globe Photos, Inc. 1997)

contestants showed up in Augusta a week early, not to practice, but to play in the Devereux Milburn Pro-Am at the Palmetto Golf Club in nearby Aiken, South Carolina. The golf course, another Donald Ross design, was built in 1896 at the end of a narrow dirt road near the equestrian estates of charming little Aiken. During construction of the National, Dr. Mackenzie took the crew to Aiken and converted Palmetto's sand greens to bermuda—"a good neighbor policy," as Roberts would later say. That act of neighborliness was not what attracted Masters contestants to cross the Savannah and play Palmetto, however. The calcutta winner at the Devereux Milburn could take home as much as five thousand dollars, which equaled the entire purse at most tour events. Over the years, winners of the pro-am have included Byron Nelson, George Fazio, Herman Keiser, Henry Picard, and Ben Hogan.

Before the 1935 invitational, by then commonly (although not officially) known as the Masters, Jones conceded his initial mistake and returned the nines to the original Mackenzie routing. While many in hindsight have praised Jones's vision for this brilliant tactical move, writing that the great champion must have foreseen the drama that would certainly unfold on the back nine, Jones made the change primarily because of morning sunshine. The sun hit the greens on the now-front-nine first, thus clearing a chilly morning's frost earlier and allowing play to begin sooner.

Jones's move was instantly recognized as a stroke of genius because of one shot in the 1935 event, one he witnessed but did not hit. Jones opened with a 74, placing him well down the list of contenders, but even though he didn't garner *New York Times* front-page headlines, he still drew substantial crowds. After Thursday's opening round, *Augusta Chronicle* editor Tom Wall wrote: "As in former years when he ruled conqueringly over the golf domain without an outstanding challenger in sight, Jones yesterday found that although his putter may fail him at times he need not fear for any disappointment from a standpoint of followers. Spectators by the hundreds trekked to the first tee and remained with the match until the eighteenth green had been written into history."

Opening-round leader Henry Picard fired a 67, placing him one shot ahead of Jones's Friday playing partner, Gene

Perhaps still smiling over the double eagle at fifteen he had recorded earlier, Gene Sarazen (center) received his $1,500 winner's check from legendary sportswriter and Augusta member Grantland Rice for winning the 1935 Masters Tournament. Sarazen beat Craig Wood (right) in a playoff. (AP/Wide World Photos)

Sarazen. The tournament moved along uneventfully until Sunday's final round. With nine holes left to play on the last day, 1934 runner-up Craig Wood had a reasonably commanding lead. Having finished his round early in the afternoon, Jones strolled down the large hill at eighteen and worked his way backward to watch the action on the last few holes.

On fifteen he caught up with Sarazen and Walter Hagen. Sarazen, the man the *Augusta Chronicle* had labeled "the money favorite" for the event, had actually changed his name from Saraceni because he wanted something that rolled off the tongue and the typewriter a little easier and didn't sound like a concert violinist. No matter how his name sounded, Sarazen needed a string of birdies in the last few holes to catch the leader, Craig Wood. On fifteen, with Jones standing alongside ten other gallery members following the group, the Italian gentleman decided to go for the five-hundred-yard par-five in two, choosing a four-wood for his second shot to the well-protected green. He needed to hit it close, and he did. Gene Sarazen holed out for a double eagle two and went on to force a playoff with Wood, which Sarazen won the next day.

Jones's "triumphant return" in 1934 had gotten the 1935 tournament off on the right foot, but it could have slipped into obscurity but for its unbelievably dramatic finish. "The shot heard round the world," as it was called, set a precedent. The "so-called Masters" would be won with style and charisma and lost with equally dramatic tragedy and heartache. "Saraceni" set the standard and many others dutifully followed suit.

Then in 1937 a charming, kind, soft-spoken Texan, who would become golf's wartime ambassador, won his first Masters by two shots over Ralph Guldahl. His name was Byron Nelson, and he became known in 1937 as Lord Byron.

"After I won in '37, [O. B. Keeler] interviewed me in the upstairs locker room that the pros used during the tournament," Nelson later wrote. "Things had kind of quieted down by then and [Keeler] said, 'Byron, I saw you play the back nine and it reminded me of a piece of poetry that was written by Lord Byron when Napoleon was defeated at the battle of Waterloo.' We did the rest of the interview then and the next day his article for the Associated Press read, 'Lord Byron Wins Masters.' "

Keeler understood that most of his readers wouldn't grasp the connection between Napoleon's Waterloo and Nelson's back nine, nor were they likely to appreciate the Romantic poet Lord Byron, but Keeler knew words and he understood the impact of a good headline. Nelson's nickname stuck.

Lord Byron shot 32 on the back nine that final day (the round that inspired Keeler's historical allusion). Nelson said of the round, "That 32 did more for my career at that time than anything, because I realized my game could stand up under pressure, and I could make good decisions in difficult circumstances." It also gave the Masters a boost. Handsome, smiling, gracious, and full of magnetic charm, Nelson had fans and reporters hanging on his every word as he heaped praise on those around him in his syrupy Texas drawl. He was a winner the National could point to with pride— someone who typified the gentleman golfer Bob Jones wanted as winner of his invitational.

Of that win, Nelson has said: "I still have the medal [green jackets were not awarded yet and the winner received a medal] and when my playing career was over, I looked back and realized that was the most important victory of my career. It was the turning point, the moment when I realized I could be a tough competitor. Whenever someone asks me which was the most important win of all for me, I never hesitate. It was the 1937 Masters, the one that really gave me confidence in myself."

That confidence would carry Nelson to a second-place finish at Augusta in 1941 and on to one of the most dramatic prewar tournaments in history: the 1942 Masters, which pitted the two greatest golfers of the era head-to-head in the first of many showdowns.

Through seventy holes of the 1942 Masters, Nelson, Augusta's most popular previous winner, led by two shots over the dour, brooding Ben Hogan, a fellow Texan and Nelson's long-time golfing rival dating back to their youthful days as caddies growing up in and around Fort Worth. In the 1938 event, when Nelson had been at center stage as the defending winner, Hogan was such an unknown that nobody bid on him at the calcutta party. Perhaps feeling sorry for his fellow Texan and looking to pry Bantam Ben's pride back up to sea level, Nelson picked him up for one hundred dollars. (In this pre–Pete Rose environment, players betting on other players was perfectly acceptable.)

In 1942 Hogan and Nelson were pretournament favorites. On the seventy-first hole of the tournament, Nelson hit a poor approach shot to seventeen that landed in the green-side bunker. He hit an equally poor third shot, leaving himself twelve feet for par. He missed. Meanwhile, Hogan hit an approach shot three feet from the flag at eighteen and sank his birdie putt. The two were tied. When Nelson missed his birdie attempt at eighteen, the Masters had its second playoff, an eighteen-hole Texas shoot-out that just happened to take place in Augusta, Georgia, between two men who played the same game but who might as well have been from different planets.

Hogan rarely spoke or smiled, and when he gave interviews, he measured his words carefully. Hogan biographer Curt Sampson said of him, "He always answered questions fully and ended with a complete stop, as if weary of the ebb and flow of normal conversation." Nelson, on the other hand, could not have been more convivial. He engaged the crowds and enchanted reporters with his dry wit and approachable persona, carving a niche as the darling of the golf world.

Nelson had a nervous stomach that Sunday night, partly because of a spicy dinner and partly because of the bitter taste of that bogey on the seventy-first hole. Weak-kneed and a little shaky from sleep deprivation, Nelson took double bogey on the first hole and found himself two down after one. That would not stand. Nelson turned the front nine one up. He then pounded Hogan on the back with birdies at twelve and thirteen. At the end of the match Nelson had earned his second Masters title, and golf had its first great rivalry in a generation. The official scorekeepers for the eighteen-hole Monday showdown had been Cliff Roberts and Bob Jones, and Roberts said of the crowds that day: "Hardly a man who had played in the tournament left town. Everyone stayed over to watch the play. I don't believe any day of golf ever had more attention from golf people themselves."

Unfortunately, as great as the match was and as watched as it might have been by "golf people," the country-at-large had other things to consider. The *Augusta Chronicle*'s headlines during Masters week 1942 included, "Japs Knifing Deep into Burma Defense—Australian Picture Is Only Bright Spot for Allied Fighters." For most people around the country another man named Nelson carried far more weight than Byron. Donald Nelson, chairman of the War Production Board, had put a halt to production of all civilian durable goods for the duration, which he predicted would lead to a "sound but lean civilian economy." It led to rationing of everything from sugar to car tires.

No one was in the mood for golf. Following the lead of the USGA and other organizations, Augusta National shut down, closing after the 1942 event until the war was over. The members were charged a hundred-dollar-a-year mainte-nance fee, and Hereford steers and turkeys were turned out to feed on the fairways. Bob Jones went off to war as an air corps intelligence officer, and a Kansas farm boy and future Augusta

National member, Dwight David Eisenhower, led the European Allied forces on a quest to turn back tyranny and forever change the political makeup of the world.

The Masters and the 365-acre golf course on which it was played would sit dormant while the entire world went to war.

CHAPTER 4

IKE LIKES AUGUSTA

You know, in the early days of the Masters, it was the most enjoyable tournament to go to in the whole country from the players' point of view. The tournament was small enough, and with the smaller number of players, you got to enjoy a lot of wonderful southern hospitality. Every year, several members would host an early evening party, with country ham and all the trimmings. Everyone felt free and easy, and we all had a wonderful time. There was a black quartet that sang each year. They'd go to wherever the party was, and that was the entertainment. They were mighty good. But as the tournament grew, it got too big for folks to have parties for all the players. It wasn't done at all after the war."

—Byron Nelson
How I Played the Game

World War II changed the complexion and makeup of the world. Augusta, Georgia, was no exception. For starters, Camp Gordon became Fort Gordon and Augusta's sleepy resort and textile economy took a backseat to an exploding military presence. The Forest Hills Ricker, once a resort hotel with one of the area's best golf courses, became

57

an army hospital and military compound. The Bon Air Vanderbilt, the other great hotel in town, had, in the words of Clifford Roberts, "ceased to be a quality-type resort." With its luster gone, members of the National found accommodations at the Bon Air unacceptable. Meanwhile, the area population expanded as GIs found the small east Georgia town of Augusta on the TDY (temporary duty) list.

Out on the grounds of the National, the turkey-raising business was doing quite well, but the two hundred head of steer had grown weary of the bland taste of bermuda fairways. They moved on to more palatable fare, grazing on the pansies, azaleas, dogwoods, and even the palm tree that's hidden behind the fourth green. The place was a mess, needing its own version of the Marshall Plan if the club expected to hold a Masters, as planned, in 1946. He wasn't Marshall, but Roberts solved the club's problems with a precise, ingenious, fastidious, and financially efficient plan that was categorical in its political incorrectness. The course was whipped back into shape when Roberts conscripted forty-two German POWs housed at Fort Gordon to shovel, mow, rake, plant, and sod everything inside the club's boundaries. Working nonstop from V-J Day until April 1946, Roberts's blitzkrieg restored Augusta National for its first Masters in four years.

Cottage construction was already underway. Roberts realized that with the Forest Hills out of business and the Bon Air below acceptable standards, the club's future hinged on creating acceptable living arrangements for members accustomed to the very best. The only way to ensure that quality, since National member Walter Marshall was no longer running hotels, was to build on-site housing. Inside the National's gates, Roberts could control the comings and goings, keep tabs on all activities, and tighten his sphere of influence. On-site apartments in an area connected to the main clubhouse and a series of cottages (Bob Jones's coming first) sprang up around the course.

A total of ten cottages (nine are visible to the naked eye, or at least the memory, although official Augusta media literature puts the number at ten) would eventually be built, but those were not the first houses constructed on the National. During the initial construction, Jones and Roberts had considered setting aside a segment of the property for residential use. Grass was not on the ground before that idea was abandoned. Although one house had been constructed just off the second fairway, it was purchased by the club and razed.

In the new round of residential construction after the war, the only cabin in

ROBERTS, ON THE OTHER HAND, CHOSE AN APARTMENT ATTACHED TO THE CLUBHOUSE. STARK AND STERILE, IT WAS AS FAR AWAY FROM THE MAIN STRUCTURE AS POSSIBLE. ROBERTS'S ONLY COMMENT ABOUT HIS LIVING QUARTERS WAS THAT "IT IS THE ONLY SUITE THAT COULD HAVE A FIREPLACE."

plain view was that of the club president and permanent icon Bobby Jones. Jones had soundly rejected any notions of erecting a monument on his behalf, and he made it clear that no such structure was to be put on club grounds after his death. But his cabin, situated a shorter distance from the tenth tee than many of the putts Jones had made while winning championships, stands as monument enough. Warm and inviting, understated and conspicuous only in its lack of anything ostentatious, the Jones Cabin perfectly personifies its namesake. Patrons get the sense they can walk up, knock on the door, and be invited into a cozy living room for a couple of stiff drinks and a few rounds of engaging talk on just about anything, from politics to world travel to the silly controversies over square grooves. Jones never lived in the cabin, if permanent or even temporary residence is the definition of living, but the place is alive with his presence. Its discriminating simplicity is a monument to both the man's mortality and the legend's immortality.

Roberts, on the other hand, chose an apartment attached to the clubhouse. Stark and sterile, it was as far away from the main structure as possible. Roberts's only comment about his living quarters was that "it is the only suite that could have a fireplace." It was a "suite" purely in an academic sense, small and unremarkably furnished. Roberts would spend as much as four months at a time living out of the little apartment at the end of the row, monitoring all the activities that passed by and controlling as many events as he could, both on and off the grounds.

In the 1946 Masters the man who had finished second in the prior event, contested four years earlier, made a tremendous surge. With one hole to play, it looked as if he would finally gain the respect his game so richly deserved. Certainly, no one in the history of the game ever worked as obsessively at perfecting the unperfectable act of hitting a golf ball as did Ben Hogan, and no one in golf is credited with a greater work ethic than the little man from Fort Worth they called Hawk. Hogan never led the 1946 Masters, but neither did pretournament favorite Byron Nelson. Nelson had played a grueling barnstorming exhibition schedule during the war, and his game was suffering from fatigue. Hogan played during the war as well, but by 1946 his game was on the rise while Nelson's had peaked with his incredible run of 1945 in which he had in one stretch won eleven consecutive tournaments en route to a season's haul of eighteen victories. In the 1946 Masters Hogan's game peaked in the final round. Herman Keiser, the leader, had not relinquished his lead since the first day. On the last hole the last day, however, Hogan stood over a twelve-foot putt. If he made it, he would win his first Masters. If he missed it and two-putted, he would force a playoff with Keiser. He did neither. Hogan's hard work, determination, and steely eyed concentration abandoned him. He three-putted. With a total score of 282, Keiser could proudly say he defeated a full field of rested and highly motivated contenders to win the Masters, but the 1946 event will forever be known as the one Hogan lost, not the one Keiser won. Herman would never repeat his win. He wouldn't even finish second. Hogan would finish second two more times, and five years later he would win the first of two Masters titles.

At the 1946 event, the members watched, applauded politely, wondered out loud about Hogan's late falter, and then adjourned inside the inner sanctum where a few of them gathered in a smoke-filled room and changed the face of the nation.

On the club's grounds and off, the members of Augusta National were ardent capitalists—free marketers, who by the late 1940s had become sick of the New Deal, the Fair Deal, and any other deal that placed government in the role of facilitator over the interests of private citizens, particularly those with large sums of capital to invest. With the new cold war emerging, the members of the National became even more actively involved in national political affairs. A group of members known as "the gang" became their own postwar clipping service, posting enough articles, opinions, cartoons, and essays to fill an Internet site. One of Cliff's favorites was a Forrest Gump precursor, "Communism Is as Communism Does," printed by the *Wall Street Journal*. Other round-table tabloid clippings included "Capitalist Comeback/France to Fight Nationalization Trend" and "Millions in Marshall Plan

Fellow Texans and long-time rivals Ben Hogan and Byron Nelson buddy up for the cameras after finishing regulation play tied for the lead in the 1942 Masters Tournament. Nelson beat Hogan in the next day's eighteen-hole playoff, 69-70. (AP/Wide World Photos)

Spark Nationalized Coal." Little humor came from this group as they mailed articles back and forth on the left-wing evils threatening America.

Roberts's long-time Dean Witter Reynolds partner, Frank Willard, wrote about the looming menace in language they all understood: "In terms of purchasing power of the investors' current income from business, a dollar today is little greater than the fifty cents of the prewar era. The investor is today the forgotten man. The capitalist free-enterprise system has never been so much as scratched by the communists, but it is being bled to death by those responsible for the endless expansion of bureaucracy."

Keynesians (economists in favor of governmental intervention), not Communists, were strangling America. That was the credo they all agreed on over drinks served by Bowman Milligan on the second floor of the National's clubhouse. They, the capitalist investors, knew that rugged individualism was being eroded and replaced with the "illusion of security" offered by an ever-expanding, ever-probing, ever-taxing-and-meddling central government. They needed a champion. They needed a man they could count on to right those wrongs, restore freedom to the individual, harness government, and put things right with the world. Yes, they decided, they needed a president they could call their own.

General Eisenhower would do nicely. In 1948, after contracting to write his wartime memoirs, *Crusade in Europe,* Eisenhower was introduced by the president of Doubleday to William Robinson of the *New York Herald Tribune.* In addition to being vice president of the *Herald Tribune* and president of the Coca-Cola company, Bill Robinson was an ardent Republican and long-time member of Augusta National. Bill and his buddies, Cliff Roberts included, decided that Eisenhower was the hero they needed to champion their ideas. They brought the general down to Augusta, put him up in Bob Jones's cabin, wined him, dined him, and Bob gave him golf clubs and, more importantly, golf lessons. Cliff offered Ike (whose military pension was just over eighteen thousand dollars a year) financial advice, including making him a shareholder in Joroberts, the Bob Jones–Cliff Roberts company that internationally marketed Coca-Cola. The gang wanted Ike, and they knew those dreaded Democrats wanted him, too, so they pulled out all the stops.

Ike, however, had plenty of other things to do, including serving as president of Columbia University. He also

An avid golfer, General-turned-President Dwight D. Eisenhower found Augusta to be his ideal getaway from real-world stresses. (*Augusta Chronicle* illustration)

had friends that Roberts and company considered enemies of the state: Lyndon Johnson, John Connally, Sam Rayburn, and Sid Richardson, to name a few. Above all, Ike abhorred petty partisan politics. He considered the rivalries and rituals to be childish and counterproductive, and he didn't have time to be annoyed with them. He was not just a statesman, he was *the* statesman—the man the world looked to for global insight in the late 1940s—and he considered his vision more than bipartisan. He thought of himself in a greater context.

The highbrows at Columbia thought of him as an embarrassment. As university president, Eisenhower attempted to permeate the campus with Ike-style patriotism. He actively attended history classes (something unheard of from presidents past) and he held rallies where he insisted that academic achievements serve practical purposes. His philosophy was simple: Columbia's goal was to help America by producing well-educated Americans. The staff considered Ike and his vision simpleminded. Eisenhower didn't understand academia, nor did he particularly want to. Staff meetings full of theoretical chatter about nothing tangible or usable drove him nuts, and after a while he quit attending. He also did what he'd always done as a general: delegate. By late 1948 Ike was playing golf with the gang every Wednesday and was making as many trips to Augusta as his schedule would allow. Columbia was good to him, and despite what the faculty thought, he was good for Columbia (Ike raised more money for the university than any of his predecessors). However, he was bored and he had other things on his mind.

In the 1948 presidential campaign, members of the gang pleaded with Ike to run. Although none of the rest of the country knew it (including some embarrassed newspaper editors) the gang knew Tom Dewey was a losing candidate for the Republicans. They wanted Ike, but Ike wouldn't run. He was content being president of Columbia. After Truman's re-election, however, he began to listen to his newfound friends. Ike modified his views on the presidency, but he never embraced the general idea of politics. In a letter to a friend, Eisenhower summed up his views on the presidency and the petty politics that surrounded it:

> I do not believe that you or I or anyone else
> has the right to state, categorically, that he will
> *not* perform *any* duty that his country might
> demand of him. Certainly, I do not see how

65

anyone could obtain a conviction of duty from a deadlocked convention that should name him as a "compromise" selection. Under such circumstances I believe that instead of feeling a call to duty, a man would have to consider himself merely a political expediency or political compromise. On the other hand, if you assume the occurrence of an American miracle, [such] that has never heretofore occurred, at least since [George] Washington, you might have the spectacle of someone being named by common consent rather than by the voice and manipulations of politicians.

There *was* common consent among the gang at Augusta National, along with more manipulation than today's scrutinizing electorate would ever allow. With the addition of Pete Jones (president of Cities Service Company), the gang was complete: Cliff Roberts—behind-the-scenes player and chief financial advisor for the candidate-to-be; Bob Woodruff—chairman of Coca-Cola and maker of men like no other; George Allen—a rotund Mississippian and the only Democrat in the group, who epitomized the Washington insider; Ed Bermingham—broker; "Slats" Slater—president of Frankfort Distillers; and Bill Robinson—*New York Herald Tribune* vice president, image maker, and spin doctor. Imageman Bill—beefy, backslapping, and the perfect political operative—suggested that no one since Benjamin Franklin had had more experience dealing with Europeans than Ike. Ike took well to that notion and Bill Robinson dutifully wrote about it, thus solidifying Eisenhower as the best foreign policy candidate in nearly two hundred years.

With help from a few ancillary Augusta members such as Lewis "Bud" Maytag and Burton Peek, Ike was assured by the gang that his expenses would be "taken care of," and that, if he did decide to run, as a good God-fearing Republican, of course, his candidacy wouldn't be hampered by the disdainful encumbrance of fund-raising. The gang also provided Ike with all the introductions he needed. E. T. Weir of Weirton Steel, a man Roberts called "a rugged individualist" in a note to Eisenhower; Charles Wilson, president of General Motors; Eugene Black, head of the World Bank and chief financier for the Marshall Plan; David Crawford, president of Pullman; Sewell Avery of Montgomery Ward; Douglas Stewart of Quaker Oats; and Robert Wood of Sears Roebuck—all became golf, bridge, and dinner buddies of Ike and his "gangsters." They successfully groomed the man most noted as "the common man's general" into a sophisticated political candidate.

> WHEN THE POLITICS GOT TOO SLICK, THE GANG WOULD SIMPLY LET IKE BE IKE, AND THE COMMON-MAN CONNECTIONS THAT WERE SO INGRAINED IN THE GENERAL'S NATURE SHONE THROUGH.

It was the perfect match. When the politics got too slick, the gang would simply let Ike be Ike, and the common-man connections that were so ingrained in the general's nature shone through. When they needed a hero, they trumped out Ike the savior of the free world. When they needed a particularly sticky political point made, they wrote a speech full of eloquent Ikeisms that became a trademark of both the candidate and the president. During one speech on the subject of government intrusion, Ike said: "The clear sighted . . . are determined that we shall not lose our freedoms, either to the unbearable selfishness of vested interests, or through the blindness of those who falsely declare that only government can bring us happiness, security, and opportunity. . . . If all

Americans want is security, they can go to prison. . . . [those that died for freedom] believed in something more than trying to be sure they would not be hungry when they were sixty-seven."

Those remarks prompted a note to Bill Robinson telling him, "For God's sake get your boy to close his trap and crawl into a hole for a while. A few more speeches and he'll be up the creek without a bucket." Ike didn't like the criticisms, telling Robinson: "I am the one person in the United States who does not enjoy the privilege of free speech. If I open my mouth on any subject from poverty to flat feet, I am accused of political aspirations." Robinson and the gang spun the spin with masterful skill. For a while, they kept Ike out of the spotlight, preparing him for the time when he would make his triumphant return to public life.

In 1949 Ike suffered an attack of chronic ileitis (inflammation of the ileum, which is part of the small intestine). In the hospital for a week and in Truman's Little White House for a week after that, the general retreated for a month to the sanctuary of Augusta National. He played golf all day and bridge at night. When he got the urge to fish, he walked Cliff Roberts out to an area behind the clubhouse that would eventually become the par-three course and showed him where to build a three-acre fishing pond. Cliff saluted smartly and built Ike's Pond. The spot would remain sacrosanct until soiled by Roberts's own hand when he committed suicide there. (Today it is a hazard for a very demanding hole on the par-three course.) Ike cherished his time at the National, and Mamie, who abhorred the thought of her husband being president, found comfort in the gentility of the town. There would be many other trips to the National but none as special as that monthlong vacation. When the Eisenhowers returned to Augusta National, they were the first family-elect, and nothing in their lives would ever be the same again.

Dwight Eisenhower shows presidential form as he tees off at Augusta.
(© Globe Photos, Inc. 1997)

Even with all the politicking and deal making behind the clubhouse doors at Augusta, Eisenhower certainly was attracted to the National by more than just his associations with the likes of Roberts and Jones. He might not have been the best golfer among American presidents—his successor, Jack Kennedy, was capable of picking up the sticks after a six-month layoff and threatening 80—but no president was more devoted to, beguiled by, and associated with the game than Eisenhower.

Ike had started playing golf in the 1930s while stationed in the Philippines, but it wasn't until after the Second World War that he was able to find the time to make golf truly a relaxing and frequent endeavor. In between NATO meetings in postwar Paris, he would often swing a club while dictating in his conveniently high-ceilinged office. By the time he joined Augusta, Eisenhower was regularly shooting in the high 80s and low 90s, although he still had aspirations of doing better. Toward that end Ike took lessons from Augusta pro Ed Dudley, who bestowed on the general-turned-president the compliment of comparing his swing to that of another famous figure, Bing Crosby. Indeed, Ike once shot a very creditable 84 at Augusta, tree or no tree at seventeen.

Although golf can be a strenuous activity for those weak of heart and limb, an aging Eisenhower found himself consistently rejuvenated by eighteen-hole jaunts. Friends claimed that Ike sometimes arrived exhausted at the first tee, but would end up relaxed and fresh after playing a secluded round with one or two companions.

"He's intent about the game," Dudley said in a 1953 *Golf Digest* piece comparing golfing chief executives. One of the things Dudley did for Ike was cure, or at least tame, a presidential slice. Dudley also said: "He takes every shot seriously. Let him blow one and he'll get pretty sore at himself. That's because he's such a competitor. But he has wonderful self-control. No cursing. No [take note, Bobby Jones] club-throwing."

While Cliff and the gang were busy selecting a presidential candidate, a handsome, quirky West Virginian who wore a fedora and spoke with an Appalachian twang won his first Masters. Sam Snead shot a 282 total in 1949 to capture the first of his three green coats. Snead had led Ben Hogan by three shots at the halfway point of the tournament, after which he was escorted into the presence of blue-blood royalty, Great Britain's Duke of Windsor, the first member of the English royal family to visit this bastion of golfing royalty.

The *Augusta Chronicle* ran a front-page photo showing the duke, nattily attired in gray pin-striped suit and a soft-collared white shirt adorned with a black knitted tie, engaged in casual clubhouse banter with Snead. If he didn't already feel out of his element trying to hobnob among the impeccably businesslike green coats of Augusta, the Slammer now found himself reaching for new heights in the area of social graces.

Perhaps someone more socially refined would have felt at home with the duke, someone like Ben Hogan. The problem was, Hogan hadn't earned a spot in that chair. He was still winless at Augusta, although that soon was to change. In 1951, five years after losing the Masters everyone had assumed he would win, Ben Hogan fired a four-round total of 280 to win the Masters by two shots over Skee Riegel, with no one else closer than six shots of Hogan. His victory was amplified by the fact that the tournament had come into its own as much more than a small invitational for Bob's friends. CBS Radio had broadcast the event starting with the first

Sam Snead had plenty to celebrate in 1952, winning the second of his three Masters Tournament titles. Here he performs a two-step shuffle after making a par-saving putt at Augusta's sixth hole. (AP/Wide World Photos)

tournament in 1934, but the network's effort had become halfhearted and it showed. Roberts replaced CBS in 1949 with a more vibrant NBC radio broadcast that helped the tournament's image. Somewhere in that move would emerge years later a subtle admonition to CBS that Roberts was *the* man to be listened to when it came to shaping a network's broadcast of the Masters. The inferred parallel between CBS Radio's fate and what could likewise happen on the television front kept CBS-TV in check, beginning in the mid-1950s and lasting well into the 1990s.

Other changes in 1951 included raising the prize money and the ticket prices. The first went over very well with the players. The second went over very poorly with the fans. It violated southern sensibilities to pay ten dollars for a ticket to a sporting event, even if it was Bobby Jones's Masters. To top it off, Jones had stopped playing. He had not been competitive in years, and after the war he was even less so. Also, he had a nagging pain in his neck, which in 1950 had been diagnosed as caused by a damaged disk, requiring surgery. Everyone wished him well before his operation, but everyone also knew that regardless Jones's playing days were over. The era of the amateur-gentleman champion had passed.

Taking Jones's place at the top of the golf world was a triumvirate of Nelson, whose eleven consecutive victories in 1945 had set an untouchable record regardless of the strength of the fields; Snead, who had come into his own in the late 1940s; and the ever-frosty, ball-beating Hogan, who, with his first Masters win, set himself on a course for stardom. By the end of his career, Hogan had won more tournaments than Jones, and unlike Jones or any other golfer past or present, Hollywood made a movie about his life. Hogan's frosty persona never melted, even after a near-fatal car crash in 1949 that would have changed almost any man's outlook on life.

With the tournament coming into its own and the club operating better than ever, Cliff Roberts and the gang turned their attention to more pressing matters. In 1950 General Eisenhower swallowed his disdain for the Truman administration and accepted a position as NATO commander. His job was to solidify and organize the loosely structured organization by bringing multinational forces under "umbrella" command. North Korea had crossed the thirty-eighth parallel and Americans were in harm's way. Eisenhower, stationed in Paris, was in his element. The enemy was real, definable, aggressive, and nasty in the same way the Nazis had been. By taking NATO from a fledgling alliance to the most powerful force in the free world, Eisenhower displayed all the mastery that had made him a worldwide hero. Right by Ike's side—coaching, counseling, spinning, and ever planning—were his trusty gangsters from Augusta National. During the NATO days Cliff Roberts flew to Paris and met with Ike at NATO headquarters. There Eisenhower told Roberts that he was "more devoted to the success of the NATO mission than intrigued by the idea of being president." Roberts knew that NATO's success was more than a springboard; it was a launching pad to the White House.

While Hogan was winning the 1951 Masters, Cliff Roberts and Bill Robinson were forming Citizens for Eisenhower, a highly organized, well-financed, and closely managed campaign organization that, because of its lack of any professional politicians, looked like a grassroots committee. The grassroots organizers just as easily could have opened campaign headquarters in the Augusta National golf shop. They were all members, all wealthy Republicans, and all committed to doing whatever it took to get their candidate elected to the presidency.

On the first Wednesday of November 1952, Eisenhower returned to the National as a welcome member and as president-elect of the United Sates. Cliff Roberts, his financial advisor and close friend (he had run the books for his campaign and continued to manage his personal finances) had set up the trip well before the election. Both Roberts and Ike had agreed, no matter what the outcome on election day, that the general and Mamie would take some time off in Augusta. During that week he played golf with Byron Nelson and, as he was quick to point out at the dinner afterward, the new resident-elect "out-drove [Nelson] twice." Nelson recalled: [Eisenhower] "would usually ride in the cart, and I would drive. But he was like a cricket; he'd jump out of the cart before it stopped, every time. It made me nervous, so I finally said, 'Mr. President, I wish you'd wait till I stop the cart before you get out, because it would look terrible in the newspapers if it said "Byron Nelson Breaks President's Leg".' "

Although he'd been there many times before, when Ike arrived in Augusta after the election, the whole town turned out. Washington Road was lined with photographers, reporters, well-wishers, and genuinely interested citizens who wanted a glimpse of their new leader. There were parades, parties, and too many speeches.

Many believe that the 1953 Masters in which Ben Hogan won the first leg in an incomparable "triple crown" was the year the Augusta invitational became a major. Others say the official "major" title came in 1954 when Snead beat Hogan in a playoff that Jones rated as "the greatest Masters ever." Either event is arguably accurate, but the event that moved the Masters into the arena of a major championship had nothing to do with the tournament at all. It was when president-elect and Augusta member Dwight D. Eisenhower chose to vacation in Augusta after being elected. Common folk had voted for Ike, people who knew nothing about golf and even less about "the majors." Those same people read newspapers and listened to radios, and a few of them tuned in on a new high-tech medium called television. When they did, they saw their president and those who had worked to get him elected all playing golf at a club in Georgia, the same club that hosted an invitational tournament every spring. It wouldn't be officially deemed so for another couple of years, but the day President Ike pulled off Washington Road and drove down Magnolia Lane, the Masters had become a major in the public's eyes.

Having two of the best tournaments ever in 1953 and 1954 helped the new major solidify its position. In 1953, after having suffered and then recovered from his 1949 car crash so debilitating that he was told he would never walk again, Hogan found himself the odds-on favorite at Augusta. He got off to a great start. He showed up in town a week early, crossed the river over to Aiken, and defended his title as past winner of the Devereux Milburn Pro-Am at Palmetto with his partner R. M. Goodyear. He didn't win in Aiken, but he did quite well in the calcutta. With his wallet a little heavier and his game a lot sharper, Hogan fired a record-setting 274, running away from the field and winning his second green jacket by five shots over his nearest challenger. The drama of Hogan's victory was magnified by the seemingly insurmountable odds he had overcome to even be there.

A man the experts had said would never walk again had beaten his crippling injuries and then beaten the greatest players in the world at Augusta—twice. The second Masters victory became even more important when Hogan also captured the 1953 U.S. and British Opens. He was golf's new hero, a man who "hit balls till his hands bled." He was also one of the grumpiest guys on tour. Hogan's victory in the

1953 Masters solidified his place in golf history and propelled him on to achievements that are unmatched in the modern era. However, all would agree with Herbert Warren Wind, the man who wrote so eloquently of Jones and also helped Hogan pen his *Five Lessons, The Fundamentals of Golf*: "[Hogan] was a very odd man."

Also in 1953 Augusta National was fenced in, ostensibly at the request of the Secret Service as protection for the president. A presidential office was added to the clubhouse and a new cabin was constructed near the tenth tee: the Eisenhower Cabin. It was financed by fifty members, who were required by Roberts to sign a nondisclosure agreement prohibiting them from divulging how much they "contributed" to the project. Ike and Mamie loved their new cabin, and they spent a great deal of time there both during and after their eight years in the White House. After all, what's not to like about the homey quarters? The upstairs to the "cabin" consists of two bedrooms on either side of an airy living room complete with fireplace, bridge table, and generously cushioned furniture. An art enthusiast, Ike also had a small studio, where the walls are filled with bookshelves, some of his paintings, and framed photos of his former residences, including his living quarters at Fort Sam Houston, Texas; Fort Benning, Georgia; and Camp Gaillard in Panama. Downstairs is another large living room with, again, a fireplace and bridge table, as well as two more bedrooms, a dining room, and a small kitchen.

Ike was not allowed to attend the Masters Tournament while he was president: It was deemed too much of a distraction. He missed some great golf drama, including the 1954 Masters when Hogan again came roaring back threatening to win for the third time in four years. However, that tournament had a new twist. Even though the Masters was openly considered a major by 1953, a large number of amateurs still received invitations, thus diluting the strength of the

The Eisenhower Cabin is more like a small mansion, but this one, unlike any other residence large or small, offers a great view of Augusta's tenth tee.

field. But that was one of the charms of the Masters and a testament to the greatness Jones had achieved as an amateur. One of the 1954 amateurs, a kid from Morgantown, North Carolina, with a funky swing, thick glasses, and a photogenic smile found himself leading the tournament at the halfway mark. Billy Joe Patton instantly became the darling of the sports media, an amateur who was beating the best in the world in the first major of the season. Patton had also gotten his week off to a great start by winning the pretournament long-drive contest, booming a tee shot some 338 yards. (The par-three course was not built until 1958, so this driving contest, coupled with a clinic for spectators, provided the entertainment on Wednesday afternoons.) After Friday's round, Cary Middlecoff said of Patton, "If this guy wins the Masters it will set golf back fifty years," apparently referring to

Patton's homegrown, backyard swing and "lowly" status as an amateur in an age when professionals had clearly taken over golf's lead.

Patton was certainly ready to turn back that clock. The National reared its head on Saturday, however, and the amateur shot a 75 to trail by five at the start of Sunday's round. Hogan led Snead by three, and everyone assumed the North Carolina amateur was out of the hunt. An amateur hadn't won a major since the war, and most pundits presumed it would never happen again. Golf had become too competitive, the field of professionals too deep, for any unseasoned amateur to actually have a chance at winning.

Determined to prove everyone wrong, Patton made his move on Sunday at the sixth hole. Over the years the Masters field has averaged 3.07 shots on the 180-yard par-three sixth, making it the fifth-hardest hole on the course. Prior to the 1954 event it had never been aced in competition. That streak was broken twice: first, earlier in the week, when Leland Gibson made a one; and again on Sunday, when five-shot-back-and-out-of-contention Billy Joe Patton hit a shot that never wavered until it landed softly on the lower tier of the green and trickled into the cup for a one.

The roar echoed back to Hogan as he walked down the third fairway. The defending winner knew what had happened, just as he would know what happened when Patton birdied eight and nine. One thing about the crowds at Augusta, as polite and proper as they are, is that the discriminating listener can follow the drama without ever looking at the leader boards. Hogan knew he was tied with Patton going to the back nine.

The turns of fate that have become commonplace and almost expected on the last nine holes at Augusta have their genesis in events such as Sarazen's double eagle, Hogan's three-putt in 1949, and the bizarre sequence of events in the final round of the 1954 Masters. Snead, playing well ahead of

North Carolina amateur Billy Joe Patton blasts out of a bunker at the first hole in the final round of the 1954 Masters Tournament. Patton later aced the sixth hole to get back into serious contention, only to falter on the back nine and finish one shot out of the lead. (AP/Wide World Photos)

both Hogan and Patton, cruised home with an even-par 72 to finish with a 289. Meanwhile, Patton played the two back-nine par-fives in thirteen shots, and Hogan pulled his second shot into the water on the eleventh. When the smoke cleared, Hogan had scraped it around to shoot 75 while Patton finished with a 71, one shot back of the two leaders—Snead, who had played well to the finish, and Hogan, who had played one of his worst nines of the year.

Patton received thunderous applause as he walked up the hill to the eighteenth green that Sunday afternoon, and his courageous showing put the tournament on the front pages of newspapers around the country. The following day Snead would beat Hogan in an eighteen-hole playoff. Today, at age eighty-four, Snead says of that Monday playoff in 1954: "I still remember all the pin placements and how many putts Hogan had on each hole when I beat him in the playoff . . . I'm proud of the fact that when Jones was asked what tournament was the greatest of all the Masters he said the Snead-Hogan playoff in '54. I could always raise my game another notch or two for Hogan."

Inspired by the storybook drama of the 1954 event, CBS came back on the Augusta scene in 1956, this time taking the Masters and Augusta National into the new medium of television. As was the case with most live television events at that time, nothing went as planned. A hearty forty-two amateurs teed off in the first major tournament of the year, once again setting a precedent for major tournament competition. Everyone hoped to see another amateur exhibition like that of Billy Joe Patton, and they were not disappointed. Ken Venturi, a young amateur and protégé of the legendary Byron Nelson, led the tournament all the way until Sunday's final

THE ARRIVAL OF TELEVISION AT THE 1956 MASTERS WAS A PRECURSOR OF DRAMATIC CHANGE FOR THE 1957 MASTERS: A THIRTY-SIX-HOLE CUT TO MAKE COVERAGE OF THE WEEKEND'S FINAL TWO ROUNDS MORE MANAGEABLE.

round. CBS viewers got to watch the formidable Venturi shoot 80 the last day, while eventual winner Jack Burke overcame a nine-shot deficit to win the 1956 Masters. Viewers got to see Burke hit all of two shots the last day. What goes around comes around and forty years later, in 1996, Venturi was in his familiar perch in the CBS booth at Augusta's eighteenth calling the shots while Greg Norman—much as Venturi himself had done in 1956—wilted on Sunday when Nick Faldo came from six shots back to overcome the Shark. If anyone ever could empathize with Norman's cruel fate, it was Venturi.

The arrival of television at the 1956 Masters was a precursor of dramatic change for the 1957 Masters: a thirty-six-hole cut to make coverage of the weekend's final two rounds more manageable. Only the low forty and ties would play on Masters weekend. The likes of Hogan, Middlecoff, and inaugural Masters winner Horton Smith didn't make it to the weekend. The tournament committee (that is, Cliff Roberts as presiding autocrat) said of the new policy: "We are as anxious as ever to have the older champions come to the party. We know that many players feel obligated to play out the full seventy-two holes even though they may not be scoring well. The new regulation automatically takes care of this particular problem. It is designed to shrink the field down to a size that could readily play two rounds, if need be, in one day and gives every contestant an afternoon pairing on the final two days."

No 7:30 tee times, but no Hogan, either.

Twelve months later a charismatic golfer destined to fill the vacancy being created by Hogan's career fade burst onto the scene at Augusta. Studio executives in Hollywood could not have created a more perfect character for televised golf than the young, chiseled faced darling of Latrobe, Pennsylvania, the guy with a blacksmith's arms and an inviting smile. Arnold Palmer made golf history at Augusta by attacking the golf course. His unorthodox swing made him look more like a fighter reeling off a string of jabs than a professional golfer. He attacked golf shots and pinned golf courses to the mat, all while smiling and hitching his trousers like a character in a John Wayne Western. Palmer's first trip to Augusta had actually been in 1955 when he was a rookie pro and the reigning U.S. Amateur champion. That year he finished tied for tenth. In 1956 he shot a final-round 79 to finish tied for eighteenth. Then in 1957 he was one of those "virtual unknowns" who made the cut instead of Hogan and Middlecoff. Palmer finished tied for sixth that year. In 1958 he won his first Masters, although not in the style that would become his trademark. He bogeyed two of the last three holes the final day and finished with an uninspiring 73. Still, even while backing into victory lane, he had obvious flair, style, and charisma like no other in professional golf at the time—and a cherished green jacket, to boot. Arnold Palmer had movie star charm in a television world, and golf fans around the country had a new hero they could now watch from their living rooms.

Palmer's father was a greenskeeper at Latrobe Country Club. Arnie, being the son of the hired help, had to sneak out and play when nobody was looking. When he and his bride, Winnie, arrived in Augusta in 1955, they were so broke they had to drag a pull-behind camper to a nearby RV park and pay eleven dollars to have power, water, and a place to sleep the week of the Masters. He made $696 for finishing tenth.

Palmer's victory at the 1958 Masters was shrouded in confusion. On the par-three twelfth, the center pew in Amen Corner, his tee shot plugged left of the bunker. It was a simple thing. The embedded-ball rule was in effect. Arnie was entitled to a free drop.

"We'd been playing that rule for the last three days," Hogan would later say. "It was announced on the first tee every day before play began."

A local rules official disagreed. He told Palmer he was not entitled to the drop. So, in accordance with the rules, Palmer played two balls—one assuming a free drop, and one not. The free-drop score was a three, and the embedded ball score was a five. It took officials three holes and a great deal more confusion than necessary to finally inform Palmer that he was, in fact, entitled to the drop and the three would stand. By that time a five had already been posted on leader boards around the course, so a collective "Huh?" went up when Palmer's score was suddenly changed to a three. Most people left the course that day bewildered, and some writers even called Arnie "the rule book champion."

A plaque honoring Arnold Palmer adorns the National's sixteenth tee, which isn't a particularly significant hole in Palmer history, but the man made such an impact on the tournament that the plaque could have been placed anywhere. Former Augusta National chairman Hord Hardin said of Palmer: "Arnold's the most special guy in golf. He had charisma about him. Golf was a country club game, but with Arnie hitching his pants and with those light-heavyweight shoulders and his warm personality, things changed completely. I can't think of anyone who's meant as much to golf as we know it today." Current chairman Jack Stephens says of Palmer: "Prior to Arnold, the Masters didn't sell as many tickets as it would have liked. After he arrived, the tournament had to limit the number of tickets it sold. Television even began to pay us for the rights. The ratings for his first victory here were up 300 percent over the year before. From the day he first set foot on the grounds, the tournament has never been the same."

After the 1958 victory, a reporter phoned Latrobe to get a quote from Arnie's father and mentor, Deacon Palmer. The elder Palmer became so choked up he could not speak. His only comment about his son's win in Augusta was, "Please accept my apologies. I'll call Arnold's mother and she'll answer your questions."

On Sunday, April 10, 1960, the South African Parliament went into an emergency session after Prime Minister Hendrik Verwoerd was shot in the head by a lone gunman; U.S. President and Augusta National member Dwight Eisenhower condemned the government of Cuba for "failing to keep its promises"; Senator John F. Kennedy took a commanding lead over Hubert Humphrey in the Democratic primaries; and down in Georgia, history was being made again by the man who brought legions of followers and new fans into the game of golf.

Arnold Palmer won his second Masters in spectacular fashion. He was one down with three to play. On the sixteenth he hit a putt from the fringe so hard that his playing partner, Billy Casper, said, "If you had missed the pin you would have had a heck of a [second] putt from the sand trap."

Arnold Palmer steps out from under an umbrella at Augusta's second hole, declares the rain over, and prepares to continue on his way to the 1962 Masters Tournament title. Two strokes back beginning this second round, Palmer later charged into the lead with a string of back-nine birdies before eventually beating Dow Finsterwald and Gary Player in a playoff. (AP/Wide World Photos)

Palmer's ball rapped the pin and rebounded a few inches from the hole. He made par, leaving him one down with two to play. He needed a birdie on either seventeen or eighteen to tie Venturi.

At seventeen Palmer made a twenty-seven-foot putt for birdie. The crowd went wild. Then on eighteen, his cotton mouth dry from the tension and the crowds deathly silent, Palmer almost holed his second shot on the fly. The ball spun back, leaving him an uphill five-foot putt for victory. He rapped it with all the fortitude of a prize fighter, and it fell in. The crowds went berserk. Venturi, watching the action on television, stood up and said, "Was that real? I thought I was looking at a Vitalis ad."

At age thirty Arnold Palmer was the crowned king of American golf, and Augusta National was his unmitigated courtyard. He finished tied for second behind winner Gary Player in 1961, blowing a victory by taking double-bogey six on the last hole. Then in 1962 he finished with a weak final round of 75 to back into a playoff with Player and Dow Finsterwald. Palmer manhandled both men in Monday's eighteen-hole playoff, winning by three shots over Player and nine over Finsterwald. Palmer finished ninth in 1963 when the tournament was won by a fat kid with a crew cut named Jack Nicklaus, but he was back in full force in 1964. Palmer became the first man to win four Masters tournaments in 1964 when he beat the favorite, Nicklaus, by six shots in a runaway victory. The *New York Times* called Palmer "golf's greatest showpiece" and a fifty-two-year-old Hogan said of the man from Latrobe, "You have to consider Arnold Palmer one of the great players. I don't know how great. You can't really compare one era with another, but I do feel that if a man is a winner in one era he could have been a winner in any era."

Arnold Palmer was a timeless winner in an era when golf needed a fearless champion. By the 1960s the country

In this get-together of legendary golf rivals, "Fat Jack" Nicklaus gets fitted for a green jacket by Arnold Palmer after winning the 1963 Masters Tournament. Palmer, the 1962 Masters winner, bounced back to win again in 1964, although Nicklaus then won in 1965 and 1966. (AP/Wide World Photos)

was at war in a little place called Vietnam, a president had been assassinated, the PGA Tour had a policy in place that restricted tournament participation to Caucasians only, and one year after the passage of the Civil Rights Act, Ike and Mamie Eisenhower celebrated their fiftieth wedding anniversary at Augusta National, a club where black servants served white members and the president's favorite caddie was named Cemetery.

Many changes lay ahead.

CHAPTER 5

ROBERTS'S RULES

THE SECOND YEAR I PLAYED THERE, I CAME IN EARLY TO PLAY SOME PRACTICE ROUNDS AND WAS STAYING AT THE CLUB. ON THE SATURDAY AFTERNOON DURING THE WEEK BEFORE THE TOURNAMENT, I GOT A CALL FROM MR. ROBERTS'S SECRETARY ASKING ME IF I WOULD LIKE TO JOIN MRS. EISENHOWER, MR. NICKLAUS, AND MR. ROBERTS FOR DINNER. I SAID, "I'M SORRY, I CAN'T GO BECAUSE I'VE ALREADY GOT PLANS." AFTER I PUT THE PHONE DOWN, IT RANG AGAIN TWO MINUTES LATER. THIS TIME IT WAS MR. ROBERTS SAYING, "I'LL MEET YOU IN THE TROPHY ROOM AT 7:00 P.M. SHARP." I GUESS I WAS JUST A LITTLE NAIVE.

—STEVE MELNYK

The skies were partly cloudy that night. The moon was hidden by cloud cover, but an eerie glow illuminated the quiet grounds. Forecasts called for high temperatures in the mid-eighties with thundershowers moving in by the afternoon. At 2:20 A.M. the air was thick and still, and the temperature hovered at around sixty-five degrees. For the late-shift security guard at Augusta National, the routine had been just that: routine.

At 2:27 the guard noticed something a little out of the ordinary. Mr. Cliff, as they all called him, was out of his suite. The guard greeted him but said very little. You said little to Mr. Cliff and he said little in return. That was the way things

THE OLD MAN HAD RECENTLY SUFFERED A STROKE, SO THE NIGHT WATCHMAN WAS CAREFUL TO PAY PARTICULARLY CLOSE ATTENTION TO HOW AND WHERE ROBERTS MOVED.

worked. One cross word and the eighty-four-year-old's iron fist would come pounding down. Former employees and more than a few former members could attest to the severity of Roberts's wrath, and people did whatever was necessary to steer clear of any run-ins with Mr. Cliff. The guard also noticed that Clifford Roberts wore a trench coat and trousers over his pajamas. The old man had recently suffered a stroke, so the night watchman was careful to pay particularly close attention to how and where Roberts moved. Everything seemed in order: odd, but in order. The guard went back to his post and Roberts disappeared.

On September 29, 1977, had he been in his suite to eat his crumpets, sip his tea, and read his normal battery of newspapers, Roberts probably would have frowned at news of President Jimmy Carter's energy plan and the warm reviews it was getting on the Hill. He would most certainly have scowled at news that the president himself had met with the Syrian foreign minister. No president of his would have met with that kind of person, and "his" president wouldn't have considered imposing an energy bill or any other far-reaching regulatory constraint on private business. Had he been there, Roberts also would have frowned at the *Wall Street Journal*'s assessment that the "Decline in the Market May Persist." On a lighter note, Roberts surely would have been intrigued by the hype surrounding that night's Muhammad Ali—"Acorn" Earnie Shavers fight. Mr. Cliff was a big fight fan dating back to the days when he and a group of Augusta members sponsored Beau Jack, one of the club's black shoe-shine boys who went off to prize fight in New York and made quite a name for himself. But those were the good ole days, the days when Bob was still alive, and Ike, and Bud, and all the others.

His Yankees had clinched the division earlier that Wednesday night. Reggie Jackson had hit a grand slam to start what turned into a 10-0 rout of the Indians. Roberts had been doing other things than watching baseball, however. There were last-minute items to prepare, a note to write, some tidying up to do. He took the gun out after 2:00, and just before 2:27, he put on a trench coat and headed out the door for a middle-of-the-night stroll.

The par-three course is situated just east of the club-house, in an area that was a parking lot until 1958 when George Cobb designed the nine par-threes. Before Cobb arrived on the scene and when the area was wooded and isolated, Ike suggested a fishing pond be added. Cliff could now take pride in having obliged his longtime friend. They had spent many hours together, Cliff and Ike, talking politics and world affairs, playing golf and bridge, and painting. Ike loved painting.

The walk down the hill to the pond was relatively short, although after Cliff's stroke, walks of any distance were more arduous than before. Then, of course, there was the cancer. Fortunately, he hadn't yet suffered its debilitating effects other than some memory lapses and a cumulative weariness brought on by a lack of sleep, which reportedly was caused by his unwillingness to take his medication. Roberts's health eventually deteriorated to the point where he was a virtual prisoner in his clubhouse apartment, the walk to his office being too much for him to bear in his weakened condition.

According to a *Golf Digest* piece by Ross Goodner:

> On what was to be his last day, he had the club barber, Johnny Johnson, come to his apartment and give him a haircut. This was late

afternoon and they talked for an hour, until about 6:00 P.M. Then he called his wife [Betty] who was in Beverly Hills, and asked her to come to Augusta. She said she couldn't come immediately because she needed a day to make arrangements for closing the house.

Roberts next called Bowman Milligan, then semiretired after forty years as the club's steward. Some time during the evening he called in a Pinkerton guard, who was operating the switchboard. Roberts produced a gun and asked the man the proper way to shoot it, saying he had heard noises outside his apartment.

It was dark, even though a floodlight shone on the path leading toward the pond. The night sounds were still as he made his way to the lower edge of the dam, wearing galoshes and no shoes, and without benefit of a cane, down the hill toward the pond. This area was safe, away from the main course where spectators would have undoubtedly discovered the spot and created some kind of macabre landmark. This was also more helpful to the staff. Emergency vehicles could access the pond with ease, investigators wouldn't disturb any of the high-traffic areas around the clubhouse or the golf course, and it would be an easy spot to clean up. He knew every blade of grass, every knoll, every trickle of water on that 365 acres, and, in every respect, this was the perfect place.

The Smith and Wesson .38 was the right choice as well: powerful enough to accomplish the task, but not overly so. He didn't want any gruesome disfiguration, but he also wanted to succeed. He always wanted to succeed. Roberts made it to the water's edge at a little before 3:00 on

Autocratic Masters Tournament chairman Clifford Roberts truly ran the show at Augusta, here getting legendary golfer Gene Sarazen to tend the pin for him while he practices his putting during Masters Tournament week of 1955. This, obviously, was happier times for Roberts. (AP/Wide World Photos)

Thursday morning. He took out the pistol, put it to his head, and in the methodical, mercurial, and cold-natured way he lived his life, he ended it with one final, resounding retort.

Roberts's body tumbled into a creek bed and was not found until 8:00 A.M. Otis Martin, the chief investigator for the Richmond County Sheriff's Department, said, "He died sometime between 2:30 and 8:00," and Dr. James Mitchener, Richmond County coroner, said that there was "no reason to believe this was anything but a self-inflicted wound,"

93

although for years, caddies at the National perpetuated the notion that something more sinister had occurred. Nevertheless, the shroud of secrecy surrounding Roberts fueled speculation of all kinds. He was a Wall Street investment banker and president of Reynolds and Company, which later became Dean Witter Reynolds. He was the chief financial advisor and campaign finance chairman for the only president to serve two full terms between FDR and Reagan, and yet, when he died, the *New York Times* had to call the *Augusta Chronicle* to get information for his obituary. He was a ghost, a shadowy unknown. Everyone saw him during Masters week: as the official voice of the Augusta National at all press conferences and in all matters relating to the club policy. But for fifty weeks a year, the steely eyed Roberts went about his business in intentional obscurity. His book, *The Story of the Augusta National Golf Club,* written just one year before his death, was intended to be his memoir and tribute to the club, to Bob Jones, and to President Eisenhower, whose every visit was chronicled. The only insightful news Roberts offered in the book was that he felt "enriched by the association with the Augusta National members," and that his eightieth birthday party, thrown at the club, provided "several highly pleasing surprises." Author Ken Bowden, who helped Roberts with the project, noted that after he completed the manuscript, he was summoned back to Augusta for some additional work on the book. When he arrived, he found that Roberts had called him back to change six punctuation marks.

Inveiglement and obfuscation in all things personal and an obsessive, unyielding control of all things relating to his club—those were the trademarks Roberts became noted for in life and were the reputation he left behind in death. Even the statement put out by the club the day Roberts's body was found reflected the cold and dispassionate legacy he left behind: "It is with great regret that the Augusta National Golf Club announces that its chairman, Clifford Roberts, died during the night. Death was caused by a self-inflicted wound. Mr. Roberts had been in ill health for several months. Funeral services will be private. No flowers are requested." No mention of Cliff's wife, Betty, his third spouse following two divorces, was offered by the men in the green coats.

The *Augusta Chronicle* ran front-page headlines the next day: "Roberts Found Dead," with heaping accolades, such as "Masters Uniqueness Stands as Tribute to Roberts's Work." The PGA Tour commissioner Deane Beman said: "The PGA Tour has lost a great friend, but more than that, the game of golf has lost a great champion." On a more genuine note, Jack Nicklaus said: "I've lost a great friend in the passing of Cliff Roberts. He was most helpful to me in my golf career and our friendship goes back many years to my amateur days." While they were printing those words, the joke (as sick as it was) around the *Chronicle* was that Roberts the autocrat had "controlled everything down to the last shot."

He was loved and hated, respected and scorned, trusted in ways only a handful of people can imagine, yet vulnerable enough to take his own life, leaving only a note of apology to his wife. Former USGA official Frank Hannigan called Roberts "a very sick old man." Nicklaus said: "I loved Cliff Roberts. He was one of my favorites . . . a great guy." There is one point, however, on which everyone agrees: From the time it opened until the time of his death, Augusta National operated under Roberts's rules of order.

HE WAS LOVED AND HATED, RESPECTED AND SCORNED, TRUSTED IN WAYS ONLY A HANDFUL OF PEOPLE CAN IMAGINE, YET VULNERABLE ENOUGH TO TAKE HIS OWN LIFE, LEAVING ONLY A NOTE OF APOLOGY TO HIS WIFE.

Sam Snead says, "Roberts was a real stickler. One time Arnold Palmer went down there with his dad to play golf. Roberts told Palmer that his dad couldn't play unless he was with a member. There was another time when a senator came there with someone to play and they just went out and played. Someone went and told Roberts that this senator was playing without a member. Roberts stayed around until the senator had finished his round, then went up to him and said, 'Mr. Senator, it's in our bylaws that you have to play with a mem-' ber here. Well, now that you've played, don't bother coming back.' He's got guts. He wouldn't let any riffraff in there."

Before the 1949 Masters, Roberts set a new rule that during practice rounds players could hit only one ball. Many players had become accustomed to hitting several balls from different locations to gauge distances and other variables. This made the practice rounds interminably slow. Amateur Frank Stranahan, who was wise enough to pick the chairman of Champion Spark Plugs as a father and who actually tied for second in the Masters in 1948, misunderstood the rule. He thought that if you were playing by yourself and, therefore, not holding anybody up, there was no harm in hitting a couple of extra shots here and there. He was wrong. Stranahan wasn't even allowed to finish his round. Roberts had him removed from the course in the middle of his back nine, his invitation rescinded. Stranahan eventually gave up golf for bodybuilding.

Roberts's rules guided the club through the depths of a depression, a world war, forty golf tournaments, hundreds of innovations that have been copied by clubs and tournaments around the world, innumerable civil rights protests, and one twelve-year-old kid getting shot while fishing in Rae's Creek. He negotiated the television deals, all twenty-one of them while he was alive, and he wrote personal notes of criticism every year to CBS executives. With pen or pencil in hand, Roberts was as meticulous with the written word as he was with every other facet of his life. One year as a Christmas gift, he sent the media a Masters-green address book with the National's logo on the front. While the address book was unexpected and a very classy touch, Roberts also sent a typewritten note that not only destroyed any goodwill he'd hoped to generate, it fueled more talk than the gift itself. The note read: "You will find that about 20 percent of your friends will annually change their address or phone number and then erasing becomes necessary; therefore, entries should not be made except with a pencil. Always use sharply pointed hard-lead pencils (No. 3), as soft-lead pencils will smear. You will need to list quite a bit of data in limited spaces, so I advise you to print rather than write. To me, the handiest place to carry an address book is in my left breast coat pocket." CBS's Frank Chirkinian vividly remembers the note and laughs heartily when he says, "I used a number-two pencil just to spite him."

There were other obsessions that bordered on neurotic. Roberts wore a variation of the same blue suit every day. His only accouterment was a red tie. He had twenty-four, all of them identical. He consumed tea and crumpets every morning and fresh peaches every afternoon, but he rarely had to place a menu order for anything. The staff knew what Mr. Roberts wanted, and they would magically appear before he had to ask. His needs were modest, but the club's menu was altered to fit his requirements. You needn't ask for french fries; Roberts considered them unhealthy and they were not included on the menu.

Nothing moved at the National without Roberts's knowledge and approval. Chirkinian recalls: "My most prominent memory of Clifford Roberts is the time I got my ass chewed out after one of my technicians drove a golf cart over Eisenhower's front lawn, although it was actually part of the golf course. I was summarily called to his office, where I got a very cold reception and a very hot reaming."

But it wasn't as though CBS had violated any established standard or written rule. Roberts's rules were in his head, dictated as he went along. Even as golf carts go, he could be very generous when the mood struck him.

Journalist John Derr, a former CBS golf announcer, wrote: "In 1970 my back and legs were causing me a great deal of pain. I asked Roberts if I might be permitted to use a golf cart to travel to and from my tower at the fifteenth hole. Those hills were steep then, worse now. He said I should check later with his secretary, Helen Harris. That was not a yes, only a hope. Later I checked with Mrs. Harris and she handed me a note: 'To whom it may concern. John Derr has permission to use this cart en route to and from the fifteenth green. C. R. P. S., John, please don't drive on the greens.'"

His office, his appearance, and his speech were remarkably mundane. "It was a spartan office," Chirkinian recalls, "very plain, totally inelegant. There were two or three pictures on the wall, but nothing to make it a very personal place. There was not a single piece of paper on the desk." Frank Hannigan in *Golf Digest* described Roberts's personal appearance as "button-faced and somber—American Gothic." An English journalist wrote that Roberts looked like "a delegate to an undertaker's convention." Later in life, with his Coke-bottle glasses perched on the end of his disproportionately large, round nose, he looked like any other octogenarian shuffling out to the first tee.

Given his total lack of charisma, it is surprising that Roberts ascended to a position as one of President Eisenhower's most influential advisers. Even more surprising is the fact that before joining Ike or meeting Bobby Jones, Roberts did remarkably well as a Wall Street stockbroker, a Texas oil speculator, and a traveling clothing salesman. Most who knew him couldn't imagine him selling water in the desert. Says Hannigan: "It took him [Roberts] forever to say anything. He just droned. He spoke in a total monotone, very slowly."

Former *Augusta Chronicle* sports editor Robert Eubanks remembers Roberts's delivery as being anything but salesmanlike: "Anyone could repeat his offerings verbatim because he delivered them in a very deliberate manner."

In spite of all that, there are pervasive rumors that Cliff Roberts had a great sense of humor. Jack Nicklaus says, "People never really seemed to see it, but [Cliff] had a great sense of humor. It was very dry." Steve Melnyk also remembers Roberts fondly: "Mr. Roberts was incredibly bright, but he had a facade he liked to project. Later, it got to where I kidded him, calling him the Great Curmudgeon." There were no great belly laughs with Roberts, but there were some well-chronicled episodes of wit, methodically planned, occasionally expensive, and always with Roberts in control. During the time in our nation's history when young Americans collectively decided to engage in the highbrow act of streaking, Roberts was asked what he would do if a streaker went racing across the course on a Sunday. He thought for a moment and then deadpanned, "I would take back his season badge."

In terms of more orchestrated humor, Roberts produced films for the members' annual Jamboree party. One time he staged himself making a hole-in-one on sixteen. After the ball was shown hopping into the cup, Roberts calmly walked off the front of the tee, stepped out onto the lake fronting the green, and, without missing a step, strolled atop the water over to the sixteenth green. He waved for his caddie to follow him, and the unsuspecting looper plunged into the pond. Long before the days of computer video editing, this little bit of film magic was pulled off by building a bridge just below the surface of the water. Cliff knew it was there; his caddie did not. In another of these slapstick classics, a large bear was shown running out of the pines scaring the dickens out of various members as they played the course. In the final shot, the bear's head came off and there was Cliff, laughing at his handiwork.

99

Deity or vicious carnivore, the metaphors in these Jamboree films hit closer to home than Roberts or any of the other members would have liked to admit. His presence made people scurry with or without the costume. A former grounds crew employee said: "Mr. Roberts was a ghost. You'd be working along and all of a sudden he'd just appear out of nowhere, and if things weren't just right, he'd get mighty hot. You never knew when he was coming or what he was going to say." Roberts retained control of his environment through power, and he retained power through fear and intimidation. Roberts's self-esteem was secure. In a late-night bridge game during one of Ike's twenty-eight visits to the club, the former general bid on a grand slam without an ace in his hand. (For those not bridge-minded, that's like going for a six-hundred-yard par-five in two after topping your tee shot.) Cliff doubled and the president went down four, at which point Roberts said, "Mr. President, now you understand why I can't let you run the country by yourself."

Eisenhower's hatred of the large tree conspicuously guarding the seventeenth fairway was well known. While most tournament players either play to the right of the tree or blow their tee shots over it, the average slicer (Ike definitely qualified) has a tough time negotiating the lone specimen. Ike publicly swore that he was going to chop the tree down, to which Roberts privately responded, "If you touch that tree you're a dead man, and not even the Secret Service will be able to help you."

The depth of Roberts's power was only eclipsed by his own perception of the depth of his power. Negotiations for television rights weren't negotiations at all: Roberts dictated what was going to happen, and the CBS brass did everything but kiss his ring. The Masters television coverage was and is as close to a commercial-free environment as exists in television. There are only four commercial minutes an hour (Roberts's rule) as opposed to eight and one-half minutes in the

U.S. Open and even more than that in an average PGA Tour telecast. Just cutting commercials wasn't enough for Cliff: In 1966 he ordered CBS to begin each Masters telecast with an announcement praising the limited-commercial policy. This announcement would take all of thirty seconds at the beginning of each telecast, but Roberts didn't want just any old announcer reciting his policy. His first pick for the assignment was Walter Cronkite. After some anxious moments and hemming and hawing, CBS finally said Cronkite couldn't make it. Cliff then commanded Alistair Cooke to come down to Augusta and plug the brilliant commercial policy. Cooke politely declined. CBS scrambled and came up with one of the most-respected and -recognized entertainers in the business who was also an avid golfer: Ed Sullivan. Roberts coldly replied, "Hell, no. Sullivan uses monkeys on his program."

Roberts's attempts to control the media extended to print reporters as well, starting with the arrogant expectation that nothing critical of Augusta or the Masters would ever make its way onto a printed page. Amazingly, for many years the writers "cooperated." After all, Augusta had included among its original membership the esteemed sportswriter Grantland Rice, whose close affiliation with a club and tournament on which he was reporting would today be deemed a blatant conflict of interest.

Roberts emphasized to the press that the Masters was a noncommercial endeavor involving a private club investing profits back into the club and the tournament. The Augusta chairman's apparent obsession to micromanage the pens and typewriters of reporters, and his incredible ability to ramble on incessantly about a matter of small significance, finally drove one writer over the edge. Grabbing a huge turkey leg left behind in the press room following a day of healthy food consumption and waving it menacingly, the reporter chased Roberts up the hill to the clubhouse and all the way to the slammed-and-locked-door sanctuary of his office.

Writer Frank Deford best summed up Roberts's estimation of his own importance: "Some men think they're God. In golf at least, Mr. Roberts was sure he was God, only he had to go around telling everybody that Bobby Jones was God. It must have worn on him. No wonder he spoke so hesitantly."

Deford was right. Roberts knew who ran things, but he had to continue to let everyone believe Bob Jones wore the ultimate green coat. The strain in Roberts's relationship with Jones festered over time and ended on a sour note when Roberts was not invited to Jones's funeral. In the beginning they were the perfect one-two punch; everybody loved Jones and everybody feared Roberts. As time went on, however, Roberts's penchant for control led to more than a few minor rifts. He would not, or could not, yield on even the smallest point. It was Cliff's way or no way.

In the late 1940s, Bob Jones struck up a relationship with the noted golf course architect Robert Trent Jones (no relation). Bob and Trent revamped Augusta's sixteenth hole—lengthening it, moving the green, moving the tee, and adding a pond. Cliff hated everything about the renovations. Never mind that in 1961 Cliff extended the championship tee even farther, and since the Jones-engineered change, the sixteenth has been the site of numerous classic Masters moments. Roberts's problem had nothing to do with golf; it had to do with control. Cliff wasn't involved; ergo, it was a bad idea.

Roberts grew stronger as Jones's physical condition worsened. The membership began to take on a more Robertsonian look as Cliff did his best to stack the club with people he deemed worthy: not Bob's old friends or the sons of existing members, but CEOs—movers and shakers and men Cliff liked to be around. Jones expressed his sardonic attitude toward these changes in a note to Cliff regarding a list of prospective new members: "About all I can say is that

A "fab five of Augusta royalty" for sure: Masters Tournament and club cofounders Bobby Jones and Clifford Roberts are seated, with Gary Player, Jack Nicklaus, and Arnold Palmer standing together behind them. Between them, Player, Nicklaus, and Palmer have accounted for thirteen Masters Tournament victories. (AP/Wide World Photos)

you appear to have picked a group of individuals who are thoroughly solvent and should be able to pay their dues."

Roberts enjoyed the company of company men, not only because it broadened his sphere of influence, but also because these CEOs came with all the trappings of their positions, including an ample supply of corporate jets that Roberts could borrow. The 1970 Masters ended on Sunday with another tie, so the green jacket ceremony did not take place until the following Monday afternoon. USGA president Phil Strubing decided that Augusta National and the Masters could conduct a playoff without him, so he informed Roberts that he would be staying home. That was unacceptable. Roberts immediately dispatched one of "his" corporate jets to pick up Strubing at his Sea Island home. Strubing was flown in for the green jacket ceremony, the world saw the USGA properly represented; and Mr. Strubing was then flown home again.

Jones, unpretentious in every thought and deed, disliked these kinds of things. Although weak in body, he never lost his disciplined, quick mind. Long after Roberts had assumed total control of the club and the tournament, Jones could verbally take his old buddy behind the woodpile when a point needed to be made. Such was the case after the printing of the 1963 Masters booklet. Jones fired off a note to Roberts: "I thought we had corrected this before, but I find on page thirty-one, last paragraph, 'Bob had always liked Augusta (his wife came from there).' Of course, Mary did not come from Augusta. Her mother did, but she was born in Atlanta." As simple as this might seem, Jones realized that a man like Roberts, who dwelled on minutiae and was obsessed by detail, knew better than to let an error like that slide. Jones also was aware that Roberts wrote and approved the copy for the booklet. Accurate or not, this was Cliff's version of the truth, and nobody was going to change it.

Perhaps the cruelest example of Roberts's manipulative skills came at the expense of Bill MacPhail, the former head of CBS Sports. An avuncular gentleman who never had a harsh word for anyone, MacPhail endured Roberts's insufferable critiques of CBS's coverage. Every year Bill would smile, respond to Roberts's bitching, and prepare for next year's event. After leaving CBS, Bill moved to Atlanta and ran CNN Sports until his retirement in 1995; but eighteen years after Cliff Roberts's death and a year after his own retirement, Bill MacPhail, the elder statesman of televised sports, lost his smile when asked about Bob Jones and the green jacket ceremony.

Jones had always been part of the post-tournament ceremony. Even after he became so weak he could no longer stand and could barely hold his cigarette holder, CBS remained content with his presence. It was touching, nostalgic, and perfect television. On the other hand, it had become increasingly obvious that while the public wanted to catch its annual glimpse of Jones the man, television viewers were being subjected to a shadow of the great champion whose enduringly boyish countenance had given way to the pained look of a sick man out of sorts with the world around him.

MACPHAIL LET JONES GO TO HIS GRAVE THINKING CBS WAS RESPONSIBLE FOR HIS OUSTING. THE TRUTH, MACPHAIL KNEW, WOULD HAVE BEEN FAR TOO PAINFUL.

Pictures and film clips from that time show a Bobby Jones with deep age lines etched across a face that was a mask of somberness that only occasionally was lightened by a forced smile. When journalist Alistair Cooke came face-to-face with Jones in 1965, he wasn't prepared for what he saw: "My first impression was . . . seeing the extent of his disability, the fine strong hands, twisted like the branches of a cypress, gamely clutching a tumbler or one of his perpetual cigarettes in a holder. His face was more ravaged than I had expected, from the long-endured pain I imagine, but the embarrassment a stranger might feel about this was tempered by the quizzical eyes and the warmth his presence gave off. (He kept on going to Augusta for the Masters until a year or so before the end. Mercifully, for everyone but his family, we would not see him when he could no longer bear to be seen.)"

Roberts thought it unseemly to have Jones's withered physical condition broadcast to the entire country. Therefore he told his old friend that CBS (specifically MacPhail) had decided Bob should not continue to be part of the presentation. Hurt to the point of tears, Jones confronted MacPhail. As he had done every year with Roberts, Bill listened, only this time he didn't smile. Instead he turned away. MacPhail let Jones go to his grave thinking CBS was responsible for his ousting. The truth, MacPhail knew, would have been far too painful.

With his power firmly solidified, Roberts spent the rest of his days piling accolades on his dear old friend Bob Jones. In his book Roberts wrote, "The basis of my association with Bob was great admiration and much liking for the person." Even though the relationship ended on a more sour note than anyone is prepared to admit, Roberts succeeded in reinventing himself as Bob's lifelong confidant and torch-bearer. Jack Nicklaus says, "He [Roberts] remained a good friend of Bob Jones's forever. He was always loyal to the purposes of [the National]."

To understand many of Roberts's idiosyncrasies, you have to look west, to the town of Morning Sun, Iowa, where in 1894 Charles Roberts and Rebecca Scott Key Roberts (a distant cousin of Francis Scott Key) gave birth to their second son, Clifford. Charles Roberts worked as a real estate salesman in various locations throughout the Midwest. While there were stories of drinking and other family vices, nothing dramatically unusual seemed afoot in the Roberts household. Then in 1913, nineteen-year-old Clifford, out on the road selling wholesale men's suits, got word that his mother had taken her own life. It was a tragic event that in hindsight offers a glimpse into Roberts's own mysterious psyche.

"The suicide of a parent more often than not suggests deeper problems in the family relationship," says psychologist Wayne Wilson, who has counseled many children of suicidal parents. "There is usually a breakdown of what we consider the normal family structure, partly because the depressed parent is incapable of parenting. In these situations, the child becomes the parent and, in effect, makes his or her own rules."

Roberts never attended college and barely made it through high school after engaging in a heated argument with the principal. Wilson says this is classic behavior among children of depressed, suicidal parents: "People like this become very rigid. They *have* to be right. They also shelter the pain from their lack of parental love by becoming emotionally detached in everything. That's why many children of depressed parents, particularly children of suicidally depressed parents, become great negotiators and businessmen."

Adds Wilson: "Men like these derive their own self-worth from outside sources—success in business, sports, or other areas—so much so that the distinction between the person and the person's accomplishments becomes blurred. When those substitutes don't successfully fill the void left by the parent, however, these children frequently slip into depression themselves, often leading them into the same tragic suicidal tendencies that plagued the parent."

A young Roberts sold suits, joined the army (where he was first introduced to Augusta when Uncle Sam shipped him to nearby Camp Hancock), and sold oil leases in East Texas. At the ripe old age of twenty-seven, Roberts—the classic over-achiever from the even more classic dysfunctional family—made fifty thousand dollars in oil speculation. The year was 1921, and the whiz kid from Morning Sun had made his mark. With the money, Roberts bought a partnership in Reynolds and Company and began earning the epithet, "the Boy Wonder of Wall Street."

He also dabbled heavily in New York real estate. In 1928 alone, Roberts bought a nine-story apartment building on East Seventy-fourth for eight hundred thousand dollars, an apartment building on East Seventy-ninth for an undisclosed amount, and a five-story home at 117 East Fifty-fifth Street. That same year he sold an apartment on East Thirty-fifth and his home on Park Avenue in the Murray Hill area. He was a high-rolling mover and shaker, with all the personal intimacy of a block of ice.

Again Dr. Wilson explains: "The pain a child has stemming from the suicide of a parent is often manifested in that child's inability to have close relationships, especially intimate relationships, if the parent was of the opposite sex. Daughters whose fathers have committed suicide find it hard to develop successful romantic relationships, and sons whose mothers have died at their own hands have few, if any, female relationships. Usually, these children either have long-distance relationships, or none at all."

Throughout his tenure as chairman of Augusta National, Roberts would spend upwards of four months a year at the club, leaving his wife behind in New York. Even more telling, while he was serving his country in France, Roberts fell into a romantic but peculiar affair with a woman named Suzanne Verdet. He visited her numerous times, long after becoming Wall Street's "wonder boy." The most memorable visit was in 1928, when Suzanne talked Cliff into staying in Paris an extra day. The plane Roberts would have taken back to London had he not accepted Suzanne's offer crashed into the English Channel, killing all on board. Roberts let it be known that Suzanne had saved his life. He never married her, never moved her to America, never formalized his relationship with her in any way; but years later when she needed twenty-four-hour nursing care, Cliff took care of all of her expenses; and he continued to take care of things after his death. Suzanne's financial needs were provided for in Roberts's will.

His obsessions weren't all negative. Through his hard work and rigid perfectionism, the Masters spawned some of golf's most lasting innovations: tee-to-green gallery ropes; grandstands; the over/under scoring system that shows how a player stands to par; pairing the field in two-somes rather than threesomes; complementary pairing sheets; and, long after Roberts's death, high-definition television broadcasts—all these were Masters firsts. Cliff had the good sense and management skills to listen carefully to suggestions, and he understood the importance of being the first on the block with a new idea. He established a series of committees to study and recommend changes, improvements, and innovations. Committee heads were members, and each reported back to him with a list of suggested improvements. The over/under scoring system, for example, was the brainchild of CBS producer Frank Chirkinian. Aiken native Bobby Knowles, who served on the scoring committee for years, then came up with the idea of making under-par numbers red and over-par numbers black. That particular innovation is usually attributed to Roberts. Granted, he thought highly enough of the idea to put the system in place, but the roots of today's most recognized scoring system lay with Chirkinian and Knowles.

All the improvements didn't come from committees, however. Future Augusta National chairman Jack Stephens, standing by Cliff during one of the par-three contests, suggested that the bunker behind the fourth green of the par-three course be moved to the side. Stephens told Roberts this move would bring the bunker into play and allow more room behind the green for patrons. Roberts grunted. A few months later the bunker was moved and the bill was sent to Jack Stephens along with a note: "Jack, you were so right."

Some changes came straight from Roberts, no committee needed. Byron Nelson recalls the first year of tee-to-green gallery ropes: "The ropes were all white. I was out on the course with Cliff, and he looked around at the white ropes and said, 'That doesn't go in this place at all. The ropes should be green.' This was just before the tournament was to start, but in a couple of days, the ropes were changed to green. That was a big improvement."

In 1966 Roberts unilaterally added two bunkers to the left side of the eighteenth fairway, right in the spot most players were hitting their tee shots. The eighteenth became a premium driving hole overnight. However, because of some semantic hang-up, Roberts referred to the bunkers as "bunker," singular. After a few years and more than a few corner-of-the-eye looks, Roberts began calling the traps a "two-section bunker," meaning he was right all along; it was the rest of us who couldn't count.

Augusta has twenty-four committees ranging from rules to public relations to first aid to finance. A total of 270 volunteers and staff members collaborate on these committees to come up with some of the innovations that make Augusta National and the Masters what it is. The committees don't exist for the sake of existing, and no one (save perhaps the ailing Hogan, who is still listed on the tournament improvements committee) serves on a committee simply as a figurehead. Members and outsiders meet, talk, and bring in all kinds of experts on all kinds of subjects. If you're an expert on the prevailing winds around the area of the National, don't be surprised if the concessions committee calls and asks you to give a presentation on how far a cup will travel when dropped in the middle of a wind gust. They even have a seven-man committee (which includes Hall Thompson of Shoal Creek notoriety) for cup and tee marker placement. A relatively new member of the tournament improvements committee said of the process: "I was surprised to find such openness and objectivity. This whole notion of continuous improvement that we, in business, only talk about is the ethos of the Masters." Another local Augusta member who serves on the transportation committee says of the process: "We strive for the utmost precision. Everything is figured out ahead of time. We also have a critique in May to see if there is something we can do better. I'm proud of the work we do, and occasionally it comes back. I remember one time I was sitting on a golf cart with my green jacket on and Greg Norman popped out of the club and said, 'Sir, may I say something? I want you to know this is the greatest golf tournament in the world.'" Roberts would have nothing less, and because of the culture he created and the taskmaster way in which he created it, his successors inherited a well-oiled, finely tuned machine.

Later in life, Cliff shared what he'd learned with a few select friends, Nicklaus being one of them. "He was tremendous to us at Muirfield," Nicklaus says. "He opened up everything to us when we started the Memorial Tournament. He was on the Captain's Club, one of the original members. He was great."

Roberts's drive for continuous improvement might have greatly contributed, but a large chunk of the Masters success in the sixties fell on the stellar play of his friend Nicklaus and the other members of what commonly became known as "the Big Three." Arnold Palmer, Jack Nicklaus, and Gary Player won seven out of ten Masters from 1960 through 1969 (with Palmer winning a victory in the fifties, and Nicklaus and Player between them adding four more green coats in the 1970s and 1980s). During that time the tournament became not just a major, but golf's favorite major. Fans identified with the course, the time of year, the history, the beauty, and the drama of Arnie's charges, Nicklaus's talent, and Player's spunky competitiveness and penchant for black clothes. The man who won the Masters didn't just win in the sense that he shot the lowest score, he rode out of the pines on horseback with his unsheathed sword glistening in the sunlight. The Masters became high drama in the same way Yankees baseball had been in the fifties. People could now follow golf on television, and, in Augusta, they could do it in a familiar setting with the same familiar faces squaring off every year.

Player won in 1961 and Palmer finished second. Palmer won in 1962 and Player finished second. Nicklaus won in 1963. Palmer won in 1964 and Nicklaus finished second. Nicklaus won in 1965 when Palmer and Player tied for second. On and on it went for much of the 1960s, although things at Augusta started to get curiouser toward the end of the decade. No Masters Tournament before or since the 1968 event has been as strange, like events elsewhere in the news. American society itself was at a crossroads with the assassinations just two months apart of Martin Luther King Jr. and Bobby Kennedy, the former instigating race riots across the nation and the latter setting the stage for the most violent Democratic Convention in the nation's history.

By contrast, golf in 1968 more than ever was seen in its true light as just a game, although classifying that year's Masters as just another game could do little to salve the pain Roberto De Vicenzo felt one Sunday afternoon in April. Roberts's unyielding disregard for any change not initiated by him was dragged into the spotlight when De Vicenzo, after apparently forcing a Masters playoff with Bob Goalby, gave Goalby the outright victory by signing an incorrect scorecard that added a stroke to his score. This was 1968 and golf supposedly was well into its modern era, yet all Augusta had to show for its official scoring area was an amateurish setup near the eighteenth green. There, a rickety table supported an umbrella and was manned by a solitary figure in a green jacket. Joe Dey, then the USGA's executive director, had warned Roberts of the inherent dangers presented by this funky setup, but Roberts had ignored the warnings. So when De Vicenzo

The man sitting glumly in a chair with his leg propped up is Roberto De Vicenzo. He has just learned that his signed incorrect scorecard has added a stroke to his score, denying him a first-place tie with Bob Goalby in the 1968 Masters Tournament. Seated at the table, at left, are Goalby, Raymond Floyd, and a Masters Tournament official. Standing to the left are Tommy Aaron, De Vicenzo's fourth-round playing partner, and two other Masters officials. Aaron's scoring error, in which he gave De Vicenzo a four at the seventeenth where De Vicenzo had actually made a three, was missed by De Vicenzo when he reviewed and then signed his scorecard. (AP/Wide World Photos)

signed a card giving himself a final-round 66 instead of the 65 he had actually fired, there was no one in the tent to insist on cross-checking the cards.

Granted, it was De Vicenzo's carelessness—not Goalby's similar presence atop the leaderboard, not even the four at the seventeen that his playing partner, Tommy Aaron,

This is Roberto De Vicenzo's official scorecard from the final round of the 1968 Masters Tournament. His score is on the bottom half of the card. Note that playing partner Tommy Aaron, in keeping De Vicenzo's score, had penciled in a four at the seventeenth where De Vicenzo had actually made a birdie three. But De Vicenzo signed the scorecard as is, thus adding a stroke to his actual score and denying him a share of the lead with declared winner Bob Goalby. (AP/Wide World Photos)

had incorrectly recorded for De Vicenzo, who had actually made birdie three—that led to his scoring blunder. De Vicenzo should have known to check his hole-by-hole score carefully before signing his card. Although De Vicenzo could not rewrite history on the spot—scoring pencils don't come with erasers—Roberts and the Masters folks had a well-staffed scorer's tent in place for the 1969 event. When later asked about the new and improved scorer's table, Roberts denied that any changes had actually been made.

Almost forgotten in the 1968 hubbub was Goalby, who should have been reaping the financial windfall normally accorded a Masters winner, even if for just the next twelve months. Hardly. Goalby's green coat turned into a straitjacket, squeezing him out of the pleasures of a one-year reign that were rightfully his. Instead, it was De Vicenzo, the balding and affable Argentinean, who emerged as the real Masters champion in the eyes of many golf fans. Goalby was cast as the villain, with hundreds of hate-mail letters to prove it.

"Roberto tells me he made $250,000 from the Masters," Goalby later said. "I made about $50,000, not including the winner's share of the purse." Goalby did receive one consolation prize: During the winter after his Masters triumph, he opened a letter from Jones that said: "You are the Masters champion. You have won it fairly. I sympathize with all that you have been through."

The decade of the 1970s got off to a great start in Augusta, although most of the country spent the first week of April 1970 glued to their television sets hoping the crew of Apollo 13 made it home alive. Back at Augusta Masters rookie and U.S. Amateur Champion Steve Melnyk was making his first of many visits to American golf's mecca. He remembers: "I was thrilled to death on my first visit in 1970. The experience is unlike any other in golf. They are especially great in how they treat amateurs. My first year there I was paired with Jack Nicklaus in the first round—I had never met him until he stepped onto the first tee. I remember being intimidated by his length, but then it was easy to be intimidated by him. That first year I stayed in the Crow's Nest [the cupola atop the clubhouse that was renovated and turned into a dormitory for amateur participants]. I ate all my meals there. It would cost a dollar for breakfast, a dollar for lunch, two dollars for dinner, and a dollar a night for the sleeping quarters. That's getting the whole deal for five dollars a day. I remember staying there for ten days and getting a bill for seventy-three dollars."

With the likes of Melnyk thrilled to be there, the Augusta of the late 1960s and early 1970s was becoming the stomping grounds for a new breed of quirky and colorful characters and of new Masters winners conspicuously lacking the charisma and notoriety of a Palmer or Nicklaus. The former group included the likes of Bert Yancey and Chi Chi Rodriguez; the latter, the likes of second-echelon talent with names such as Brewer, Goalby, Archer, Coody, and Aaron. Augusta had crowned its share of nonmarquee winners in previous decades, but this was beginning to look like a near-annual onslaught of Average Joes crashing services at Augusta Cathedral.

For Masters week each year Chi Chi was officially referred to as foreign guest Juan Rodriguez of Puerto Rico. In 1970 Cheech annoyed Frank Beard during the Friday round with such comments as, "Ave Maria! I don't see how the ball can take it. When I hit it, smoke comes out." For local color, there was Tommy Aaron of Gainesville, Georgia, who hovered near the lead but could never mount a substantive charge, regardless of whose scorecard he was keeping. Then there was Yancey, who was actually tied for the lead midway through the tournament and who personified Masters heartbreak.

Yancey had an intense love for all that was Augusta and the Masters. Back home he had constructed clay models of all eighteen of Augusta's greens and brought them with him to his rented house (for a number of years his host family's last name was, ironically, "Masters") during Masters week. Yancey was one of the informally chosen few who wore the albatross labeled "one of the best golfers never to have won a major." He came close a number of times, most notably in U.S. Opens

Bert Yancey, an Augusta fanatic, came close on several occasions to winning the Masters Tournament. Here he is in 1970 blasting from a trap at the fifteenth. (AP/Wide World Photos)

and the Masters. In 1967 he led after two rounds and did well in shooting even par over the weekend, leaving him alone in third behind Gay Brewer and runner-up Bobby Nichols. The 1967 tournament began a four-year span in which Yancey finished fourth or better three times at Augusta with no coveted green jacket to show for his admirable efforts. After finishing tied for twelfth in 1972—he had been in second after thirty-six holes, two shots behind Nicklaus—Yancey disappeared from Augusta's radar screen, his golfing career sidetracked by his worsening illness, eventually brought under control with lithium.

"Bert was called eccentric, but I call it obsessed," says Frank Beard of his friend Yancey. "Augusta and the Masters were his number-one obsessions among the tournaments. It was an obsession that got more damaging for him the closer he came to winning. There were a number of times that he had chances to win at the Masters but couldn't pull it off. Then the obsession would get darker and deeper. It's too bad he couldn't have enjoyed this quest instead of being a part of it. Bert had a marvelous sense of humor but his heart never smiled. Any time you're mired in an obsession, it's no fun. I know, because I'm a recovering alcoholic."

In the end it would be another Masters playoff in 1970, but this time the Big Three sat out. Gary Player was the only member of the triumvirate who had a legitimate shot, but his putt on the seventy-second hole to tie the leaders stayed high. Gene Littler and Billy Casper teed off on Monday. Casper won.

Third-place finisher Player went on to win two more Masters. Aaron won one in 1973, but he played so poorly during the late 1970s and 1980s that he considered giving up golf entirely. (Like many, Aaron has since discovered new life on the Senior Tour.) Melnyk went on to play in four more Masters and then served as a CBS broadcaster for ten tournaments.

Roberts watched it all and aged a little more. When it finally dawned on him that he was not going to live forever, he bestowed the ultimate compliment on himself: He picked his own successor. Unfortunately, the man he picked, Hord Hardin, a great amateur player and former USGA director, turned Roberts down. Hardin knew that as long as Cliff was alive, Roberts's rules would be in effect, so he politely declined the offer, citing the demands of his career and family.

Unaccustomed to rejection, Roberts picked Bill Lane, a successful Texas businessman without much of a golf background. Because Hardin never let anyone know about Roberts's initial offer, everyone assumed Cliff had snubbed his heir-apparent for a more docile Lane. That was not the case, and even after Hardin became chairman, he didn't speak about Roberts's original offer out of respect for Bill Lane and the Lane family. Hord had been right to turn Roberts down, however. At the press conference to announce Lane as successor, Cliff did not allow Lane to say a word. The message was clear: Roberts still ran things, no matter what.

Tragically, Lane suffered a stroke and only served as chairman for the 1977 and 1978 seasons. Hardin replaced him, because prior to Lane's last year in office, Roberts pulled the trigger of his .38. Clifford C. Roberts was cremated and his ashes are buried on the grounds of Augusta National, although the exact location is unknown and all club officials involved were sworn to secrecy—a final act of recalcitrance.

The .38 caliber Smith and Wesson sat in a room untouched until it took a journey that, in some ways, mirrored the bizarre life of its victim. In 1988 Augusta National general manager Jim Armstrong came across three old guns during a routine physical inventory. One of them happened to be the

THE .38 CALIBER SMITH AND WESSON SAT IN A ROOM UNTOUCHED UNTIL IT TOOK A JOURNEY THAT, IN SOME WAYS, MIRRORED THE BIZARRE LIFE OF ITS VICTIM.

pistol Roberts had used eleven years earlier to commit suicide. Assuming they were excess baggage, Armstrong sold the guns to his chief of security, Charlie Young, who was a gun dealer. Although Armstrong had no idea that the Roberts gun was part of the transaction, Young knew what he had. "Of course, we didn't know that it was *that* gun when we sold it and two other pieces," Hardin said of the sale. "Had we known, we never would have sold it. . . . The price was very modest, something like two hundred dollars for all three pieces."

Young made a sizable profit when he sold the gun to official Augusta National photographer Frank Christian Jr. for a thousand dollars. At the time Christian said of the transaction: "[Young] approached me and said, 'I have something you might like to have. I have the gun that Mr. Roberts killed himself with.'" Christian, whose father had also been the club's official photographer, had known Roberts for years and didn't want the gun to end up on display or at auction. To keep it off the open market, he bought it himself.

Enter golf collectibles dealer Bob Burkett, who offered to buy the gun. Said Christian: "He [Burkett] came down to buy my golf ball collection and a number of other things. He asked if I would consider letting him sell the gun. He said he had a source that could put it where it would never be seen. He said it would be very confidential."

Burkett, owner of Old Sport golf antiques and collectibles in Atlanta, still says of the deal: "Frank didn't want it out on the open market. At the time I was representing a Japanese museum group that had agreed to purchase the gun and move it into a private museum in Japan. Unfortunately, when things got tight in Japan, the group stiffed me, leaving me with over a hundred thousand [dollars' worth] in collectable merchandise, some of which I still own."

Along came a New Jersey man named Richard Ulrich, who approached Burkett with a claim that he had some Japanese investors who would buy the gun if Burkett would allow Ulrich to represent it. Anxious to get rid of his excess inventory, Burkett agreed.

"The guy didn't have any Japanese clients," Burkett says. "What he had was an auction catalogue, printed in English, that he sent to Japan. A week or so later, the catalogue filters back to America, and Frank Christian and Charlie Young lose their jobs."

The club terminated both men's affiliation with it in early 1991, even though it had actually been the National itself that had started the chain of events by selling the gun. Hardin called the auction catalogue "distasteful," and said of Christian, "The guy made a mistake." Burkett claims he was contacted after the terminations of Christian and Young by several greencoats who, in his words, "tried to play hardball" to get the gun back. However, none of them made an offer to purchase the piece.

Hardin later resigned his chairmanship, citing ill health. His replacement, Jack Stephens of Little Rock, brought the issue of the gun to a close. Burkett says: "Frank [Christian] came back to me and explained his situation. I sold him the gun back for exactly what I paid for it. After Jack Stephens was in, Frank and Charlie were rehired."

Frank Christian is still defensive about the topic: "I was only gone for two months. [The *Augusta Chronicle*] never published an article when I was rehired, only when I was fired." Of the incident itself, Christian will say only: "I agreed not to talk about it; they [Augusta National] agreed not to talk about it, and I'm keeping my end of the bargain."

Burkett is a little more open. About the gun and the entire episode he says, "As far as I know the damn thing's in the bottom of Ike's Pond. Christian got his job back, Augusta got the gun back, and all I got was the blame and a lot of crap."

Roberts ruled well past his time, as the incident with the gun clearly demonstrated. On matters of tournament policy, however, his passing precipitated almost instant change. A shake-up in the caddie ranks was soon to come, as were wholesale changes in the golf course. The eighties witnessed a transformation in the way the Masters was played and a reformation of the tournament's glory. The go-go eighties saw the greatest players, the greatest drama, and the single greatest golf tournament in the history of the game. It didn't come a moment too soon. The decade of the seventies had been marred by the death of Bobby Jones, the suicide of Clifford Roberts, and the untimely death of Bill Lane. It ended with the first sudden-death playoff in Masters history being won by a curly headed Augusta rookie named Fuzzy.

Mr. Roberts must have been spinning in his grave.

CHAPTER 6

YOUR DESTINY IS RIGHT HERE

YOU KNOW, IT'S HARD TO SPAR WITH HISTORY AND TRADITION. YOU HAVE TO BE ABLE TO KEEP IT OUT IN FRONT OF YOU LIKE IT'S A PUNCHING BAG AND YOU PUNCH AT IT. I COULD NEVER QUITE GET THE RIGHT PERSPECTIVE. BUT NICKLAUS CERTAINLY COULD. I KNOW IN MY HEART THAT JACK NICKLAUS IS AFFECTED BY THE MASTERS IN A WAY THAT IS MORE INTENSE THAN ANY OTHER PLAYER. FOR ME, I DON'T THINK I EVER FELT LIKE I WAS WORTHY ENOUGH TO WIN A MASTERS. I DREAMT OF IT, BUT I DON'T THINK I EVER SAW MYSELF IN THE WINNER'S CIRCLE. IT WAS LIKE LIFE IN GENERAL. WHEN WE WENT TO AUGUSTA, NICKLAUS BECAME SOMEONE DIFFERENT. HE WAS WORTHY. HE WAS A CHAMPION.

—FRANK BEARD

The eighties will be remembered as the decade of Ronald Reagan, Donald Trump, leveraged buyouts, and the disintegration of communism. Music, culture, technology, and sports leapt forward at breakneck speeds. Arnold Palmer became the world's richest athlete, while Michael Milkin continued to reign as the world's richest alleged crook. Two nerdy computer guys from the West Coast, Steve Jobs and Bill Gates, battled it out to see who would be the world's richest man. Amid this backdrop, while the world map was changing faster than a downhill putt on the ninth green, Augusta National and the Masters Tournament underwent its own series of transformations.

The first metamorphosis occurred when the members unanimously elected a former banker, lawyer, and USGA president as the club's new chairman. Hord W. Hardin, a burly man with a gentle smile, had been elected president of the USGA and, two years before ascending to the chairmanship, was elected vice chairman of Augusta National. Cliff Roberts had never been *elected* to anything. Hardin was unlike Roberts in a number of other ways as well. He was a known quantity, a businessman who lived in Florida most of the year and who was very open about who he was, where he was from, and what he thought about life, politics, and the new metal wood craze. He laughed and joked openly (you didn't have to search the archives for his sense of humor) although no one ever accused Mr. Hardin of being a backslapper. He was also a very good player, having qualified for the U.S. Amateur four times and the U.S. Open once. He won the club championship at his home course in St. Louis a stunning twenty-two times. Whereas Roberts had lived on Augusta's premises four months out of the year, Hardin managed by phone, fax, and modem. He came two weeks before the tournament and always made special trips for the five yearly parties, but Hord preferred to set the direction and policy from a distance, then to manage by checking in. He knew golf outside the cocoon of Augusta National, and while he continued to rule the club as an autocrat, he had the good sense and managerial skills to consult with others before passing law.

Hardin let the professionals do a professional job. Jim Armstrong, the club's general manager, and his staff of highly qualified, highly trained professionals, along with the hundreds of committee members and volunteers, saw the new chairman as a refreshing change. But many quickly realized that Hardin the teddy bear had very sharp claws. Ken Green, the first player to break the sex barrier in the Masters when his sister caddied for him, squared off with Hardin, not over the issue of bag-toting but over the matter of badges and his desire to buy more than the usual player allotment. Green lost. Writer Frank Deford saw a somewhat lighter side of Hardin while discussing an innocent misuse of terms: "When I was chatting with Hardin at the club in Florida where he winters, I referred to Augusta National as a 'number-two club,' which is a common enough expression in affluent sporting company, meaning that a man belongs to a country club where he resides and a number-two club where he goes to escape the winter." A bemused Hardin told Deford, "I don't think anybody ever calls us a number-two club. My God, if Mr. Roberts heard that, he'd roll over in his grave."

Ripping up the greens at the National had been a common occurrence prior to 1980. With the club conveniently closed during the summer months, such drastic measures weren't all that difficult, and the club could do whatever it deemed necessary in the summer to get the greens in shape for the following season. But the 1981 transition to bent-grass greens actually had more to do with pride than any overwhelming agronomic need. It started at the last Masters Cliff Roberts presided over as chairman. That year, 1976, reformed playboy Raymond Floyd shot a then-tournament-record-tying 271, sending shock waves through the magnolias. Nicklaus had held the record alone since 1965. And prior to that, Hogan had held the record of 274, which he fired during his amazing 1953 run. After Nicklaus destroyed Hogan's twelve-year-old mark, bunkers were added to eighteen (right where Jack liked to drive the ball) and a bunker was inserted in the landing area of number two.

To have Nicklaus's record matched after "toughening" the course was troublesome indeed. Even more disconcerting to the greencoats was the fact that from 1970 to 1979, all but two of the Masters winners broke the 280 mark. In the

Eighty-two-year-old Fred McLeod, who for many years joined Jock
Hutchison as honorary starters for the Masters Tournament, cranks his
drive off No. 1 to kick off the 1965 Masters. (© Morgan Fitz
Photographers, Globe Photos, Inc. 1997)

thirty-three tournaments prior to 1970, only seven winners
broke 280. The National could, as Hogan had suggested to
Roberts, let the roughs grow, but that was anathema to Bob
Jones's ideals and most members' handicaps. So Hord Hardin
ripped up the greens and replanted them with bent grass,

immediately making the putting surfaces harder and slicker and placing even more of a premium on shot placement and a steady putting stroke.

"I thought we'd made a mistake," Hardin said of the decision. "We got a bad break with the weather. It stayed too hot too long in the fall when we planted. I thought we were going to have the first Masters ever on sand greens." They didn't. The greens came around, and by Masters week they were firmer and faster than ever before. From 1981 through 1989, only two Masters winners broke 280.

The caddie situation was a little less auspicious. It had long been tradition at the Masters that everyone, including tour players, used the Augusta National caddie staff. It consisted of a group of locals—all black men, some of whom had worked at the club since its inception. The caddie corps was a proud group, including such colorfully named people as Pappy, Lambchop, Cemetery, and Iron Man. They wore the white jumpsuits, carried the bags, and, as Jariah Beard, who guided Fuzzy Zoeller to victory in 1979, said: "We knew that golf course and we loved what we were doing. We were so proud to be a part of it. . . . The Monday of the Masters I was somebody in this community."

Jariah Beard, now fifty-six, still admires the numerous trophies on display in his Oakland Avenue home as he recalls those glorious days. Up until the 1979 event, Beard had been Don January's caddie, and prior to that he worked for Doug Sanders, Tommy Bolt, and Bob Toski. Then he got the call of a lifetime: "Fuzzy had never seen the course. He came in the first day and played nine holes—the back side. He asked me, 'Do you know the yardage?' I clubbed him on ten and eleven, and then he asked me if I could read putts. At twelve I read the putt and he knocked it in for birdie and he says, 'It's your game. I want you.' "

Beard still remembers every Zoeller shot from that year. "I read every putt and pulled every stick . . . I take that

> "WE GOT SCREWED. A LOT OF PEOPLE SAID IT WAS SEGREGATION, LIKE BLACK PEOPLE WERE VICTIMS OF PREJUDICE AND BLACK-ONLY CADDIES WAS A SYMBOL OF IT, BUT THAT WASN'T SO." THEY WERE HEROES.

back . . . He pulled the last stick on the playoff hole. We had 136 yards to the front of the green and I wanted him to hit nine-iron. He said to me, 'I knock an eight-iron down better than anybody in the world.' So I said, 'Hit your shot!' The birdie putt [which Zoeller made to win] was maybe ten feet uphill. It broke a little left. I told him to putt it that much [he holds up his index finger and thumb an inch apart] right of the hole. It was tracking all the way. I looked away when it was about four feet from the hole, because I knew it was in. . . . Those were some magical times."

That all stopped for Beard and other caddies in 1982. Gun-shy from two decades of being branded as racists, many of the members winced at the images of black men in white coveralls catering to white men in plaid golf slacks. Members of the Black community agreed. "In old African movies the natives carry guns for the white hunters and masters," says Mallory Millinder, former publisher of the *Augusta News Review*, a Black-owned newspaper. "It is the same analogy for the caddies. It is an obvious projection of the plantation mind-set."

The caddies and other members of the Black community disagreed with Millinder's take on the issue. Says Jariah Beard: "We got screwed. A lot of people said it was segregation,

Longtime Augusta National caddie Jariah Beard helps golfer Fuzzy Zoeller study a putt during Zoeller's successful bid to win the 1979 Masters Tourament. (*Augusta Chronicle* photo)

like black people were victims of prejudice and black-only caddies was a symbol of it, but that wasn't so." They were heroes. Carl Jackson, who still caddies for Ben Crenshaw at Augusta, signs almost as many autographs as his famous boss during Masters week. Their association with the club gave them clout. They were Masters caddies. "I've caddied out there a few times," says one local Augusta attorney. "When the rules changed on caddies, there were people standing in line wanting to do anything they could to get out there."

The racist claims might have been the powder keg for change, but an incident in the 1982 Masters lit the fuse. That year, after torrential rains, many of the caddies went home assuming the round was rained out. At 7:30 the next morning, when play was to resume, the bag room was a mess. Golfers' bags were still wet. Clubs weren't cleaned. Caddies weren't at the club, and Mr. Hardin and the members were embarrassed beyond belief. "It was pitiful," Carl Jackson remembers. "I was here. I don't know what the other guys were thinking. The clubs were still wet, the bags weren't drying out . . . it was a mess."

Changes were swift and massive. Tour caddies were allowed on site the next season, and many of the older caddies were forced to quit the only job they'd ever known, thus losing the only opportunity that offered them hope and a week's worth of glory. "We were brushed aside," says Leroy Shultz, who worked for Lanny Wadkins. "When Mr. Roberts died, we all went downhill." Of course Shultz labors under the assumption that Mr. Roberts would have tolerated the bag room incident, which, given his penchant for perfection, was anything but true.

Hardin made other changes for the good of the tournament and, for the first time, shared with the media the logic and reasoning behind Augusta National's decisions. He pared down the number of amateur invitations from as many as sixteen to around five, and he explained the reason Masters invitations are limited to eighty players:

> April is a rainy time in Georgia with short daylight hours. We have ninety-eight acres of fairway which have to be cut morning and evening; it takes time. We can do things right and have the best show. . . . With eighty players, fifteen players comes to almost a sixth of the field. In the early days, the amateurs finished high. Charlie Coe finished second. Ken Venturi was so far ahead he had to shoot

80 in the final round to lose by one stroke when he was an amateur. The game has changed since then. We want to keep amateurs in the tournament and I felt that five out of eighty was a pretty fair shake—more than in most tournaments.

Hardin's decision hasn't quieted critics who say the Masters field is laughably weak for a major, but it has opened invitations to more professionals while still allowing players like Tiger Woods and Justin Leonard to compete as amateurs. If Hord experienced heartburn over changing over the greens and the caddies, imagine how he must have felt in late October 1983 when he got a call that a gunman had crashed the gates and taken hostages. Augusta National member George Shultz, who just happened to be secretary of state at the time, had brought several guests in for the weekend. That Saturday afternoon, Shultz and his guests, White House chief of staff Don Regan and President Ronald Reagan were teeing off on the par-three sixteenth when the crisis broke out.

In the presidential scheme of things, it wasn't much of a crisis at all. The gunman, forty-five-year-old Charles Raymond Harris, was in the middle of a pretty tough year. His father had died, his wife had left him, and he'd recently lost his job as a welder. Heavy drinking caused two of those three, but Harris was a good ole boy who hunted, fished, camped, watched Georgia Bulldog football, and didn't see anything wrong with sipping a little George Dickel and Coke every now and then. When Charles heard that President Reagan was in town playing golf, he decided a chat with the commander in chief could perhaps straighten a few things out. After all, the president worked for the people. Charles was a citizen and, by God, he had his inalienable rights as an American. The Saturday afternoon of October 22, 1983, Harris extended those rights to include crashing gate 3 (one gate east of Magnolia Lane) and driving his four-wheel-drive Dodge pickup to the front door of the golf shop. He just wanted to talk to the president. The gun (a .38 caliber pistol) was just to get everybody's attention.

It did.

Club manager Jim Armstrong, along with White House staffers Robert Fischer and Lanny Wiles and club employees Robert Sullivan and Kris Hardy, paid very close attention to Mr. Harris as he demanded a summit with the president. Two other club employees, golf pro Dave Spencer and Louise Cook, heard what was happening and locked themselves in a small room off the main golf shop. Armstrong handled himself and the situation in heroic fashion, keeping everyone as calm as possible, even when Harris fired a shot into the golf shop floor, just to make sure he was being taken seriously.

Harris never met Reagan, and all the hostages were released except Armstrong, who escaped when Harris excused himself for a little nip of whiskey. Later, after his capture, Harris had to be rushed to University Hospital where he was diagnosed as having suffered from hyperventilation. "He might be aware of his situation more so than he was earlier in the day," doctors said. If not, he was certainly aware of his situation when he was sentenced to ten years in prison for threatening the president. He served three and a half years in the Columbia Correctional Institute and was released with a note of uncharacteristic praise from Judge Albert Pickett, who called Harris "one of those rare cases in which the probationer is worthy of early release from his sentence." Sober and a good deal more lucid, Mr. Harris went home where his three daughters and son, Bubba, strung a homemade sign over the door of their small brick house saying "Welcome Home, Daddy."

The story quickly faded away. The National didn't need or want that type of publicity, so in that sense Hardin and the members were happy to see it die. If the lack of extended press coverage had a downside, it was that Jim Armstrong and the other staffers never received adequate praise for their handling of the crisis. They displayed exemplary courage and professionalism in the heat of the moment. For them the crisis could not have been more serious. But, if the men of Augusta National were happy to see their names off the front pages, they, like the rest of the country, were saddened by what took their place. That same Saturday evening, while Charles Harris was "becoming aware of his situation," 147 U.S. Marines were killed when a suicide bomber plowed a truck full of explosives into their barracks at the Beirut airport. Charles Harris's attempt at rogue terrorism took an ugly backseat to the murderous acts of organized madmen. Like the rest of America, citizens of Augusta and the men at Augusta National viewed their incident in its proper perspective, and they mourned.

While all this was going on, the Masters Tournament was undergoing its own metamorphosis. Palmer and Player remained the nostalgic favorites, but the only member of the original Big Three who was still truly competitive by 1980 was Nicklaus. There were other heavyweight contenders by then with names like Watson, Stadler, and Crenshaw. But there were other names, too; names common folk in Augusta had trouble pronouncing—for instance, Severiano Ballesteros and Bernhard Langer. The 1980s would become known as the decade foreigners invaded Washington Road and took control of the Masters tournament. In the sixteen years from 1980 through 1996, non-American competitors won ten green jackets prompting some writers to muse that "the days of American dominance in golf" were over.

Sure, Gary Player had won three Masters titles, and players such as Bruce Devlin, Tony Jacklin, and Bob Charles consistently made good showings; but until the eighties, most experts considered the large foreign contingent at the Masters tokenism. Writers, players, and politicians who knew nothing about the game criticized the inclusion of so many foreigners, not that they thought the Masters should be a totally American event, but because they thought the foreign and amateur players weakened the field and displaced many capable American professionals who actually had a chance at winning. Since 1980, however, the suggestions that foreign players somehow weaken the Masters field have ceased, the critics relegated to the press building where they are chewing on a steady diet of crow.

In the mid-1980s the pretournament favorite was a foreigner, not from the Scottish motherland or the golf-rich regions of South Africa or Australia, but from the coast of Spain. Seve Ballesteros, the dashing, aggressive, fiery young golfer who had the charisma and style of Arnold Palmer and the chiseled features of a Hispanic Cary Grant, had only one problem when he won the 1980 Masters at age twenty-three—he couldn't speak English. By the time he won in 1983, Seve knew enough to say "thank you" and could grope through a few softball questions at the green jacket ceremony. But as a former tour player remembers, "When things weren't going Seve's way, he had a great knack of pulling the *no hablo inglés* line." A member of the transportation committee has vivid recollections of Seve's communication problems. "He could speak no English. A translator helped him. I was responsible for giving out Cadillacs to players and VIPs at the tournament. Seve wanted to know if he could take a Cadillac and leave it at the airport. I said sure, assuming he meant [Augusta's] Bush

Field. Turns out the car was left at the Atlanta airport [some 150 miles away]."

By the time the 1986 Masters rolled around, Ballesteros had earned two Masters titles. Bernhard Langer had one. Odds were even money on a foreigner winning again in 1986. No American blazed golf's trails as had been the case in the sixties and seventies with Palmer and Nicklaus. There were the critics who spat the same old saw, "Golf has no personality anymore," which seemed to be the standard mantra when the game went longer than two months without anyone dominating. Watson had a chance, as did Kite, and the always-crowd-pleasing Australian Greg Norman. But no one, not even the most imaginative oddsmaker or the most lovesick golf writer, could have possibly dreamed of what would come in the 1986 Masters. It was just too unbelievable.

The Masters is the world's greatest golf tournament in large measure because of Cliff Roberts's obsessions and Bob Jones's legacy. But if the tournament did not attract the world's greatest players, and if the drama of the event were not more compelling than any other sporting event of its kind, the Masters would have long ago fallen into the scrapheap stockpile of "good golf tournament . . . lots of fun . . . lots of history . . . nothing special." The tournament is what it is because from the moment Gene Sarazen nailed a four-wood into the hole on fifteen, the Masters has produced more great golf moments than any other event of any kind. The Super Bowl would kill for anything remotely resembling Masters drama, and baseball would be a better game with a Cliff Roberts or Hord Hardin at the helm. But the magic that is the Masters is more than just one moment; it is the combination of years of moments that have become almost

135

expected. Ken Venturi says of the Masters, "The tournament doesn't start until the back nine on Sunday." In 1986 he couldn't have been more right.

It was the fiftieth Masters, a golden anniversary milestone for the youngest of the four major championships, and nostalgia ran thick. During Wednesday's par-three contest, Player scored a hole in one on the fifth, prompting the loudest roar of the day and lining more than a few gamblers' pockets. (The par-three contest has become a haven for closest-to-the-pin bets ranging from twenty-five cents to one hundred dollars. Augusta officials don't encourage the practice, but they don't do anything to stop it either.) Gary Koch won the par-three event with a four-under 23.

Masters rookie Ken Green, who would later become a thorn for Hord Hardin, led after Thursday's round with seven birdies and a score of 68. In recalling that first Masters experience, Green has some less-than-obsequious things to say about the club, the course, and his 1986 experience: "I thought it would be something incredible. Well, there I was going down Magnolia Lane and it's like What the hell is so special about these things? There must be five thousand drives in Connecticut prettier than this. The second thing that struck me was that the players had to share lockers—two to a locker. That's not something you would expect at a Masters, but I guess they don't make enough money. [He chuckles.] The only reason it's never cramped in the locker room is that there's never a time everyone is in there. It must be a nightmare during a rain delay. As for the greencoats, they're pretty stuffy. They won't say hello to you unless you say it to them first. But I was ready for that because people told me to expect it. It makes no sense to me to treat people that way. It's not like the Masters tournament is being forced on the people at Augusta. I mean, it's not like the president came in and insisted that Augusta be used as the venue for the Ryder Cup. Why pretend you're better than anyone else?"

Whether playing backyard chipping games among Augusta's residential neighborhoods or teeing off in Masters Tournament play, Ken Green always puts a little extra body English into it. (AP/Wide World Photos—Rusty Kennedy)

The coleader after Thursday, Georgia's own Bill Kratzert, had nothing but great things to say about the entire Augusta experience, but Green still recalls that even the golf course was not what he'd imagined: "The first impression I can remember about the golf course is how bizarre the greens are. TV doesn't do them justice, especially the front side. Perhaps that's why they've never been crazy about televising the front nine during Masters coverage. There are four or five greens on the front nine that are absolute abortions. If anyone built a course like that today, they'd be crucified."

Could the 1986 event possibly be won by such a "heretic"? At least Green's sister Shelly added diplomatic levity to her brother's brutal frankness. She said of being the first female caddie at the Masters: "It was very exciting. I was just there so he'd have somebody to talk to. I was very proud of him." Green, honest and opinionated as ever, still can't understand what the fuss is all about. "People will criticize the USGA for this and that, but they never criticize Augusta. Why? I have no idea."

Shelly Green wasn't the only relative wearing white coveralls and replacing the old guard Augusta caddies. Vicente Ballesteros caddied for his younger brother, Severiano, and twenty-four-year old Jackie Nicklaus caddied for his dad, the elder statesman Jack Nicklaus who, at age forty-six, was playing in his twenty-eighth Masters. Ballesteros shot an opening-round 71 while Nicklaus shot 74 to tie with a couple of good-humored guys named Burns and Lewis—George Burns III and Robert C. Lewis Jr. Of the round and his chances, Nicklaus said, "If I can get any putts to fall, I can shoot some good scores out there." Reporters smiled, nodded, and moved on to Seve, Norman, Kite, and other contenders.

On Friday Bill Kratzert hung on to shoot an even-par 72 that trailed Seve Ballesteros, who fired a 68 of his own. Ballesteros led by one. Ken Green followed his opening-round lead with an ugly 78 that could have easily been an 80.

On the eighteenth, Green hit his second shot into the green-side bunker, a cavern so deep that all that can be seen when standing in it is the top of the flagstick. The pin was cut on the front edge, just over the bunker. Green hoped to get it close and have a reasonable putt to save par (and face) by breaking 80. Instead, he holed the sand shot, although he never saw the ball go in the hole.

The foreign invasion saved its charge for Saturday. Zimbabwean Nick Price (who, for the record, claimed to play out of South Africa since few sportswriters could spell Zimbabwe and even fewer could find it on a map) broke Augusta's equivalent of the four-minute mile by firing a stunning round of 63. The record of 64 had been challenged by the likes of Nicklaus, Player, Palmer, and even such notables as Maurice Bembridge and Miller Barber; but, like a glass cover, the final putts that would break the record had remained sealed until that Saturday in 1986. It could have actually been better. Price's birdie putt on eighteen for what would have been a 62 disappeared and then spun out, leaving him an inch-long tap-in for the 63.

Greg Norman, resident of Jupiter, Florida, but Australian to everyone in the golf world, led after the third round with a total of 210. Price, who had opened the tournament with an uninspiring 79, had climbed back to within one. Nicklaus finally broke 70 in the third round with a birdie at the sixteenth and pars on seventeen and eighteen, putting him three under for the day, two under for the tournament—four back but still hanging around.

Before Sunday's round, Greg Norman would say of Augusta National, "You still have to respect the old girl. When the pressure's on you still have to be careful."

No, Greg Norman is not waking up from a nap, and this isn't just a bad dream. This tumble took place in front of the fifteenth green on Sunday in the 1996 Masters Tournament moments after the Shark's eagle chip had lipped out, leaving him two shots behind eventual winner Nick Faldo. Norman had started the final round with a six-shot lead, only to see it gradually disappear in one of the most notable meltdowns in major tourament history. (AP/Wide World Photos—David Martin)

Those words should be tattooed on Norman's forehead, for in addition to a loss in 1986, Norman would suffer the ultimate heartbreak in 1987 when, on the second hole of sudden death, Larry Mize made an "impossible" chip-in for birdie to win. Then in 1996, after finishing tied for third in 1995—his best showing since 1989—Norman would suffer an even more debilitating defeat. He was leading by six shots going into the final round, and it appeared the Shark would finally don the green jacket his game so richly deserved. The crowd was with him. The course suited him. And he had led from the first hole on the first day. On Sunday the train derailed . . . very, very slowly.

THE 1986 MASTERS WOULD NOT BE LOST THROUGH CARELESSNESS, HOWEVER. IT WOULD BE WON THROUGH SOMETHING APPROACHING DIVINE INTERVENTION.

"It was unlike any Masters I've ever seen," Augusta writer Steve Hale says of the 1996 event. "The sounds were different. It was like a funeral out there. Nobody said anything. We were all just stunned."

Norman shot 78 that Sunday, losing to Nick Faldo by five shots and draining the blood out of fans all over the world in the process. Hale summed up everyone's feeling: "It hurt to watch."

"There's no reason to say anything when a television picture is already telling the whole story," Frank Chirkinian says. "Some members of the print media criticized us for not saying on the air that Greg Norman was choking. That really ticked me off. I mean, why say it? The viewers could see for themselves what was happening. It's obtuse."

The 1986 Masters would not be lost through carelessness, however. It would be won through something approaching divine intervention. It started on number nine. Nicklaus had played the first eight holes even par on Sunday and, at nine, he knew it was time to get something going. He did just that with a birdie. That birdie started a chain of events

141

that will be remembered and repeated forever by golf historians and lovers of the game. Nicklaus birdied ten and eleven sending shock waves through the pines and implanting a hint of nervousness into the swings of his fellow competitors. A sleeping bear had awakened and rediscovered his den. At the twelfth Nicklaus made a bogey and many hard-hearted skeptics wrote him off. Nice try, Jack. Thanks for the memories. But when he birdied thirteen and made a good par at fourteen, the rumble again started to grow.

Ballesteros looked as though he had the tournament in hand when he rapped in a five-foot eagle putt on the thirteenth.

Nicklaus stood on the fifteenth tee four shots down. He had four to play. In the fifteenth fairway, site of Sarazen's "shot heard round the world," Nicklaus turned to his son, Jackie, and asked, "How much good do you think a three would do?" Jackie didn't answer. When the twenty-foot putt went in on fifteen, Jackie leapt higher than Willie Patterson, Jack's rotund Augusta caddie for all five of his previous Masters victories, had ever jumped. The crowd erupted and continued to cheer as Jack and Jackie made their way to the sixteenth tee. CBS commentator Ben Wright summed up the moment well when he said, "The battle is joined."

Ballesteros parred fourteen and proceeded to blast a 301-yard drive at the par-five fifteenth, guarded in front by water. Meanwhile, Nicklaus stood on sixteen, the hole he had owned more than any other in his career. In 1963 a young, overweight Nicklaus had likewise started the week with an opening-round 74 only to battle back to eventually take the lead with a fifteen-foot birdie putt on the sixteenth. He won by one shot and became the youngest Masters winner ever, until Ballesteros came along in 1980, then Woods in 1997.

Again in 1975 Nicklaus turned the sixteenth into his special place for fourth-round theatrics, making a forty-foot birdie putt that highlighted a back-nine battle with

Tom Weiskopf and Johnny Miller and propelled Nicklaus on to his fifth green jacket. Now it was 1986 and Weiskopf was providing color commentary for CBS from within the cozy Butler Cabin. As Nicklaus stood on the sixteenth tee with a five-iron, announcer Jim Nantz asked Weiskopf what he thought might be going through Jack's mind at that moment. Weiskopf aptly replied, "If I knew how he thought, I would have won this golf tournament." Then, as Nicklaus addressed his tee shot, Weiskopf gave Nicklaus these prophetic words of encouragement: "Make the swing you are capable of making. Your destiny is right here."

Nicklaus came within inches of making an ace. His ball landed just to the right of the flagstick, then rolled down the slope of the green, just missing the cup on the abbreviated return trip and finally stopping three feet away. It was birdie time again. The crowds erupted. Nicklaus recalls: "The ovation was unbelievable. The sound was deafening. I couldn't hear a thing." With the crowds clearly with him, who could stand against him? Nicklaus clearly had the home-field advantage. Tom Watson and Tommy Nakajima had to rush their putts on the nearby fifteenth green because of what they knew was going on with Nicklaus over at sixteen. Sixteen and fifteen are closer than they appear on television, and any attempt to play while Nicklaus was on sixteen would have been thwarted by the thunderous ovations Jack received. Watching from the fairway, waiting by his monstrous drive, was Ballesteros. Nicklaus made his birdie and the cheers reverberated through the pines.

Printed on every badge at the Masters tournament is the following admonition:

> In golf, customs of etiquette and decorum are just as important as rules governing play. It is appropriate for spectators to applaud successful strokes in proportion to difficulty,

but excess demonstrations by a player or partisans are not proper because of the possible effect upon other competitors. Most distressing to those who love the game of golf is the applauding or cheering of misplays or misfortunes of a player. Such occurrences have been rare at the Masters, but we must eliminate them entirely if our patrons are to continue to merit their reputation as the most knowledgeable and considerate in the world.

Bobby Jones wrote those words, ironically, when in 1967 a Palmer-crazy crowd cheered when "Fat Jack" Nicklaus missed a putt. Furious, Jones wrote the message and insisted it be printed on every ticket. In 1986 almost every member of that "knowledgeable and considerate" crowd pulled against Seve as he stood over his four-iron second shot in the fifteenth fairway. He was cursed before he ever took the club back. Conditions were ideal. The wind, as Ben Wright said, "was a mere zephyr." The crowd was quiet, and Seve had less than two hundred yards to the flag. He hit what all will agree was the ugliest shot of the day: a low pull-hook that never had a chance at finding anything but the water. Before the ripples reached the edge of the pond, a roar went out as fans, who obviously had forgotten to read their badges, let Nicklaus know that his destiny was, indeed, right there.

"I heard this cheer or roar," Nicklaus remembers. "I told myself, he's either hit it in the water or holed it."

Nicklaus would later stand on the seventeenth tied for the lead. At the seventeenth green, he faced a seventeen-foot birdie putt that gave him an opportunity to move to six under for the back nine, seven under for the day, and nine under for the tournament. When the putt dropped, Nicklaus, in old familiar form, raised his putter and stepped toward the hole, knowing right then and there he had snared sole possession of

A golden moment if ever there was one: A young Jack Nicklaus and an aging Bobby Jones, arguably the two greatest golfers of the twentieth century, share some insights on the occasion of the Golden Bear's Masters Tournament victory in 1966. (© Morgan Fitz Photographers, Globe Photos, Inc. 1997)

the lead. Said Jackie Nicklaus, "When the putt went in, you could have heard it in Atlanta."

Jackie would hug his dad on the eighteenth green after Jack tapped in for par. Then, as the five-time winner,

145

The Golden Bear watches his birdie putt at Augusta's seventeenth drop, putting him one hole away from clinching the 1986 Masters Tournament title at age forty-six. (AP/Wide World Photos)

about to win for the record-extending sixth time, watched from the Butler Cabin, Tom Kite missed an eighteen-footer for a tie. Norman, the last person who could have spoiled history, then missed a ten-footer for par after having blocked his approach shot at eighteen well right, into the grandstand.

Jack Nicklaus had become only the second winner to break 280 after Augusta's conversion to bent-grass greens. He had been the youngest man ever to win the Masters in 1963 and on April 13, 1986, at the age of forty-six, he had become the oldest Masters champion and the only man in history to win six green jackets. It was his twentieth major title, including two U.S. Amateurs.

In a professional career that has spanned four decades, no win of his had or has equaled Nicklaus's victory in the 1986 Masters. The only surviving knight of the Big Three, Nicklaus struck down the foreign invasion and breathed new life into a game that sorely needed him. MacGregor Golf Company would sell a record number of the putter Jack used that year. Artists from around the world did their best to capture on canvas the images of that day; Jack leaping on fifteen, raising his putter on seventeen, rolling his eyes skyward as he walked to the eighteenth tee. It was a moment that everyone could remember; one of those rare moments in sports and in life when those who witnessed an event became keenly aware of place and time and history.

The drama didn't stop there. In 1987 Augusta native Larry Mize won the Masters with an incredible chip-in on the second playoff hole to defeat Norman. In 1988 Sandy Lyle of Scotland entered the special club of Masters winners when he made a downhill birdie putt on the eighteenth green, set up by a wonderful eight-iron shot out of the double fairway bunker, to beat Mark Calcavecchia by one shot. The next year England's Nick Faldo kept the British tradition alive by winning the first of his three Masters titles in the playoff that Scott Hoch actually lost by missing a thirty-inch putt on the first playoff hole. Faldo did it again in 1990, this time defeating Ray Floyd in a playoff and becoming only the third man in history to win two consecutive Masters titles. And in 1991 the Europeans made it four in a row when a former amateur boxer from Wales, Ian Woosnam, beat Spain's José Maria Olazàbal by birdieing the eighteenth.

All the while, Hardin continued to manage as he always had, but there were a few annoying crises. The first concerned that candid rebel who had briefly led in 1986, Ken Green.

Here is how Green tells it: "The year I had the fracas was 1989. My friends and I had two houses rented that year, across the street from each other. I had about a dozen friends and relatives in with me that week, but my wife—now my ex-wife—and I had a fight that week and she still had seven of the tickets back home in Florida. She wouldn't send them up to me. The amazing thing is, four of those dozen people were from her family. Everyone tried to talk her out of what she was doing, but it didn't work. So, there I was stuck with only five tickets for twelve people. I told them I was going to go into the club, tell them the truth, and see if I could get replacement tickets. On Wednesday I go to the club and speak to the lady in charge of all this. I told her the whole truth about my wife, and all the lady said was, 'You've got to get better control of your wife. There is nothing we can do.' I was willing to pay [full price] for the tickets, but it didn't make any difference.

"What we ended up doing was pretty bizarre. I had a big Cadillac as a courtesy car and got my people into Augusta by hiding them in the car, on the floorboards and in the trunk. Some of these people had traveled about a thousand miles to be there and I was going to get them in one way or the other. Once they got in, the trick was for those without tickets to stick close to those with them and keep a sharp eye out for on-course security guards checking for passes. One guy got caught— my wife's brother—and got kicked out. On top of that, I get a call from her ripping me for not giving her brother one of the five tickets. The irony is, it was my best Masters ever. I tied for eleventh."

AFTER HARDIN AND OTHER AUGUSTA NATIONAL OFFICIALS PIECED TOGETHER THE CIRCUMSTANCES OF GREEN'S DRIVE-IN ANTICS, THEY QUICKLY PUT PROCEDURES IN EFFECT TO HALT SUCH FRATERNITY-LIKE HIJINKS.

After Hardin and other Augusta National officials pieced together the circumstances of Green's drive-in antics, they quickly put procedures in effect to halt such fraternity-like hijinks. Green recalls: "The next day, Mark Calcavecchia—one of my best friends, and they knew it—gets stopped at the front gate by a security guard who checks out Calc's car. When Calc asked what was going on, the guard said, 'This is what we call the Ken Green Rule.' Me and all my friends managed to get in the rest of the week by doing it differently, making several runs with the car. I didn't enjoy doing this, but I felt I needed to do it for all those people there supporting me. I would much rather have paid another seven hundred dollars for replacement tickets."

Green continued to be Hord Hardin's fly in the Augusta ointment for the rest of his tenure as chairman. Of their relationship, Green now says: "Hord was kind of a weird duck. One thing I will always remember about him is what a friend told me based on what he had seen in the clubhouse. Hord was sitting in the grill room with Frank Chirkinian and I was out playing on the golf course. It was the first round and I was five under at the turn. When my score flashed inside, Hord looked up and said, 'Ahh, he's coming to haunt me.' It just so happened that's the last time [1991] that I played there."

Hardin would retire as chairman in May 1991, passing the reins to Little Rock investment magnate Jack Stephens. But before he left office, Hardin had to deal with one more management crisis: a continuing problem that had plagued the National since the early sixties and was brought into focus again. On June 20, 1990, a general-assignment reporter for the *Birmingham (Alabama) Post-Herald,* Joan Mazzolini, sat down for an hour and a half with Augusta National member and Shoal Creek founder Hall Thompson.

Thompson, a Caterpillar tractor dealer and one of Birmingham's richest men, answered all of Mazzolini's questions openly and candidly, including a question about an ad in the PGA Championship program that a city councilman wanted to pull because Shoal Creek didn't allow black members. Augusta National member Hall Thompson said: "Bringing up this issue will just polarize the community . . . but it can't pressure us. We have the right to associate or not to associate with whomever we choose. The country club is our home and we pick and choose whom we want . . . I think we've said that we don't discriminate in any other area except for the Blacks."

All eyes turned toward Augusta as the race card had been turned up once again.

CHAPTER 7

FROM CLAUDE TILLMAN TO TIGER WOODS

PLEASE ACCEPT MY SINCERE THANKS FOR PROVIDING ME THE OP-
PORTUNITY TO EXPERIENCE THE MOST WONDERFUL WEEK OF MY
LIFE: IT WAS FANTASY LAND AND DISNEY WORLD WRAPPED INTO
ONE. I WAS TREATED LIKE A GENTLEMAN THROUGHOUT MY STAY
AND I TRUST I RESPONDED IN KIND. THE "CROW'S NEST" WILL AL-
WAYS REMAIN IN MY HEART AND YOUR MAGNIFICENT GOLF COURSE
WILL PROVIDE A CONTINUING CHALLENGE THROUGHOUT MY AMA-
TEUR AND PROFESSIONAL CAREER. I'VE ACCOMPLISHED MUCH HERE
AND LEARNED EVEN MORE. YOUR TOURNAMENT WILL ALWAYS HOLD
A SPECIAL SPOT IN MY HEART AS THE PLACE WHERE I MADE MY FIRST
PGA CUT AND AT A MAJOR YET! IT IS HERE THAT I LEFT MY YOUTH
BEHIND AND BECAME A MAN. FOR THAT I WILL BE ETERNALLY IN
YOUR DEBT. . . . WITH WARMEST REGARDS AND DEEPEST APPRECI-
ATION, I REMAIN

> SINCERELY,
> TIGER WOODS
> (WRITTEN TO THE MEMBERS OF
> AUGUSTA NATIONAL AFTER THE 1995
> MASTERS)

For three decades no one questioned the racial makeup of Augusta National members or Masters Tournament participants, and no one batted an eye at the color of the hired help. Golf was a white man's game where black men served as stewards and caddies. It was that way over much of the country, and Augusta, deep in the heart of Dixie, was no exception. Throughout the 1930s, 1940s, and 1950s race wasn't an issue. Not at Augusta, anyway. Golf clubs were for white men: no women, no Jews, no Asians, and no Blacks. Segregation was the law of the land, and clubs were simply a magnified extension of the era's prejudices.

The PGA of America left nothing to the imagination. In 1943 golf's professional ruling body voted to add an article to its constitution. It read: "Professional golfers of the Caucasian Race, over the age of eighteen (18) years, residing in North or South America, who can qualify under the terms and conditions hereinafter specified, shall be eligible for membership." The amendment became known as the "Caucasian Clause." Years later, all heads would turn toward the South to find the roots of discrimination, but it was Michigan's PGA delegation that proposed the Caucasian Clause, thus making a declarative highbrow argument: "Show us some good golf courses established by Negroes."

Perhaps there weren't any good "Black" golf courses, but there were some better-than-good golfers who were excluded from competition by the rule. Ted Rhodes, golf's version of Satchel Paige, could have been a superstar at any level, but because of golf's exclusionary policies he could only compete on the mostly black United Golf Association tour, where he won a staggering 150 tournaments.

"People like Jimmy Demaret and Sam Snead spoke highly of him," Rhodes protégé Lee Elder said of his mentor. "They were always commenting on how great Ted would have been had he been allowed to play [the white tour]."

Charlie Sifford, who became the subject of heated Masters controversy in the 1960s, said of his predecessor, "I owe my career to [Ted Rhodes]." So do players such as Calvin Peete, Jim Dent, Jim Thorpe, and golf's star phenom of the 1990s, Eldrick "Tiger" Woods. Nike's golden-boy-in-golf-shoes is able to smile because Teddy Rhodes was able to smile.

"He was a gentleman," South African golfer Gary Player, whose background had amply exposed him to apartheid, said of Rhodes. "When you see a man smile in the kind of adversity he was under, that's the true sign of a great man. Every time you saw [Ted] he had that glowing smile."

Oddly enough, the game that maliciously excluded Blacks owes a tremendous indebtedness to Blacks in the form of players such as Rhodes, Sifford, Elder, and Peete, players who overcame the odds and demonstrated to a legion of Blacks that golf was their game, too. It also is indebted to men such as Dr. George Grant, a Boston dentist and black man, who patented the first golf tee, and to John Shippen of Shinnecock, Long Island, who is widely acknowledged as the country's first golf professional. Shippen competed in five U.S. Opens and was the first Black ever to lead the country's national championship.

As Shippen and a fellow black Shinnecock professional by the name of Oscur Bunn prepared to begin play in the 1896 U.S. Open, a group of foreign entrants threatened a boycott if Shippen and Bunn were allowed to tee off. Theodore Havermyer, USGA president at the time, would have none of it. He said to the field, "We are going to play this thing today even if Shippen and Bunn are the only people in it." No one boycotted, and Shippen ultimately finished fifth.

Even with such performances, white America continued to ignore the talent at its feet, not just in golf, but in baseball, football, medicine, engineering, and the arts. The only difference with golf is that its narrow-minded behavior lasted longer than the rest. It wasn't until 1962, with

Charlie Sifford, pictured here sometime in the sixties, probably was the greatest African-American golfer of his era, yet he never got to play in the invitational Masters Tournament for what he claimed were racist reasons. (AP/Wide World Photos)

cigar-chomping Charlie Sifford drinking from golf's prover-bial white-only fountain, that golf became integrated. That year the PGA chose the prestigious Brentwood Country Club in Los Angeles as the host club for its championship, one of golf's majors. The members of Brentwood were de-lighted by their good fortune, and the staff feverishly pre-pared for their moment in the sun.

All went as planned until Stanley Mosk, California's attorney general, received a copy of the PGA constitution and read Article III, Section One—the Caucasian Clause. Mosk couldn't believe it. Not only was the clause an affront to common decency and good sense, it violated the U.S. Constitution and the Constitution of the State of California. Mosk sent a very simple message to the PGA: Abolish discrimination or get out. Either Blacks played in California or nobody did. The PGA chose the latter. They moved their championship, not to Birmingham, Alabama, or Jackson, Mississippi, but to the city of brotherly love, Philadelphia. No Blacks played. However, later that year the PGA finally relented and voted to repeal the Caucasian Clause.

Even though Sifford has enjoyed success on both the regular and senior PGA Tours, and even though he's been called "the Jackie Robinson of golf," he remains bitter about those exclusionary years.

"I don't know what's more disturbing," Sifford says in his book *Just Let Me Play,* "the fact that the PGA was so ignorant and arrogant that it thought it could keep the game alive in modern times while keeping it segregated, or the fact that it didn't seem to make a damn bit of difference to the corporate sponsors and general public." Stanley Mosk cared, and although you won't find his name among the plaques in golf's Hall of Fame, he made more than "a damn bit of difference" in 1962. Charlie and the others would get to play . . . well, sort of.

After the PGA belatedly saw the error of its ways, tournament organizers became incensed. How could anyone tell the sponsors, patrons, and organizers that they *had* to allow "coloreds" into *their* events? Good ole boys from the rest of the country didn't give a damn what they did in California; they would run their tournaments as they saw fit. Almost overnight, tournaments that had historically been "open" suddenly became exclusive "invitationals." Only those who conformed to very specific criteria were invited. Amateur and even junior tournaments quickly jumped on the bandwagon even though the PGA had no governing effect on amateur events. The Future Masters, a junior golf tournament in

Dothan, Alabama, required its "invitees" to submit pictures with their applications. One could assume those looking at the pictures weren't checking for photogenic appeal or good haircuts. The term "invitational" became code for "segregation." Blacks need not apply.

The Masters was an invitational, always had been, always would be.

Perhaps the reason Augusta National received, and continues to receive, so much attention regarding race lies in the fact that Augusta, the town, is ensconced in the traditions of the South, and Augusta National is, for many, the stereotypical epitome of antebellum society: a big white house at the end of a long drive where white folk mingle and black folk tend. The look and feel of the Old South can be found in every detail at the National, and with those images come the negative stereotypes of white masters and black slaves. It isn't a historical allusion, it's a time warp. In the early days the cozy plantation environment appealed to everyone, but by the 1960s, as society integrated and cultures had to learn to coexist, the idea of a plantation oasis in the center of a divided nation rubbed a great number of American civil sensibilities. Throw in the fact that Augusta's main claim to fame (other than Godfather of Soul and North Augusta native James Brown) remained a lily-white "invitational" golf tournament, and the recipe for racial unrest was written.

In fact, the Masters had been an invitational since 1934 and the National had for years provided steady employment to a number of Augusta residents, both black and white. That is not to say the attitudes at the National weren't racist. Former Georgia governor and pronounced segregationist Lester Maddox was a member. Blacks didn't play the National, even as guests. Cliff Roberts and, to a lesser extent,

Bob Jones, were part and parcel to the southern racial culture: Roberts because his rigid belief system made him suspicious of anyone unlike himself and Jones because of the time and place where he grew up.

THE LOOK AND FEEL OF THE OLD SOUTH CAN BE FOUND IN EVERY DETAIL AT THE NATIONAL, AND WITH THOSE IMAGES COME THE NEGATIVE STEREOTYPES OF WHITE MASTERS AND BLACK SLAVES.

If you're in reasonably good shape, you can walk from Tuxedo Road in Atlanta where the Jones's house still stands to Tenth Street where Margaret Mitchell penned *Gone With the Wind*. A few more miles south is the Martin Luther King Jr. Center for Non-violent Social Change, a sprawling complex devoted to the ideals of the great civil rights activist. Jones lived, metaphorically if not physically, somewhere in between the two. He was a man who hated no one and who thought himself no better than any other human being, black, white, or otherwise. He also had a butler and a housekeeper (both black) his entire life. His caddies at East Lake and Augusta National were black, as were the waiters, stewards, and maids in the clubhouses. As a child Jones would lie in bed eagerly anticipating the reading of his favorite bedtime stories from *Uncle Remus: His Songs and Sayings,* written by fellow (white) Georgian, Joel Chandler Harris. These stories sported such passages as: "Brer Fox went ter wuk en got 'im some tar, en mix it wid some turpentine, en fix up a contrapshun wat he call a Tar-Baby en he sot 'er in de big road, en den he lay off in de bushes fer to see what de news wuz gwineter be." Although Jones could never philosophically or intellectually be accused of racism in any form, the practicality of his life and the era in which he lived was (by today's standards) demeaning to minorities.

Roberts harbored more practical day-to-day feelings of bigotry. According to Frank Hannigan, in his writings for publication, "[Roberts] thought that Blacks should be cared for decently, so long as it was understood they were servants or entertainers. . . . This confidant of the president of the United States thought there would be trouble in both the United States and England wherever people of color converged in large numbers." Hannigan is quick to point out, however, that Roberts's innate suspicions weren't confined merely to Blacks or Hispanics or other people of color. "He regarded shortened Italian names as evidence of sinister behavior."

The best example of Roberts's pejorative view of Blacks is the story of Augusta National employee Claude Tillman and the way in which Tillman came to work at the club. In Roberts's own words:

> [Claude] came to us shortly after the death of our member Tom Barrett, of Augusta. . . . During that [early] period I developed a very strong liking for Claude, Tom's faithful helper. . . . The little black fellow couldn't read or write, but he was able to drive a car, mind the children, keep the yard clean, mix drinks, relieve the cook when necessary, shave and dress Tom in the morning, and give him a rubdown if Tom had a morning-after feeling. I recall one occasion when Tom got into a heated argument with a friend from Macon as to who had the better servant. After another drink of corn, the question of who loved his man the most nearly precipitated a fight.
>
> Tom Barrett's war injuries were credited with bringing on a fatal illness, and during that time he told me that he wanted me to have Claude. He apparently made a stipulation to

that effect, because Tom's widow, Louise, placed a Christmas wreath around Claude's neck, tied a card to it bearing my name, and sent Claude to me. After conferring with Bowman [Milligan, the club's steward—also black] I passed along my gift to the club by placing Claude in charge of the kitchen. After arrival in Augusta from New York some six weeks later, the following conversation took place between Claude and me:

"Claude, how are you doing in the kitchen?"

"We is doin' jus' fine."

"Are we doing a good volume of business?"

"We is doin' lots of business."

"But are we making any money?"

"Yes, suh!"

"But, how do you know? Give me an example."

After scratching his head for a bit, Claude said, "You takes my milk. I measures it out very careful and I serves five glasses from a bottle at fifteen cents a glass, and a bottle only costs us fifteen cents. And on that basis, Mr. Cliff, we is 'bliged to show a profit."

Roberts didn't write this during the 1930s Al Jolson period, not even during the 1950 *Amos and Andy* times (although by then many Americans saw Kingfish and Andy as degrading stereotypes); Roberts wrote that description—dialogue included—in 1976, *eight years after Martin Luther King Jr.'s death.*

The National to this day defends Roberts. Granted, many of the accusations thrown Roberts's way are patently untrue, but the statement by current Augusta and Masters chairman Jack Stephens that he "knew Cliff Roberts very well [and] there was not a prejudiced bone in his body" is, if not demonstrably untrue, at least suspect. The charge that Roberts was a racist, the club refutes by saying, "For people to infer that twenty years after Roberts has been dead is not fair. As far as Clifford Roberts was concerned, golf had no boundaries: no geographic boundaries, no social boundaries."

It is true that applying 1990s standards to 1930s, 1940s, 1950s, and even 1970s behavior is skewed and maybe even unfair. However, the charges being leveled while Roberts was alive were more vicious than anything people have said since his death. Sifford, the most outspoken and blunt of the early black players, said of Roberts: "I'll tell you why I knew that I'd never get into that tournament [the Masters]: they told me so themselves. In the late fifties, when I was playing a limited PGA Tour schedule and was the perennial champion of the Negro tournaments, it was suggested to Augusta National that I receive a kind of goodwill bid to play. . . . Word came back from . . . Clifford Roberts: 'As long as I live, there will be nothing at the Masters besides black caddies and white players.' "

Sifford's accusations were at least as skewed as Stephens's assertions that seemed to suggest that Roberts was pure, tolerant, and ready to sing "We Shall Overcome." Both viewpoints are wrong. The big difference is, while Stephens is looking at Roberts through the scope of friendship, Charlie was seemingly speaking out in detached bitterness.

Probably chomping on a cigar at the time, as is his trademark, Sifford mused: "One of the great disillusions of my life in golf is that the Masters has become a tournament so revered by golf fans and media, with all the fanfare on television every year when it's played. As far as I'm concerned, it has long been the most racist and hateful spot on the golf globe. . . . I'm positive that they changed their rules more than once to exclude me from playing, because for many years I was the only Black man good enough on the PGA Tour to come close to getting an automatic bid. Quite simply, they didn't want a Black, specifically me, on their golf course. The most prestigious golf course and tournament in America were also the most conniving and the meanest."

Not true. Yes, Clifford Roberts "gave" a black man to the club who had shown up at his doorstep with a wreath around his neck; and yes, the National employed black caddies and black servers while accepting only white members (until 1990), but the accusations that the Masters committee systematically changed its invitation policies just to exclude Blacks is debatable. In fact, many players believe that being a white American was equally as great a handicap when it came to getting into the Masters. Frank Beard remembers: "There used to be kind of a joke going around that white American-born professionals couldn't get into Augusta, but if you were a foreigner or of mixed race, you could get in. It was a sore point with many of the players. Chi Chi Rodriguez throughout the year was known [rightfully] as an American, but when it came Masters week he was Puerto Rican and got in. You had guys from Australia who had been living in the U.S. for years getting invites as foreigners. [For

SOME IN THE MEDIA ACTUALLY SUGGESTED TO ROBERTS THAT LEE ELDER SHOULD RECEIVE A FOREIGN INVITATION AS AN AFRICAN, ALTHOUGH AT THE TIME IT'S UNCLEAR WHETHER OR NOT ELDER HAD EVER SET FOOT ON AFRICAN SOIL.

example] Bruce Crampton [a native Australian] was living in the U.S., but he would go and play something like three tournaments a year back in Australia and he would get a foreigner's invitation to the Masters. That rankled a lot of the rest of us. We knew in our heart he was an American tour player. I'm not blaming him—it wasn't his fault. But it was a bone of contention."

Some in the media actually suggested to Roberts that Lee Elder should receive a foreign invitation as an *African,* although at the time it's unclear whether or not Elder had ever set foot on African soil. Roberts was not amused. Then in 1973 eighteen members of Congress took time out on the floor of the House to "insist" that Augusta National arbitrarily invite a Black into the Masters. They sent a telegram to that effect; and Roberts responded that he was "a little surprised as well as being flattered that eighteen congressmen would be able to take time out from trying to solve the nation's problems to help us operate a golf tournament."

The most noteworthy claim Sifford ever made alleging racist-motivated manipulation of Masters invitational criteria concerned his play in the 1962 Canadian Open. Leading the tournament with nine holes to play in the fourth round, Sifford says he was abruptly told by an official arriving on the scene that word had just come down from Augusta that the Canadian Open winner would not be invited to the 1963 Masters. The way Sifford tells it, the story rings of blatant racial exclusion, if it were grounded in truth.

A check of Masters invitational criteria for that period shows that, yes, winning the Canadian Open brought with it a ticket to the first tee at Augusta, *provided the winner was actually a Canadian,* which Sifford certainly was not. Note, too, that the Canadian Open clause fell within the Masters' special foreign section criteria, meaning that not even Ted Kroll, a white man who ultimately came from behind to beat Sifford at the 1962

Canadian Open, could get a Masters invitation. Kroll didn't meet the *foreign section* stipulation and neither did Sifford.

Despite the desires of the press, Charlie Sifford, and members of Congress, American qualifications for invitation to the Masters haven't changed significantly over the years. In 1969, just after the height of the civil rights movement and during one of the years Sifford groaned that he was "unfairly" excluded, the qualifications were clear, concise, and available for everyone to see. There were fourteen ways to get into the Masters:

(1) Win a Masters and you got a lifetime exemption, which, of course, didn't do black players much good in the 1960s. Since none were invited, the chances of a black player winning were not good.

(2) Win a U.S. Open, which has been possible for anybody of any race at any time in American history.

(3) Win a U.S. Amateur.

(4) Win a British Open.

(5) Win a British Amateur.

(6) Win a PGA Championship.

(7) Earn a spot on the Ryder Cup team, which in 1969 was an opportunity as available for a deserving black man as being asked to accompany Neil Armstrong on a moon walk.

(8) Earn a spot on the World Amateur Cup or Walker Cup teams, which for Blacks in the 1960s, made the moon walk look easy.

(9) Finish in the first twenty-four players, including ties, in the 1968 Masters Tournament. Of course, for golfers not invited to the 1968 Masters Tournament, this qualification didn't mean much.

(10) Finish in the first sixteen players, including ties, in the 1968 U.S. Open.

(11) Finish in the top eight, including ties, in the 1968 PGA Championship.

(12) Finish in the top eight, not including ties, in the 1968 U.S. Amateur Championship.

(13) Be the one player selected by the past Masters champions.

(14) Finish in the top sixteen on the tour's money list for the year spanning the week after the 1968 Masters until the week before the 1969 Masters.

There was no hidden agenda then, and there is no hidden agenda now. To get an invitation in the mail for the 1998 Masters, you need only:

(1) Win a Masters. Tiger Woods has shown himself to be an odds-on favorite in every tournament he plays, so there's a very good chance that a black man will not only play, but win—again.

(2) Win a U.S. Open.

(3) Win a British Open.

(4) Win a PGA Championship.

(5) Be a finalist in the most recent U.S. Amateur.

(6) Win the most recent British Amateur.

(7) Win the most recent U.S. Public Links Championship.

(8) Win the most recent U.S. Mid-Amateur Championship.

(9) Finish in the top twenty-four, including ties, in last year's Masters.

(10) Finish in the top sixteen, including ties, in last year's U.S. Open.

(11) Finish in the top eight, including ties, in last year's PGA Championship.

(12) Win a PGA Tour cosponsored event deemed by the Masters committee to be a "major" event from between the time of the previous year's Masters and the current year's Masters.

(13) Finish in the top thirty on the PGA Tour money list for the previous year.

Roberts and the Masters committee did not openly practice discrimination in their invitation policies, nor, apparently, did they modify their policies to exclude Blacks or other minorities. However, they also did not modify their guidelines to make it easier for Blacks to qualify. A black player could have qualified under any of the aforementioned criteria, but it wouldn't have been because of any affirmative action program, even though Roberts and the Masters committee were pressured to make it happen.

Sam Snead remembers: "There was a senator that called the club asking them to let [Lee Elder] in the tournament, that it would be good for the game. Roberts's response was, 'Senator, I don't know if Lee Elder is black or white, but if he earns his way here, he's welcome to play.' Roberts was right in saying that the club shouldn't allow someone to play there who didn't deserve to be there. Clifford didn't care about who played as long as that golfer got in there the right way."

Still, pressure continued to mount. When Lee Trevino decided not to play for a few years even though he was eligible and received an invitation, cries went out that white Augusta had made life too uncomfortable for a Mexican-American, a charge even Trevino denies. "I didn't like the golf course," Trevino told *Golf* magazine. "Everything is a dogleg to the left. You have got to hit a high hook to play Augusta. I hit the ball low."

There were also stories that Trevino was mistreated and made to feel like a second-class citizen, so much so that he had to change his shoes in the parking lot.

His rebuttal was: "That was simply because they let the media in the locker room. You couldn't sit down without five hundred of them pouncing on you like a dog with a piece of meat. I went in there to put my shoes on, bent down to lace them, and hit my head on five tape recorders. I took my stuff and ran. That's the reason I never went in that locker room. Had nothing to do with Augusta."

Augusta was not Lee Trevino's favorite golf course, nor was the Masters his tournament of choice, but he still was able to entertain the crowds at the National. (*Augusta Chronicle* photo)

In reflecting on the whole issue of race at the Masters, Trevino, in his typical style, cut right to the quick: "They asked me one time about a Black never playing there. I said, 'No one has ever qualified. Do you have a history of a Black qualifying that they turned down?' No."

One finally did qualify, and others followed. It was poetic justice that the first black man to play in the Masters was not the acrimonious Charlie Sifford, but a more reserved man who accepted his invitation with grace and withstood the prejudices of his day to become a leading money winner and one of the most respected men on tour: Lee Elder. By winning the Monsanto Pensacola Open in 1974, Elder qualified to be the first Black to ever play in the Masters Tournament, and a collective sigh of relief went out across the country and inside the gates of the National. It was finally over. The charges of conspiracy were finally dismissed.

Elder rode through the gates in April 1975, not as a servant or a caddie or a deliveryman but as a golfer, just like Jack Nicklaus, Johnny Miller, Lee Trevino (who came back after Jack Nicklaus convinced him that sitting out of a major was just plain silly), and Arnold Palmer. Nicklaus won in 1975, and Miller and Weiskopf tied for second. Trevino tied for tenth and Arnold Palmer finished tied for thirteenth. Elder, amid a barrage of media, shot 74, 78 and missed the cut, but forever established himself as a man with a colon after his name—Lee Elder: first black man to play in the Masters.

Elder's momentous journey to Augusta in 1975 wasn't exactly a tournament of roses and well-wishes, however. In a 1995 HBO *Real Sports* special about Augusta and the Masters, in which it was suggested that he had been "snubbed" by Roberts, Elder said, "I think that when I qualified, it really put him in such an embarrassing position that he [Roberts] wanted to do everything that he possibly could to, maybe, not make it comfortable for me there."

Lee Elder got plenty of attention at the 1975 Masters Tournament, becoming the first African American to tee it up in the prestigious tournament. Elder qualified by winning the 1974 Monsanto Open on the PGA Tour. (AP/Wide World Photos)

Today, Elder, a leading supporter of junior golf and children's charities, sees the Masters not as a black man, but as a golfer, having said: "The history and traditions of that tournament make it the greatest. Even though we were discriminated against as players, the Masters is still to me a much more important and emotional experience than the U.S. Open or the PGA. . . . With the possible exception of the Ryder Cup, it's the most important golf tournament to me. . . . If you ask every golf pro what tournament is most important to him, 75 or 80 percent will say the Masters. People talk about the weak field and say, 'It's easy to win the

Masters.' Sure, it's easy to win, if you beat the best players in the world!"

Elder didn't compete in 1976, the year of Ray Floyd's runaway, but the tournament did invite a sporty young Brazilian amateur named Priscilo Gonzalez Diniz, who faded into obscurity after shooting 78 and 77 and missing the cut. That year, however, the National had to deal with another racial crisis. Fortunately, it had nothing to do with members, guests, or tournament participants. Unfortunately, it had to do with trespassers, and how three of them (all black) ended up in University Hospital with gunshot wounds after fishing in Rae's Creek on the back nine.

Trespassing has always been a problem at the National. Even before the club opened, people wandered onto the grounds hoping to catch a glimpse of Bobby Jones or to sneak in a shot or two while nobody was watching. In 1947 a group of teenagers slipped down from the ninth fairway at Augusta Country Club, crossed the twelfth green, slid out of their clothes, and jumped headlong into Rae's Creek. The incident was fondly recounted by Reverend Bert Hatch, a native Augustan and one of the eight trespassing teens, who wrote about his escapade in *Golf* magazine: "At the very spot where many a professional golfer has lost a tournament, four young men gained a small foothold in their journey toward manhood." Twenty-nine years later, however, three young men came close to losing a lot more.

On a Tuesday afternoon in late October 1976, Augusta National nurseryman Rogers Bennett, making a routine pass on the back nine, saw three black youths fishing Rae's Creek in front of the twelfth green. The boys knew where they were and they knew they weren't supposed to be there.

169

Signs were clearly posted. The boys were obviously local. They should have known better. Mr. Cliff had made it clear that trespassing needed to be stopped, and Mr. Wahl (the club general manager at the time) had made it clear in a memo to the maintenance staff that "we will prosecute to the letter of the law and will continue to do so until such time as . . . vandalism and trespassing ceases." His memo went on to say: "Any youngsters caught on our property will, hereafter, be immediately taken into custody and, in turn, arrested by the Richmond County Sheriff's Department. Whatever legal action is necessary to prosecute will be done."

These youths weren't vandalizing anything—they were just fishing. Bennett didn't want to call the sheriff and spend the rest of the day filling out reports, so he confronted the boys and told them to hit the road. Then he saw the gun. It was a .410 shotgun the kids had brought, ostensibly to shoot any snakes or other nefarious creatures that might sneak up on them. After a few tense moments and a few wisecracks, the boys packed up their fishing poles and left the property. Bennett took a deep breath and went on about his business.

Later, when Bennett made another pass through Amen Corner, he saw the black youths again. They had come back, this time with a few more of their buddies. Bennett assumed he'd been lucky the first time, and he wasn't about to push that luck. And Mr. Wahl and Mr. Cliff had made it clear: If they're trespassing, call the sheriff. Bennett did what he cursed himself for not doing the first time: He fetched the security guard.

Bennett found Charlie Young, the guard on duty, and quickly apprised him of the situation. Young, who had taken a security job at the National after being laid off as a salesman at Stereo City, had no law enforcement experience, but he was a gun collector and the pay at the club was better than the $150 a week he'd made selling turntables and speakers. He also knew how Mr. Cliff and the others felt about trespassers, especially black kids on the grounds of an all-white club. He, too, had gotten a memo:

> Where possible, we should apprehend any person entering our property by means other than admittance through the Main Gate. Youngsters, in particular, cause mischief and vandalism but may also have the capability of committing theft. Any youngster found on the grounds, who doesn't belong, should be brought to the office and "booked"—the first offense, given a warning and listed on the special file; a second time should result in apprehension and retention until a parent claims the delinquent—and again posted on the list; a third offense and the Sheriff's Department is to be summoned and charges proffered as necessary. The final step is not too harsh a measure when one considers the consequences of a constant offender—the purposes of entry could hardly be termed as casual or mischievous.

Charlie grabbed a pump action riot gun and some magnum buckshot. These boys were going to be brought in, one way or another.

At that point the story takes a vague turn. The club general manager, Philip Wahl, reported: "The guard [Charlie Young] was in the act of loading his shotgun with the thought of firing over the heads of the boys as a means of causing them to stop and identify themselves. Unfortunately, the gun was discharged, quite by accident."

Nineteen-year-old Charles Avery was shot in the chest while his brother, twelve-year-old Robert Avery, was shot in the upper right arm and the right thigh. Justine Jackson, age

CHARLIE GRABBED A PUMP

ACTION RIOT GUN AND

SOME MAGNUM BUCKSHOT.

THESE BOYS WERE GOING

TO BE BROUGHT IN, ONE

WAY OR ANOTHER.

nineteen, was also shot in the right leg—all, according to Young, with one misfire from a distance of fifty yards.

The Averys sued. They didn't deny trespassing, although they vehemently denied any malicious or even mischievous intent. According to court documents, the Averys said they "were doing no harm to the defendant or its property, and there is no reason or justification for the use of such violent weapons and tactics by the defendant and its employee." Three of the boys' uncles worked at the National: Horrace Avery, the caddie master; Palmer's famous caddie, Iron Man Avery; and President Eisenhower's caddie, Cemetery. Their father, Henry Avery, was caddie master at Augusta Country Club and their brother David was an occasional caddie at the National, so the boys knew the property well. While they may not have fully appreciated the historical golf significance of Rae's Creek and Amen Corner, they knew there was some mighty good fishing down there. They also knew that because of a bloody race riot in Augusta six years before, lots of security guards carried big guns. The suit also claimed "the attack made upon the plaintiff and his young black companions was based primarily, or at least in part, upon their race." The Averys claimed that in spite of the fact they were on posted property, if the boys had been blond-haired, blue-eyed rednecks instead of poor local Blacks, the gun never would have discharged.

As for the .410 shotgun the boys had with them earlier, it was later recovered from a friend's house. The gun was not on the National's grounds when the shooting occurred. The Averys settled before trial. Each of the two Avery boys received fifteen thousand dollars, a sum that the Averys say "was far, far less than they should have gotten." Jackson received close to six thousand dollars. As for the claim that Charlie Young's riot gun went off "quite by accident," the Averys say: "It was a lie. Everybody was in their own space. . . . He never warned them. He snuck up on them through the bushes and just started shooting."

The other thing that irks the Avery family, aside from the fact that two of their younger members were shot, is that in their view the National shrugged the whole thing off. "He [Young] wasn't fired, wasn't suspended . . . wasn't anything," the family said. Charges were never filed, a fact the Averys claim had more to do with politics than with procedure. The club's attorney, William Calhoun, had numerous connections in local political circles, and according to the family, "things were just dropped."

In fact, Charlie Young was eventually fired, but not for shooting the Avery and Jackson boys: He was fired for selling Cliff Roberts's suicide gun, although he was later rehired by Jack Stephens. Young eventually retired from the club and in October 1994 died of a heart attack, almost exactly eighteen years to the day of the incident.

After the ruckus with the Averys, the National continued to operate as it always had, and the Masters continued to uphold its honorable policy of inviting all players who qualified under their prescribed guidelines. Lee Elder finished tied for seventeenth in 1979. In 1980 Elder was joined by fellow African American Calvin Peete. The guy with the permanently bent left arm, who apparently also rates as the first Masters participant with diamonds embedded in his teeth, Peete played every year from 1980 through 1987 and finished as high as eleventh. Jim Thorpe, another talented African-American player, finished as high as eighteenth.

Then in 1990, with a new chairman, new greens, and a new crop of champions, the National was again thrown into the racial fray when Hall Thompson's racial-exclusionary comments leading up to Shoal Creek's hosting of the PGA Championship caused a nationwide uproar, ultimately forcing private clubs to reevaluate their membership policies. "It was a wakeup call," said Southern Christian Leadership Conference president Joseph Lowery of the Thompson–Shoal Creek affair. That call extended farther south to Ponte Vedra, Florida, where PGA Tour commissioner Deane Beman said, "Looking back, it was inevitable that racism in golf would become an issue, but we were not preparing for it. We never saw this coming. Black players never complained about their treatment at clubs, and no civil rights groups were complaining. We weren't focused on it at all."

Shoal Creek caused everyone to "focus" on it. Thompson apologized for his comments and Shoal Creek quickly added an African-American member to quiet the controversy. It didn't work. Vendors outside the Birmingham club sold T-shirts with images of the Little Rascal's Buckwheat character saying, "Shoal Creek is Oh-Tay." Another hot-selling souvenir was a shirt with a Black caricature playing golf at "Soul Creek—Site of the PGA Championship." Television hyped the controversy and pundits argued the constitutionality of private clubs and the freedom of association. For weeks, programs ranging from *This Week with David Brinkley* to CNN's *Crossfire* aired discussions on Shoal Creek, Hall Thompson, and race and golf in America.

Angered by the accusation that Augusta National was simply reacting to the Shoal Creek incident, Hord Hardin issued a statement: "We have been discussing [adding an African-American member] for a year. We concluded at least a year ago that there were more black people playing golf, more black people climbing the business ladder, more climbing the scientific and educational ladders, and we realized that there were people in that group who would enjoy being with people we have as members. I don't want to create the impression that all of our members are enthusiastic about this. Shoal Creek perhaps expedited something that we would have liked to do in our own way. The ideal way, in my mind, would have been that we would bring in a Black with no announcement, just as we bring in all our members. And then, two or three years down the road, someone would come up to me and say, 'You mean you got a black member and he's been in two years and you never told anyone?' "

This time, they had to tell everyone. Within weeks of the Shoal Creek debacle, Augusta National announced that Ronald Townsend, president of Gannett Television Group and a prominent African-American businessman, had accepted an invitation into membership. As for the implications of becoming Augusta's first black member, Townsend in 1991 told *Golf Digest*, "It's satisfying. . . . I do remember that when I went down there and sat there in my green jacket with a couple of my friends, one of them said, 'Do you realize what you've just done?' And I said, 'What do you mean?' He said, 'Well, you're sitting here at Augusta National with a green jacket on, and you're the first black person to do that.' I said to him, 'That's kind of heavy.' "

Hall Thompson, Shoal Creek's founder, continued as an Augusta National member as well. We know this because his bill kept coming. A few years later the National was able to "bring in" another black member under the relative obscurity Hardin had wanted from the beginning. Bill Simms, president of the Reinsurance Division of Transamerica Occidental Life in Charlotte, North Carolina, and part owner of the National Football League's Carolina Panthers, accepted his invitation to join Augusta, becoming the second black member in the club's history.

HALL THOMPSON'S POLITICALLY INCORRECT STATEMENT ULTIMATELY MADE GOLF A BETTER GAME. THE FACT THAT HE HAPPENED TO ALSO BE A MEMBER AT AUGUSTA NATIONAL ADDED WHAT IS ARGUABLY ANOTHER BLEMISH TO THE CLUB'S RACIAL RECORD.

Shoal Creek took on a life of its own, and the attention and reactions from the incident opened more opportunities for minorities than had ever been available before. In that sense, Hall Thompson's politically incorrect statement ultimately made golf a better game. The fact that he happened to also be a member at Augusta National added what is arguably another blemish to the club's racial record. Sure, they shot three black kids in the Roberts era; but at the time of Shoal Creek, Augusta National's racial makeup was commonplace, not the exception. Many famous golf clubs—including Hazeltine, Baltusrol, Oakmont, Shinnecock Hills, Crooked Stick, Bellerive, and Aronimink—still had no African-American members. In fact, Los Angeles's exclusive Sherwood Country Club, which had no Blacks, scrambled to add a minority to its roster. Their choice, as it turned out, was a questionable one. "I must admit I wondered about why I was asked to join and why my name came up," said O. J. Simpson of his 1989 invitation to join Sherwood.

Attempts to right racial wrongs have been made by at least one Augusta National member. Tom Cousins, an Atlanta real estate developer, has spent more than twenty million dollars revamping the deteriorated East Lake Country Club (where Bobby Jones played his first and last rounds of golf) in what is now a mostly Black, predominantly poor, area of

Atlanta riddled with crime, drugs, and poverty. Cousins has developed one of the nicest clubs in town right in the middle of an area the Atlanta Police Department calls "Little Beirut." As part of this effort, the Augusta National member provides junior golf programs and community redevelopment programs for minorities. East Lake's goal for these programs, as summed up by their general manager, is: "We want the kids [black and white] in this community to be known for what they shot, not who they shot." Tom Cousins, one of the greencoats, is a hero in Atlanta. Because of him, a new group of minority youngsters have a chance at golf, and more importantly, a chance at life.

Still, old memories die hard. Even though there are now two African-American members, race and Augusta National still have a very dividing effect. In October 1992 the club took its broadest and most open step ever. On a sunny Wednesday afternoon, at a table alongside the putting green behind the stark white clubhouse, Jack Stephens and Billy Payne, chairman of the Atlanta Committee for the Olympic Games (ACOG), announced plans to bring men's and women's golf back in the 1996 Summer Olympic Games. Olympic golf hadn't been played since the 1904 St. Louis games, and Payne saw this as a chance to separate the Atlanta games from all others over the previous ninety years. Augusta National was, in Payne's words, "the only choice." However, the National had never held an outside tournament other than the Masters, and they had never even considered a women's event. Even more exciting and intriguing was the seeming openness of Stephens's gestures. In addition to subjecting the club to the inconvenience of crowds, a television network other than CBS, and countless Olympic organizers,

Augusta National also had to restructure its operating schedule. The Olympics were slated for July and August, months when the club is closed. Maintenance plans would have to be restructured (at substantial costs) and the golf course would not only have to be ready for a spring Masters, but gear itself back up for a summer tournament.

In spite of all the negatives, Stephens and the members of the National put all that aside and agreed to open their doors to an awaiting world. "We're trying to send a message that we're for both men's and women's golf," Stephens said at the press conference. Then came the predictable questions about exclusionary membership practices, to which Stephens curtly responded, "We have no prohibition for any member or any type member. . . . That's always been the policy of the club." That sounded a little suspiciously like saying Cliff Roberts didn't have a prejudiced bone in his body. As good as Stephens's intentions were, he seemed to be ignoring any and all racial strife in the club's varied history.

It's not clear if Stephens could have thwarted the problems that were to come even if he had been more open. Certainly, he could have disarmed many of the club's critics had he simply acknowledged that Augusta National has done some good things and some not-so-good things when it comes to racial and sexual tolerance. As it was, Stephens's good-hearted, well-meaning intentions rang hollow to many who couldn't look past the white plantation building and the tuxedo-clad black waiters.

Reaction was unyielding. Atlanta city councilwoman Jabari Simama said of Augusta National: "There are certain institutions and places in this state that are symbols of the Old South and a period many of us have worked our entire lives to eradicate. To award this particular golf course with an Olympic venue would send out the wrong message to many Blacks and minorities who have suffered and still suffer at the hands of institutionalized racism." Jabari failed to be specific about who in particular was suffering out at the National, but the symbolism was more important than the substance: Augusta National, a white plantation with one token Black thrown in for television, provided an easy and high-profile target. That symbolism, in the view of the Atlanta City Council, was more than unacceptable; it was a travesty.

Loud, vicious cries went out. Reverend Timothy McDonald, executive director of Concerned Black Clergy, called the idea of Augusta National hosting the Olympics outrageous and said, "It would be a mistake, a serious mistake for them to do this, and I can't believe they would [go through with it]." In an unprecedented move, the Atlanta City Council passed an "Anti-Augusta National" resolution condemning the club as a racist symbol. Even the honorable and ever-present Joe Lowery piled on, suggesting (in not-too-subtle fashion) that the National might win favor among minorities if it would just make "major concessions" by assertively recruiting black members and doing business with minority firms.

"All these things need to be initiated prior to accepting them as a venue," Lowery said in a borderline blackmail statement. He added: "I have difficulty believing they would stubbornly refuse to continue their movement into the twentieth century. If they want to have the tremendous benefits of the Olympics, then it is inconceivable that they would refuse to take the necessary steps."

What Jack Stephens found inconceivable was the fact that anyone made a fuss. "It's puzzling to me," he said. "It was my understanding from the beginning . . . that the [International Olympic Committee] had accepted Augusta National's composition of membership, and that everyone knew what we are. We have no discriminatory policy." He also answered Lowery's blackmail by saying in so many words, If you come, fine; if you don't, fine.

"We've offered the venue," Stephens said. "The rest is up to them."

Not all minority leaders saw Augusta National just in terms of black and white. Atlanta mayor Maynard Jackson refused to sign the city council's anti-Augusta National resolution, and he held a series of meetings to try and "resolve the differences" between civil rights activists and Atlanta organizers. Dr. LeRoy Walker, president of the U.S. Olympic Committee and the grandson of slaves, said of the National: "Birmingham sort of opened up our eyes to all of the clubs that they must look at this issue. I believe that [the Olympics] are going to be something that—not tomorrow, but maybe before the 1996 Games—might make a difference."

Billy Payne, who, like Jack Stephens, presumably never practiced or even understood the tenets of racism, found himself mired in a controversy he didn't understand. He said: "I have the same goals [as those who were calling for greater minority inclusion]. In some respects I understand and appreciate the historical symbolism. I think, however, that Augusta is moving forward. I know for a fact they are, and I view this as a significant positive step. The refusal to take advantage of this opportunity and choose rather to penalize for a historical perspective would be a mistake."

No matter, the cries were too great, and only months after that fateful press conference on the lawn at Augusta National, the idea of golf in the Olympics died an ugly, painful, and, for the city of Augusta, a financially devastating death. The city estimates it lost $165 million and a once-in-a-lifetime opportunity. Metro Augusta Chamber of Commerce president Al Hodge said bitterly: "We were able to offer something not only to the country but to the world and the Atlanta City Council turned their backs on us. People here pay state taxes that support Atlanta and the city's infrastructure and then the Atlanta City Council worked against us. They should have been elated that Augusta National opened its doors without barriers. And instead they undercut us."

The greencoats opened their arms to the world, and black politicians—some of the same politicians who had petitioned for minority participation in the Masters and protested the all-white status of club memberships around the country—effectively spat in the members' faces. Jack Stephens, a firm but genuinely enlightened chairman, felt betrayed. "We felt an obligation to golf, and an obligation to the state of Georgia, an obligation to the city of Augusta and to golf fans. And we really concluded it would be unduly selfish on our part to deny the use of the club for an Olympic event."

Today the club says of the Olympic incident: "Everyone was disappointed it didn't work out. The Olympics were a unique situation and it is unlikely that the club would consider hosting another event."

That's a shame. A member who chooses to remain nameless said, "There is no way Clifford Roberts would have supported this." And so Jack Stephens and the current members of Augusta National paid for the sins of the fathers, and the whole world suffered a great loss.

But if the wounds suffered from years of distrust heal slowly, that knitting process began in 1995 when in a Tuesday practice round at the Masters, a nineteen-year-old Stanford freshman teed it up with Greg Norman, Fred Couples, and Raymond Floyd and found himself the star of the group. Greg Norman said of Tiger Woods's skills and potential at the Masters: "He can win it. His game is that good." He also outdrove Greg on more than one occasion.

"It's just another tournament," Woods said. "It just happens to be a major. . . . When I first arrived here I thought, 'Magnolia Lane, is that it?' It was a short drive. . . . The clubhouse is a lot smaller than it appears on TV, and the golf course is jammed together, all the holes running right next to each other, with the tee boxes right next to the greens." These weren't the bitter words of a man who had to sleep in a hotel away from town or eat at the "colored" counter in

Amateur sensation Eldrick "Tiger" Woods, nineteen at the time, removes his appropriately fashioned head cover as he prepares to warm up for a practice round preceding the 1995 Masters Tournament. (AP/Wide World Photos—Curtis Compton)

back of the corner diner. This was an upper-middle-class kid with God-given talent, loving parents, and a smile that won the hearts of millions.

As for his negative comments, they weren't made maliciously, just matter-of-factly. He smiled, shrugged, and then teed off in "just another golf tournament." In the process, Tiger Woods changed the face of the Masters. He made the cut that first year and shot three even-par rounds while finishing as low amateur, something Palmer and Nicklaus had been unable to do. He also dazzled the crowds with staggering tee shots of unbelievable length. On number two, the course's first par-five, Tiger hit short-iron second shots into the green every day, and during one practice round he actually had a nine-iron second shot into the 555-yard hole. Then there's number fifteen, the hole where Nicklaus had made eagle with a four-iron in 1986 and where Seve hit his second shot in the water, where Gene Sarazen made double eagle with a four-wood and gave Masters drama its beginning, and where Chip Beck chose to lay up short of the water in 1993, thus sealing the victory for Bernhard Langer: During Thursday's opening round in 1995, Tiger Woods hit the fifteenth green in two shots with a driver and a *seven-iron.*

Woods turned pro in late 1996 after becoming the first man in history to win three consecutive U.S. Amateur Championships. Before the year ended he already had racked up two tour victories. "I want to win," he says, a smile growing on his still-boyish face. "I can't help that. That's just who I am."

Behind the gates of Augusta National, men in green coats, most white, a few black, some Jewish (although that, too, is a post-Roberts innovation) sit and ponder the implications of their tournament and their club on the game, on its past, and on future generations of golfers. For all the unfair accusations and self-inflicted blunders, the National remains a poised and distinguished, stuffy and pretentious, secretive and hard-nosed, friendly and romantic place where history has been made and will continue to be made. On the grounds where an army once roamed, and a Bear once prowled, a Tiger has been surveying his territory and patiently stalking his prey. Patient, that is, to a point: Woods picked right back up in 1997, winning the first PGA Tour event of the year—the Mercedes Tournament of Champions—for his third Tour victory in only *nine* starts. What came next is changing the face of Augusta and complexion of golf in ways that the likes of Tillman, and possibly even Tiger Woods, never thought possible.

CHAPTER 8

TIGERBEAT

PEOPLE ASK ME TO COMPARE TIGER TO WHEN ARNOLD PALMER
FIRST BURST ON THE SCENE, ELECTRIFYING THE GALLERIES AND CRE-
ATING "ARNIE'S ARMY," AND BRINGING THE TELEVISION REVOLU-
TION OF GOLF INTO THE LIVING ROOMS OF THE WORLD. I SAY THAT
ARNOLD PALMER WAS THOMAS EDISON AND BENJAMIN FRANKLIN,
AND TIGER WOODS IS BILL GATES.

MARK MCCORMACK

CHAIRMAN, IMG

Two black men were invited to play in the 1997 Masters. One was considered by his peers as one of the Tour's better ball strikers, if not the hardest-working man in golf—Vijay
Singh. The other was proclaimed by international media, as
well as most of the public, as the hottest athlete on the planet,
a man *Gentleman's Quarterly* had already dubbed "Sport's
Next Messiah"—Tour newcomer Tiger Woods.

While few outside his island home of Fiji had paid
much attention to Singh's first foray to Augusta, the whole
world waited in breathless anticipation as Woods's private jet
landed at Bush Field. Whether or not the Augusta National, a
golf course commonly called the "Cathedral in the Pines,"
was seeking a new messiah, many believers speculated that
Woods's God-given talents would propel him to victory in
1997. Others were more skeptical.

Defending champion Nick Faldo, paired with Woods during Thursday's opening round, had played with Woods eleven days prior to the Masters in the final round of the Players Championship (where Woods had his worst showing since turning pro). When asked if he thought it presumptuous to assume Woods would waltz in and tear up Augusta, the three-time Masters champion emphatically answered, "Yes. There is a route around Augusta, and you have to follow it." Faldo went on to say, "I think there's a learning curve to playing Augusta and a discipline to playing the golf course."

Tiger had experience at Augusta, only most of it was bad. In two previous Masters appearances, Woods's lowest score had been even-par 72, and in the 1996 Masters he fired two uninspiring rounds of 75 and missed the cut. "I've made a lot of mistakes playing Augusta," Woods admitted prior to his 1997 appearance. Woods's Georgian blunders hadn't been limited to Augusta, either. Barely six months earlier, he sent organizers and fans of the Buick Southern Open (Pine Mountain, Georgia) into a tizzy by pulling out on Tuesday of tournament week, citing fatigue and near-burnout. After turning pro in August 1996, on the heels of winning his third consecutive U.S. Amateur title, Woods had embarked on a whirlwind schedule of autumn PGA Tour stops hoping to earn a Tour exemption as well as invitations to the Players Championship and the Masters. One of those stops had been the Southern Open, which had reserved a sponsor's invite especially for Woods.

Pulling out of the Southern Open wouldn't have been so bad, but Woods further snubbed organizers of the Fred Haskins Award dinner, which honors America's best collegiate player. The 1996 dinner was scheduled to coincide with Woods's Southern Open appearance. By the time his agent, Hughes Norton, read a prepared statement announcing Woods's withdrawal, young Tiger had checked out of his rented house and was aboard his private jet bound for Orlando.

The shock of betrayal quickly escalated into apoplectic fury. Buick had flown more than two hundred dignitaries to Pine Mountain for the Haskins dinner. A video had been produced. Promises had been made. Decorations, flowers, food preparation—all the ancillary logistics that go into such a presentation had cost the tournament more than thirty thousand dollars in hard cash and immeasurable time and energy.

"Tiger should have played, and he should have gone to the dinner," Arnold Palmer said. "You don't make commitments you can't fulfill unless you're on your deathbed, and I don't believe he was." Said Tom Kite, "I don't remember ever being tired when I was twenty." Curtis Strange, himself a former Haskins honoree, thought Woods had become too big too quickly: "This tournament was one of seven that agreed to help Woods when he needed his card. How quickly he forgot. I'll bet the Buick people don't forget."

After realizing what a PR disaster he had created, Woods, to his credit, exercised his first venture into damage control. He wrote a public apology in *Golf World*. He showed up at the rescheduled Haskins dinner and apologized to the group of assembled dignitaries, saying, "I was wrong and I'm sorry for any inconvenience I may have caused. I have learned from it, and I will never make that mistake again." All was forgiven, but Curtis Strange was right—folks in Georgia rarely forget.

Because of the Southern Open flap, Woods might have expected a cool reception when he landed in Augusta. Fortunately for him, a few things had changed since his leaving Pine Mountain. By now, Woods had won three Tour events, including beating American top gun Tom Lehman in the season-opening Mercedes Tournament of Champions. He had appeared on the cover of *GQ*, the first golfer ever so recognized. Beneath the glitzy cover and wide smile, however, *GQ* revealed a kid with a frat-house sense of humor who told lesbian jokes and poked fun at the mythical size of black men's private parts. On the other hand, here was a golf prodigy who Jack Nicklaus predicted would win more Masters green jackets than Jack and Arnie's combined ten. Nobody took Jack seriously.

Woods took Nicklaus's prediction to heart, however. The week before the Masters, he hustled friend and fellow Orlando resident Mark O'Meara out of sixty-five dollars by shooting what O'Meara would later call "a pretty easy 59. He should have shot 57, really. A sixteen-footer was about the longest putt he made, and he parred two of the par-fives."

By virtue of the color of his skin, Woods was being hailed as the standard-bearer for minorities around the world. As Thursday's opening round approached, the pressure on Woods began to show. "He was very tight," said Butch Harmon, Woods's swing coach. "He was coming into the biggest tournament in the world, and everybody was picking him to win the doggone thing. I'd be nervous, too."

The man responsible for managing that nervousness on the course was the affable, unflappable Mike "Fluff" Cowan, Woods's forty-nine-year-old caddie. A Tour veteran and former Peter Jacobsen looper, Cowan had joined Woods the previous August, pulling the clubs, reading the putts, and offering snippets of advice throughout Woods's meteoric seven-month rise. Regardless, nothing could prepare Cowan for that first round. Just before 1:30 P.M., Woods made his way to the first tee, lined by security guards and swarmed by a sea of fans. Experts estimated the 1997 Masters crowd at forty-two thousand people a day. At least one out of ten lined the first hole waiting for the next twosome. At 1:41 P.M. that Thursday, a white caddie removed a tiger-shaped headcover, and handed a driver to the first black man in history ever favored to win the Masters.

The groans came early. Woods pulled his first tee shot into the left rough and proceeded to bogey the first hole. An unseasonably cool wind had transformed hard, fast greens into harder, faster, and, some said, unfair tests. Jack Nicklaus said of conditions, "The last time I remember the course playing this difficult, Deane Beman was on the leader board." Colin Montgomerie said, "These greens are better than any ride at Disney World." On a day of four- and five-putts, Woods had no three-putts and no score higher than a bogey. He had four bogeys on the front nine, making the turn in 40 and driving away a few cynics nodding their heads and thinking, *I told you so.*

JACK NICKLAUS SAID OF CONDITIONS, "THE LAST TIME I REMEMBER THE COURSE PLAYING THIS DIFFICULT, DEANE BEMAN WAS ON THE LEADER BOARD."

Champions in sports are made at defining moments: Michael Jordan's game-winning shot for North Carolina in the 1982 NCAA finals; Cassius Clay/Muhammad Ali's knockout victory over Sonny Liston to capture his first heavyweight crown; and Bjorn Borg's first of five consecutive Wimbledon championships, for instance. For Woods at Augusta on a Thursday in 1997, the defining moment came on the tenth tee. He willed himself to make a swing change that anyone else at his level would have saved for a lonesome hours-long session on a driving range. Woods realized his backswing was going past parallel, so he geared it down a notch. On the spot, just like that.

"I was pretty hot at the way I was playing," Woods said later. "I couldn't keep the ball on the fairway. I was playing real defensive golf."

Splitting the tenth fairway with a two-iron, Woods birdied the tenth, parred the eleventh, birdied the twelfth, and birdied the thirteenth. At fifteen, the site of Sarazen's miraculous four-wood double eagle in 1934 and Nicklaus's incredible three-iron eagle in 1986, Woods reached the green with a driver and a wedge, and rolled in a six-foot putt for eagle. He then birdied the seventeenth, before finally lipping

189

out a birdie putt on the eighteenth that would have given him a 29. He settled for a 30 and an opening round of 70, two under par. That night at dinner in downtown Augusta, Butch Harmon made one of the week's most prophetic statements, telling friends Tom Crow, president of Cobra Golf, architect Tom Fazio, and real estate developer William McKee, "The kid's going to win this week."

As the week progressed, Woods picked off four of the era's toughest head-to-head competitors one by one, starting with Faldo. Paired with Woods, Faldo opened with a 75 and followed with an 81 on Friday, missing the cut and leaving the course "flabbergasted." Paul Azinger was Woods's playing companion for Friday. Too bad for Azinger: After opening with a 67 that left him a shot out of the lead Thursday, he slumped to a 73. Similar fates would follow on Saturday for Colin Montgomerie, Europe's top-ranked player four years running, and on Sunday for 1995 British Open runner-up and Ryder Cup hero Costantino Rocca of Spain.

Woods was poison ivy for the games of Faldo, Azinger, Montgomerie, and Rocca. With Azinger on Friday, Woods followed up his opening 70 with a six-under 66, driving the ball an average of 323.1 yards and taking a three-shot lead into the weekend. "He never had a mental lapse out there," Azinger said. "I just got out-concentrated."

Nicklaus paid the ultimate compliment to his young heir-apparent, recalling a comment made by an aging Bobby Jones about a then-young, long, and dominant Jack Nicklaus. Jones had said of Nicklaus, "He plays a game with which I am not familiar." About young Woods, Nicklaus, the elder statesman and ultimate American golf icon, said, "It's a shame Bob Jones isn't around. He could have saved the words he used for me for this young man."

Like Jones, Woods elevated his game to an elite level when the moment in history demanded it. Like Jones, he felt he had accomplished everything he could as an amateur, in his case winning six consecutive USGA titles; and, like Jones, Woods defeated over half the field just by showing up. Woods opened golf to a new generation of players, and through character, will, and charisma, he elevated his own celebrity beyond anyone in golf in at least two decades. Jones had been the gentleman-hero for a country mired in the depths of depression and despair. Woods was the courteous, soft-spoken, and attractive hero of a generation plagued by drugs, poverty, crime, and social decay. Like Jones had been in the 1920s and 30s, Woods was now a role model and hero for the 1990s.

He also had a short fuse when he felt he'd become smug with his game. Like Jones, Woods was not above slamming a club into the ground and spewing obscenities at himself anytime he'd made a mental lapse. During the break between eighteens in the 1996 U.S. Amateur (where Woods was five down with eighteen to play), he threw his hat and began swearing at himself. Of the outburst, Woods said, "I could feel myself getting complacent. I had to snap out of it. If you do it right, you can channel the anger." Jones learned to channel his anger into the only Grand Slam in golf history.

The two men shared a unique, if not privileged relationship with the USGA. Jones was able to write instructional books, star in Warner Brothers shorts, and negotiate a golf club deal with A. G. Spalding and Brothers, all without losing his amateur status. Woods's dad Earl worked as a "scout" for Woods's eventual agency, the International Management Group, where Earl and others at IMG hashed out the details of Woods's Nike and Titleist agreements before the young champion left the amateur ranks. Neither man broke the rules, and each approached the USGA before entering into any deals. The USGA did what it could to preserve the amateur status of both Jones and Woods, even when the impressions left behind were suspect.

Jones and Woods also had their marked differences. Jones grew up in well-bred, white southern society; Woods brought a multiracial, multinational, multicultural acceptance

JONES AND WOODS ALSO HAD THEIR MARKED DIFFERENCES. JONES GREW UP IN A WELL-BRED, WHITE SOUTHERN SOCIETY; WOODS BROUGHT A MULTIRACIAL, MULTINATIONAL, MULTICULTURAL ACCEPTANCE TO A GAME WHITER THAN MOST.

to a game whiter than most. Helping create the ultra-exclusive Augusta National, Jones perpetuated the lingering caste system in golf; Woods grew up playing the municipal courses of greater Los Angeles. Jones would never have considered missing the Haskins Award dinner. The most obvious difference: Bobby Jones never turned pro.

Montgomerie didn't think Woods's thirty-six-hole lead was insurmountable. Monty made no bones about his desire to meet Woods in the Ryder Cup. He even made a few subtly disparaging comments about all of Woods's victories coming on resort courses. Before their Saturday pairing, Montgomerie said of Woods, "I have a lot more experience in major championships than he has, and hopefully I can prove that." Montgomerie could have used a lesson from fellow Brit, Sir George Everest, explorer of the wild and surveyor of what we now know as India. Sir George would have advised Monty it is unwise to stick your finger in a tiger's eye.

With Montgomerie along as his playing companion, Woods shot a bogey-free 65 on Saturday for a record-tying, three-day total of fifteen under par, good for a nine-shot lead. After the round, a beaten and red-faced Montgomerie stomped into the press room and announced, "There is no chance humanly possible that Woods is going to lose this tournament." Added Jesper Parnevik, "If they don't make a set of Tiger tees fifty yards behind us, he'll win the next twenty green jackets."

Like any twenty-one-year-old killing time before winning his first major championship as a professional, Woods spent Saturday night eating fast food and playing Mortal Kombat and ping-pong with friends at his rented Augusta home. He had assembled a pretty good pick-up basketball game, but Harmon stepped in and nixed the game.

Sunday's final round of the 1997 Masters turned out to be the most-watched golf telecast in history, even though the outcome was long a foregone conclusion. The only remaining drama on CBS was whether or not Woods would break the tournament record of seventeen-under-par 271 held since 1965 by Jack Nicklaus and tied by Raymond Floyd in 1976. Tiger went to the eighteenth tee at eighteen under, only to pull-hook a monstrous drive well left of the left rough. After hitting his approach shot twenty feet above the hole, Woods calmly two-putted for par, making a testy four-footer that broke Augusta's fabled seventy-two-hole scoring record by one. He pumped his fist in his trademark uppercut, then tearfully embraced his waiting father in a scene President Bill Clinton called "the best shot of the day." On the week that marked the fiftieth anniversary of Jackie Robinson's triumphant breakthrough as the first black in major-league baseball, a man of color changed the world by winning at the Masters.

Controversy arose a week later in the delayed airing of an impromptu interview with Fuzzy Zoeller, although a foreshadowing of Fuzzygate occurred before Woods teed off on Sunday. As hordes gathered around the practice green to

As CBS's Jim Nantz said, it was a win for the ages. (AP/Wide World Photos)

watch—among them, CBS commentator Jerry Pate and Harmon—Zoeller, the 1979 Masters champion, joined those rolling tune-up putts. In a edgy attempt at what was obviously politically incorrect humor, Zoeller, in anticipation of Woods's victory-to-be, said, "Tell [Woods] not to serve fried chicken and collard greens next year [at the Champions dinner]."

Had Zoeller realized that it was the content and not the timing that kept his audience from laughing the first time, the incident would have passed unnoticed. But later that Sunday afternoon, after Zoeller had finished his final round and Woods was still out on the course lapping the field, one of CNN's international sound men was gathering sound bites to be edited into the evening Masters coverage. Zoeller meandered over to the cameras and repeated the lame joke about fried chicken and collard greens, only this time referring to Woods as "that little boy."

The CNN sound man, who was from South Africa, didn't get it. He took the footage to Jim Huber, a CNN sports reporter and longtime friend of Fuzzy's. Disturbed by how harsh the statement looked on tape and aware of the flap it was likely to generate, Huber told others that airing the tape would serve no purpose. The footage went back to CNN's Atlanta headquarters where it sat, untouched, for almost a week. Huber forgot about it.

When someone else at CNN happened to see the raw footage, Fuzzygate was born. On the April 20 edition of CNN's *Pro Golf Weekly*, exactly one week after Zoeller actually uttered the remarks, the whole world heard him say, "That little boy is driving well, and he's putting well. He's doing everything it takes to win. So, you know what you guys do when he gets in here? You pat him on the back and say, 'Congratulations and enjoy it,' and tell him not to serve fried chicken next year. Got it?" Then walking away, Zoeller turned back to the camera and quipped, "Or collard greens or whatever the hell they serve."

Reaction was swift and massive. Kmart, Zoeller's long-standing corporate partner, issued an immediate statement distancing itself from Zoeller while criticizing his comments. Zoeller said he was joking, that he was taken out of context, that he didn't mean it, that he was sorry he said it, and that he wouldn't say it again. That wasn't enough. Kmart dropped him. Zoeller subsequently withdrew from the Greater Greensboro Chrysler Classic, an event he hadn't missed in twenty-one years. Terrance Moore, a columnist for the *Atlanta Journal,* writing in *Golf World,* and who happens to be an African American, opined, "To the majority of us darker than a golf ball, there is nothing funny about a white man using racial stereotypes to refer to a black man."

Only days before Fuzzygate broke, Woods reiterated his staunch ambivalence toward any ethnic labeling. Appearing on *The Oprah Winfrey Show,* Woods said he considered himself "Coblinasian," a self-created combination of Caucasian, Black, American Indian, and Asian. When Winfrey, a professed non-golfer, asked Tiger and Earl Woods what race the young champion belonged to, the answer was "the human race."

On April 24, a full four days after the Zoeller brouhaha was launched, Woods finally responded, reading from a prepared statement: "At first I was shocked to hear that Fuzzy Zoeller made these unfortunate remarks. His attempt at humor was out of bounds, and I was disappointed by it. But having played golf with Fuzzy, I know that he is a jokester; and I have concluded that no personal animosity toward me was intended. . . . We all make mistakes, and it is time to move on. I accept Fuzzy's apology and hope everyone can now put this behind us."

Joe Lewis Barrow, president of Izzo Systems and one of the premier African-American executives in golf, summed up Fuzzygate when he said, "When you think of Fuzzy Zoeller, you're going to think of his comments at the 1997 Masters. I think that's unfortunate for a man who has contributed a great deal of personality and enjoyment to the game."

For two decades Fuzzy Zoeller had been one of pro golf's most popular humorists, but there was nothing funny about his Tiger Woods comments at the 1997 Masters that were construed as blatantly racist. Zoeller is seen here a month later at the 1997 Mastercard Colonial in Fort Worth, where he met with Woods for the first time since the CNN incident to discuss and settle the issue. (AP/Wide World Photos)

Color ruined more lives in 1997 during the Masters, only it was the color of money at the only one of golf's four major championships that, ironically, makes no provision for corporate hospitality. Because Masters badges are doled out to selected "patrons" who have been on the National's "list" for decades, a huge secondary market for Masters badges has mushroomed over the years. Those who fill that secondary market range from smarmy street hustlers who simultaneously sell Masters badges and Swiss watches, to highly organized, licensed ticket brokers and corporate hospitality specialists. Even a close relative of a prominent Augusta National employee has been selling badges out of the trunk of his car for years.

"Masters badges are just like anything else," says one national ticket broker. "Scarcity breeds demand. Whether you're talking about Masters badges or those stupid little Beanie Babies, when you can't get something, it drives up people's desire to get it. In the case of the Masters, you don't even have to like golf; it's the status of *being there* that's the thing."

With all the hoopla surrounding Woods's professional Masters debut, that "status of being there" drove the 1997 ticket market to obscene levels. Tom Patania, president of the East Coast Ticket Brokers Association, says, "Even from a broker's perspective, the Masters is the toughest ticket to obtain in sports. Ten or twelve years ago there were only about a dozen of us [brokering badges] and cumulatively we might have needed one hundred badges. Then some tour operators and travel agents and other people started getting involved and even if they only needed four badges apiece, that was more added to the list. All of a sudden nobody knew what was available in the market."

That uncertainty steadily drove prices up to a point where, prior to Woods's 1:44 P.M. Thursday starting time, 1997 badges were going for ten thousand dollars apiece. While leaving the grounds after Thursday's opening round, Steve Hale, a local, was approached by a young man offering him nine thousand dollars for his ticket for the tournament's last three days. "He told me that if I really loved golf, I could go golfing in Scotland with what he was willing to pay me," Hale said. "It was very tempting. But even as poor as I am, I couldn't do it. I have this sad vision of me sitting in front of my television drinking beer in my underwear and watching the 2016 Masters on CBS because I sold my tickets for a short-term gain and lost the privilege."

Before patrons receive their coveted badges each year, they must sign a "patron agreement" with Augusta National. Part of that agreement reads, "The Augusta National Golf Club is the only authorized source of tickets to the Masters. No other vendors such as travel agents, tour groups, etc., have permission to sell Masters tickets. Sales through such vendors are in violation of the sales agreement and such ticket holders are subject to denial of admission and/or prosecution." Furthermore, ticket scalping is a misdemeanor under Georgia's penal code.

Don't tell that to people like Fred Moir, owner of the Sports World Group. Moir moved his corporate headquarters to Augusta to accommodate corporate clients who wish to entertain during the Masters. According to Moir, "[Augusta National] has been aware for many, many years that the Masters is a prime target for corporate hospitality and [the members] don't really frown on that, provided everybody maintains the decorum and understands the protocol. The attitude of Augusta National has been, 'Provided you don't advertise, don't put it on the Internet, and don't scream it from the rooftops, we're going to turn something of a blind eye and let you get away with it.' "

Turning a blind eye in 1997 was virtually impossible. Directly across the street from the National's entrance, the old Green Jacket restaurant, freshly painted and newly designed, was reopened for business as the Clubhouse. Instead of serving the public, however, it now housed a corporate hospitality pavilion. In nose-thumbing proximity to the greencoats, the Clubhouse offered packages for twenty-two thousand dollars that included lodging, transportation, dining, and golf. In addition to all the ancillary perks, when corporate guests arrived at the Clubhouse for breakfast during Masters week, they were treated to fine southern cooking . . . and Masters badges underneath their napkins.

Technically, this sort of arrangement circumvents the state's scalping laws. According to Moir (who said his company had nothing to do with the Clubhouse or its clients),

THE RESPONSIBILITY OF ACQUIRING THE MASTERS BADGES FELL ON THE SHOULDERS OF WORLD GOLF HOSPITALITY'S NEWEST PARTNER—AUGUSTA NATIVE ALLEN F. CALDWELL III. IT WAS NOT A GOOD MATCH.

"We don't sell badges *per se*. But, if you want lodging, a chauffeur service, tee times at some of the area's finer golf courses, and oh-by-the-way access to the Masters thrown in . . . that's what we do."

World Golf Hospitality, one of the companies that organized the Clubhouse, intended to do likewise. Although company president Brendan Lillis was a known hustler in the ticket world and had been sued for ticket fiascoes at the Olympics, the 1996 Super Bowl, and the 1997 Ryder Cup, companies such as New York's Lehman Brothers didn't hesitate to book their hospitality and ticket arrangements through Lillis's World Golf Hospitality. The Clubhouse arrangement was supposed to be simple: World Golf Hospitality would arrange lodging and transportation, then market and sell the packages. The responsibility of acquiring the Masters badges fell on the shoulders of World Golf Hospitality's newest partner—Augusta native Allen F. Caldwell III. It was not a good match.

"Allen owned a liquor store and ran the local child development center," Chris Nickelson, an Augusta attorney, recalls. "He was always dealing a few badges here and there out of his liquor store, but this was his one chance at the big time. Everybody loved Allen, and Allen loved golf and the Masters. He saw this as his big break."

"Ticket brokering is not a paint-by-numbers exercise," an East Coast broker says. "It's about setting a limit and knowing what it takes to be competitive. If you set a number and know you can go out and buy twenty or thirty badges, then you sell twenty or thirty packages. Anything more than that and you're risking your reputation."

Patania, a ticket broker with New Jersey-based Select-a-Ticket, says one rule of thumb in buying Masters tickets is getting them ahead of time—before the unpredictable and emotionally charged events of Masters week throw reason out the window. "We go into an event knowing that we're going to take orders against the badges we already have," Patania says. "That's how we determine what prices we will charge and how many orders we place. [For the 1997 Masters] the last three badges we needed, we had pre-sold at a price of $2,750. Two of them cost us $5,600, and the last one cost us $6,300. On one order we lost $13,000, but we committed to a price and we stuck to it. It's like playing the stock market. You've got to know your business."

Lillis and World Golf Hospitality oversold the 1997 Masters to the tune of 142 badges, then relied on Caldwell to cover the shortfall. According to locals in Augusta, Caldwell approached his friends and golf buddies, who, weeks prior to the event, had committed to sell their badges to him, only now to find the badges already gone. According to a Caldwell family friend, "He was liked by everybody, so all his buddies said, 'Sure, Allen, you can have my ticket for $2,500,' but when other people came along and offered between $3,500 and $5,000, they forgot about Allen, went after the money, and left poor Allen hanging out to dry."

"He was stressing out," Caldwell friend Walter Clay told the *Augusta Chronicle*. "[Allen] said he hadn't slept in two days. I told him his friends would help him." Clay, in fact, offered his badges to Caldwell, but it was too little, too late. By Thursday morning it was apparent World Golf Hospitality couldn't honor their ticket commitments. Clubhouse clients, like Lehman Brothers, panicked, hitting the streets to find a way into Augusta National.

Allen Caldwell was a popular Augusta resident who got in way over his head in trying to arrange deals for Masters tickets for the 1997 event. He ended up taking his own life before the tournament was over. (*Augusta Chronicle* photo).

"The market did not get to ridiculous levels until Thursday, when Allen announced he was short 142 tickets," one broker says. "[Ironically] it was World Golf's corporate clients that drove [the price of badges] up." Adds Moir, "When you have a Fortune 500 corporation down here with clients and they're in a potentially embarrassing situation of not being able to fulfill their needs, they send people out onto the streets to do whatever it takes to buy tickets."

As part of that whatever-it-takes strategy, many company representatives camped outside the Caldwell family home in nearby Martinez. About this time Lillis abandoned Caldwell, leaving Caldwell to fend off the angry mob on his own—a task Caldwell was ill-equipped to handle. By the time Woods lipped out his putt on eighteen and tapped in for the amazing opening round of 40–30—70, Caldwell was looking at a debt in excess of four hundred thousand dollars and the losses of his business, his home, and probably most of his friends.

In the misty, early-morning hours of Friday, April 11, ten hours before Woods moved to the top of the Masters leaderboard, Linda Caldwell slid open the glass door leading onto her back deck, and she knew. Her husband—a family man, a businessman, a well-liked local citizen, and the father of their ten-year-old son—lay dead. The twelve-gauge shotgun he used to end his life lay beside him, a testament to the cold reality that accompanies the beauty and majesty of Augusta National and the Masters.

On Saturday, Allen F. Caldwell's friends and family laid the man to rest. Meanwhile, clients of the Clubhouse had either found access to the tournament through other means or gone home disappointed and angry. Brendan Lillis was nowhere to be found. As of July 1997, World Golf Hospitality had litigation pending in excess of one million dollars.

"This isn't the first time since 1934 something tragic has happened," Moir said. "Everybody will get over it. [The Masters] is going to be here next year, and the year after that. But Augusta National is eventually going to have to embrace some kind of corporate policy, certainly not a carnival as is the case with the British Open, but perhaps like a Muirfield or a U.S. Open. That will bring prices back down and keep Fortune 500 companies from using their deep pockets to drive prices out of control."

When the final putt of the 1997 Masters fell, as did a lot of scoring records and a lot of tears, one conspicuously quiet member of the gallery felt a weight lift from his shoulders. Lee Elder, who had accepted an invitation by club chairman Jack Stephens to attend the final round, watched every shot, walked every step, and shared every moment with the newest honorary member of Augusta National.

"This is more significant to me than Jackie Robinson breaking the color line," Elder said. "It's a great day for all people. I'm a part of history in the past, and now I'm a part of history in the present. After today, we will have a situation where no one will ever turn their head to notice when a black person walks to the first tee."

During the Butler Cabin ceremony of awarding the green jacket to Woods, staged especially for television, Woods paid tribute to great golfing Blacks who had blazed the trail before him. "People like Lee Elder, Charlie Sifford, and Ted Rhodes made it possible for this to happen," Woods said to CBS's Jim Nantz. "Without them, I might not have had a chance to play golf. I might not have had the chance to be here." Then in the soft-spoken manner of a champion, Woods thanked the members of Augusta National and made history by slipping into a forty-two–long green jacket presented by defending champion Nick Faldo and emblazoned with the logo of Augusta National.

On the way from the Butler basement to Augusta's putting green for the official green-jacket ceremony, Woods, surrounded by security and the deafening roar of cheering fans, looked up and saw Lee Elder, and he stopped.

"Lee!" he shouted, motioning for Elder to come to him. Woods then put an arm around Elder and whispered into his ear, "Thanks for making this possible."

"It made me feel wonderful," Elder said. Then looking out over the grounds, the sun hanging low over Amen Corner, Elder said, "We needed to get rid of all those ghosts hanging in those trees."

Jack Stephens led the members of Augusta National in a standing ovation to welcome their newest honorary member. A new record-holder prevailed at Augusta; a man of color; a man of mixed heritage; and a man to make Mr. Jones proud. When he slipped into his jacket, Woods said to no one in particular, "I'll probably sleep in it." Later that Sunday night, *Golf World* columnist Pete McDaniel, who had recently ghost-written *Training a Tiger* with Earl Woods, showed up at the Woods's rented home for the victory celebration.

"Where's Tiger?" McDaniel asked Tida Woods.

The new champion's mother smiled and motioned McDaniel to follow her to one of the rear bedrooms. When she cracked the bedroom door, McDaniel saw that Woods had indeed fallen asleep clutching the forty-two–long Masters green jacket.

After the sun set that Sunday, when the members had all retreated to the confines of their cabins, questions began to rumble about what changes would be made to the golf course. After all, Nicklaus's record-breaking round produced Cliff Roberts's famed "two-section bunker" on eighteen. The tying of that record by Ray Floyd resulted in the conversion from rye grass to "ride at Disney World" bent-grass greens. Did Woods's dismantling victory warrant changes to the famed Jones-Mackenzie design? Jack Stephens said no. "I'm not at all embarrassed that the record was broken by one shot after thirty-two years," Stephens said. "It has withstood the test of time."

Still, subtle changes to the National after Woods's victory were certain. Then again, there were changes made after Faldo had won in 1996. The first hole was lengthened by four yards, making it slightly more difficult for the average tee shot to carry the bunker at the corner of the dogleg. The putting green was moved closer to the Eisenhower Cabin, and the mounds on the right of the fifteenth fairway—players sometimes used them as springboards to gain extra yardage—were flattened before 1997's opening rounds.

Other changes will certainly come, but don't expect the men in green coats to grow the roughs or dig moats in the fairways. Unless Washington Road is re-routed, or adjacent Augusta Country Club becomes a sixteen-hole layout, lengthening the National in any substantive way probably won't happen. Meanwhile, whispers of Woods-influenced change persist:

"Lengthen it."

"Grow the rough."

"Create more forced carries." On and on.

The members have never gone to such extremes, and nothing about Woods's record-setting tournament suggests a change in that attitude now. Woods summed up many of the misconceptions about the National's apparent gentility before he teed off in 1997. "You stand on the tees and the fairways look fifty yards wide," he said. "It takes a while to realize there is only ten yards of that fairway you want to be on."

The dawn of a new era has begun, and those who aren't ready should get out of the way before they are devoured by Tiger. As 1996 Player of the Year Tom Lehman said, "Tiger Woods is probably the player of the next two decades." Augusta and the world should stand ready. There will be no shortage of the tired old calls to toughen the golf course and strengthen the field in the future. For if there is one of Lee Elder's so-called ghosts left "hanging around in those trees," it's probably the pale, shackled spirit of Clifford Roberts, who is pointing a quivering, bony finger at the site where he wants the new Tiger tees.

CHAPTER 9

EYE ON AUGUSTA: THE CBS STORY

THE REALLY SAD THING IS THAT TOM WATSON HAS THE ABILITY TO GET GARY MCCORD KICKED OFF CBS'S MASTERS BROADCAST WHEN ALL GARY WAS SAYING ABOUT THE GREENS [THE "BIKINI WAX" REMARK] IS TRUE. BUT THAT'S THE MENTALITY AT AUGUSTA: THEY HAVE A TENDENCY TO PUT THEIR LOVE FOR HISTORY AND TRADITION ABOVE REALITY, WHEN THAT'S NOT THE WAY THE GENERATION OF THE NINETIES EXISTS. WE CAN APPRECIATE IT, BUT YOU HAVE TO BE ABLE TO DEAL WITH OTHER FACTORS AS WELL.

—KEN GREEN

The "bikini wax" comment during the 1994 Masters, which prompted a scathing letter from Tom Watson to Augusta, could have been the least offensive thing Gary McCord had said all year. It was certainly the second least offensive comment he'd made that day. Earlier in the telecast McCord attempted not to say that José Maria Olazàbal was "dead" when he hit his second shot long on the seventeenth. Instead, as the ball rolled long, McCord said that if the ball "rolls any further it will be down there with some body bags." A few minutes later McCord looked for a way to describe the speed of Tom Lehman's downhill putt. He said, "These greens are so fast, they don't mow them, they bikini wax

207

them." A fair number of citizens residing east of California had no idea what that meant. Whether Tom Watson knows bikini wax from candle wax remains a mystery, but Watson knew enough to find McCord's comments distasteful. As the tour's self-appointed defender of tradition, virtue, and the Augusta way, Watson fired off a letter in which he strongly suggested that the National and CBS, "get rid of him, now." It worked. Jack Stephens informed CBS's Frank Chirkinian that McCord was persona non grata. If CBS wanted the Masters telecast again in 1995, it would conduct its program without Gary McCord.

"My problem is that I don't like clichés," McCord said of the incident. "Sure I use them, but I try not to. That's what got me into all this trouble. I have all this time on my hands and I've got software in my computer that has a thesaurus. I wish I wasn't computer literate."

At Augusta National there has always been an autocrat hanging around to pass judgment on all things, including which commentators work, what they can and cannot say, and, in some cases, how much they will be paid. Such was the case with the late, great English announcer Henry Longhurst, who was famous for a lot of things, not the least of which was his prophetic statement that Tom Weiskopf would "either hit a wooden club or an iron club," leaving many to wonder what else Weiskopf had in his bag. According to Frank Hannigan, writing in *Golf Digest*, "Longhurst learned he would be on the commentary team at Augusta when he was so advised in a note saying the Jones-Roberts pair had 'informed' CBS they wanted Longhurst, and he was to advise them if CBS tried to be 'niggardly' in the financial arrangements."

According to Frank Chirkinian, booth announcers came and went at the whim of Mr. Roberts and his committees: "As equipment got more sophisticated, we began to expand our coverage. In '61, we covered back to [hole number] thirteen, and so forth. Eventually, we were able to do all nine

Former CBS sportscaster Jack Whitaker was a Masters Tournament coverage fixture until his on-air use of the word "mob" to describe a scene involving exuberant spectators got him removed from CBS's broadcast team for a few years. This is Whitaker pictured in the seventies. (AP/Wide World Photos)

holes on the back side. . . . But every time we added a hole, I had to go out and find another announcer to position at that hole, and that was more of a problem than any technical considerations. One year we had a Scot, a writer, foisted upon us. We put him out at thirteen to cover play at that hole, but his brogue was so bloody thick that even the English announcers couldn't understand what he was saying."

Byron Nelson also recalls how he was summoned to the booth at Augusta: "Cliff Roberts was having a discussion [in 1957] with Frank Chirkinian. They got to talking about the color commentator Cliff and Bob Jones wanted to use for the Masters. Frank had used various ones, both on radio and then on the first telecast in 1956, but Cliff wasn't satisfied with any of them. . . . So Frank asked Cliff, 'Well, who do you want to use?' And Cliff finally said, 'I know Nelson pretty well. He won't go off half-cocked and he'll do what you tell him to do (which was code for "he'll do what *we* tell him to do"). Why don't you ask him?' Frank called right away and asked me and I said yes, though I was quite nervous about it."

Rightfully so. While Roberts didn't dictate the exact script of the live telecasts (which he certainly would have done had he been able to predict the action out on the course), everyone knew that Roberts analyzed, scrutinized, and criticized every syllable uttered during the Masters telecasts. One critic told *Golf Digest*: "The list [of dos and don'ts] bordered on breaking the First Amendment, but it made the telecast great. Through the years the commentators sounded better at the Masters because of all the things they're not allowed to say. They have to think before they talk, which they're not used to doing. So they end up saying less."

John Derr, one of the original cast who covered fifteen and sixteen, recalled in a column that the restrictions were more of a laundry list than a few incidental dos and don'ts: "We were discouraged from using too many superlatives about any particular player or the Masters itself—they didn't want it to look even remotely like the Open. We could mention a player's previous wins, but only briefly, and we could not utter the vaguest reference to how much money he had won. And we didn't call him the greatest golfer in the world, even if he was. . . . We were discouraged from applying an actual number to the size of the gallery, because they [the greencoats] felt that would be a guess, and a guess, of course, isn't accurate. And we were not to dwell on a player's bad shot. Augusta felt that these were invited guests and we were there to show the public what they were doing—we were not in a position to criticize."

A CBS camera captures the action at the thirteenth green, where off in the distance Jack Nicklaus surveys a putt en route to his winning the 1965 Masters Tournament. CBS and the Masters were usually ahead of their time in golf coverage, although in the sixties, awkward long-range shots such as these were the norm. (© Morgan Fitz Photographers, Globe Photos, Inc. 1997)

The one rule on which there was no ambiguity was the money, or the absence of the mention of such. At Augusta, you never, ever talk about money. Says Chirkinian, "There was only one rule: Don't talk about the money."

Masters money was off the table, but so was reference to *any* money. The Masters was to be broadcast as if all those fine athletes were competing for love, honor, and country. Melnyk found the restrictions tough, but he also feels the telecasts were better because of them: "Working at Augusta is both the hardest and the easiest event to cover. It's the hardest in the sense of being careful to choose just the right words to describe what is going on, yet it's the easiest because the

THE ONE RULE ON WHICH THERE WAS NO AMBIGUITY WAS THE MONEY, OR THE ABSENCE OF THE MENTION OF SUCH. AT AUGUSTA, YOU NEVER, EVER TALK ABOUT MONEY.

viewer already knows so much about Augusta and the tournament. The trick for an announcer there is to stay out of the way of the telecast. Describe the shot and then keep quiet. A lot of announcers would be better off saying less at the events they are covering."

One announcer who could have used that advice is Jack Whitaker, who was issued his own kind of "body bag" for not letting a picture tell the story.

Chirkinian remembers: "It occurred on a Monday. There was a good number of [first-time] spectators out that day using passes they had gotten from regular ticket holders who had left after the seventy-second hole the previous day to return to work or whatever. It was an unruly scene when they came to eighteen on Monday, with the crowd bursting forward to rush toward the green. Whitaker, who was in the tower at eighteen, at that point said, 'Here comes the mob!'

"We didn't have any immediate reaction to what Jack had said because everyone knew exactly what he was describing. It was quite true, but it was one of those things that all broadcasters need to learn—there's no reason to say anything when the television picture is already telling the whole story."

Whitaker, the epitome of stoic traditionalism and the antithesis of Gary McCord, was hurt and angry at his dismissal: "It really stung. I was more angry with CBS than I was with the Masters for not notifying me about my so-called fall from grace until a month before the following year's tournament. . . . In retrospect, there may have been two things that led to my discharge. . . . Playoffs are disastrous for TV. We were running over [by] an hour and the network wasn't about to let us do that. So as darkness came on and Nicklaus sank the winning putt, I called the gallery a mob because they were rushing up the hill and looking like a mob. But the Masters people were also upset with me because I failed to mention that the green jacket ceremony would take place immediately afterward on the putting green. The evening news came slamming right in and my last word was cut, so I obviously didn't have time. I don't know which of the two mishaps sealed my fate."

WHITAKER RECEIVED A MUCH-DESERVED REPRIEVE IN 1972 BY NONE OTHER THAN CHAIRMAN ROBERTS HIMSELF. HENRY "WOODEN CLUB OR IRON CLUB" LONGHURST FELL ILL AT THE LAST MINUTE, AND WHITAKER HAPPENED TO BE IN THE GALLERY AS A SPECTATOR.

"The thing with Gary McCord seemed to be a matter of taste," Whitaker added years later. "It's ironic to me that I was taken off there because I used a cliché; Gary was taken off because he was trying to avoid a cliché."

Whitaker received a much-deserved reprieve in 1972 by none other than Chairman Roberts himself. Henry "Wooden Club or Iron Club" Longhurst fell ill at the last minute, and Whitaker happened to be in the gallery as a spectator. Bill MacPhail approached Roberts with the news that it was either Whitaker or dead air. Roberts raised his eyebrows and, without hesitating, said, "How fortunate we are!" When Whitaker approached Roberts for the official commuting-of-sentence, Roberts said to him, "Young man, we are very happy to have you back. We are very lucky to have you back."

213

As close as the comment from Roberts came to an apology, the Masters was never "lucky" enough to have Frank Beard at all. Beard writes in his book *Making the Turn: A Year Inside the PGA Senior Tour*:

> I hadn't signed a contract with CBS, but I had done seven or eight tournaments as a color man. Frank Chirkinian was the CBS golf producer then, and he told me at the beginning of the year that he wanted me on the team. He called me for this and called me for that, worked my appearances around whatever tournaments I was playing in. . . . I was recognized as a CBS part-time guy, and I expected to be in the booth in Augusta, since I wasn't going to be invited as a player that year. . . . I was writing my *Golf Digest* column at the time. We were doing some articles for the annual Masters issue, and Robert Trent Jones, the architect, had just made some . . . changes to Augusta National.
>
> Traditionalist that I am, I wrote a column, the sum and substance of which was that Bobby Jones, the golfer and codesigner of Augusta National, was probably turning over in his grave. I said, How dare they? I said, Bobby Jones and Alister Mackenzie are gods of golf! I said, I don't care if the players shoot thirty under for the week, you don't touch Augusta National! It's sacrilegious!

You'd think the greencoats would have given Beard a standing ovation for his passionate defense of their 365 acres. You'd think that he was the kind of man of low-key sincerity and deep respect for the game the Masters wanted in the booth. You'd think Roberts would have dispatched one of the many corporate jets he controlled to pick up Mr. Beard and deposit him at the front gates of the course he so reverently worshiped.

Wrong on all counts.

Beard writes: "Cliff Roberts, who ran the Masters with an iron fist, didn't like that. He got on the phone to Chirkinian. He said, 'We don't want Beard down here doing this tournament. In fact, we really don't want Beard on CBS at all.'

"Chirkinian told me himself. And of course the Masters was the jewel in the CBS crown, the most prestigious event in their sports lineup. Chirkinian was apologetic. He said, 'I can't take a chance, Frank.' I understood. I wasn't fired, because I never had a contract in the first place. I just never worked for CBS again."

Roberts "yanked" the CBS chain at least once per annum. He was able to do this because there were no extended contracts and the broadcast rights for the Masters were renegotiated every year. Bill MacPhail said of the one-year deal: "You could call it a threat, you could call it good business, but I think the whole purpose of that one-year contract has been to say to CBS, 'You play ball correctly or you're out on your tokus.' "

Frank Hannigan, a commentator for ABC, agrees: "This type of thing didn't happen anyplace else. . . . This was part of a philosophy that said, 'The tournament is important; you are not important.' Augusta understood very early on how important TV was. Cliff knew of its potential to influence what people thought."

Cliff also knew that if CBS didn't comply with his edicts, there were plenty of other folks waiting in line to jump through whatever hoops he set up. Jim Nantz, a Butler Cabin regular since Brent Musburger's departure, said, "If we weren't televising this tournament, NBC, ABC, ESPN, and Turner would be lined up to take our place."

Steve Melnyk agrees: "ABC [where Melnyk now works] would love to be able to televise the Masters—any major network would. Having worked at CBS for ten years, I have a good sense for how things should be done, and I believe there are some things ABC could offer in making it better.

"Coverage in terms of pictures and camera angles could be better. It now comes across as a very flat presentation of Augusta—first-time visitors to Augusta are usually struck by the severity of the contours, such as at ten and eighteen. That severity isn't conveyed well by the current television coverage. One suggestion I would make is to place a camera high above eleven, twelve, and thirteen so that the viewer could get a good perspective of Amen Corner and how those holes relate to each other. Then again, the club—that's capital T-H-E C-L-U-B—might not want that and I would certainly respect that."

Dave Marr also believes ABC could do a great job with the Masters but he doubts they will ever get the chance, having said: "I know ABC would love to have the Masters, but I don't think anyone has a chance of getting in there because it's not a question of dollars. I think they [Augusta and CBS] have one of those rare business relationships that works. But if CBS messes up, NBC and ABC are standing in the wings licking their chops."

That's exactly what CBS doesn't want to hear, and that's exactly why, since the days when Roberts insisted that CBS turn off the air-conditioning in the executive suites and have Oreo cookies with the cream scraped off waiting for him at the negotiating table, the network has smiled, nodded, and taken it.

Chirkinian says: "CBS doesn't make money off the Masters. We break even. What it does do is add prestige to the

An elevated camera and cameraman give viewers back home a more panoramic view of Augusta's green splendor. (*Augusta Chronicle* photo)

network. It has become a corporate tapestry. To lose the rights to the Masters would be like losing one of our children. It's important to maintain that kind of relationship. CBS has been with it for more than forty years and we've learned to live with it. . . . The value of the relationship is more than just intangible."

That relationship has become much more cordial in recent years, but the greencoats could afford to make it so; Roberts had set the tone and whipped CBS into shape many years before.

Every year Mr. Cliff would review hours of tape and critique every aspect of the broadcast. Marr said: "I've been told that one year, while he was reviewing the telecast on tape, [Roberts] pointed at an announcer and grumbled that his hair was 'askew.' Can you imagine? *Askew!*"

From out-of-place hair to out-of-character shots, Roberts never missed a thing. "Whenever there was a problem, I would get a phone call," Chirkinian remembers of Roberts. "And it was never him calling to say, 'Have a nice day.' One time, I got chewed out for showing on camera a player cleaning off his spikes. I remember it clearly: It was Bruce Devlin. When Cliff saw that, he made it clear to me he would prefer a shot of the flowers behind the thirteenth tee to a player scraping dirt out of his spikes. You never really had much of a defense when it came to talking to Cliff."

Roberts also wrote down his complaints about television. In his trademark fastidious fashion, Roberts showed his genuine distrust for the "unfiltered" medium in his annual letters to Bill MacPhail. Excerpts of one such letter, dated April 30, 1963, and written three weeks after Jack Nicklaus won his first Masters by one shot over Tony Lema, showed Roberts's attention to detail:

Dear Bill,
. . . On the whole we felt it was a definite improvement over the telecast made last year.

. . . Once again the pictures were especially good and clear and in fact, better than at any other golf tournament. . . . There were, of course, a few minor errors and a few places where improvements can be made in 1964 . . .

(1) At one point I believe the CBS scoreboard showed Boros to be seven under par at No. 17, while he was in the process of playing No. 15.

(2) One of the commentators spoke of "humps" in the fairways, whereas "mounds" is a better word, I believe . . .

(3) After Nicklaus holed out his final putt on the eighteenth, it was announced that he was the winner, and immediately thereafter, the viewers were switched to a commercial. I believe it was a mistake not to have had something more to say at that point about the accomplishment by Nicklaus . . .

(5) A bungle was made in connection with the time available for the ceremony in my room. Apparently, the signal was given by a CBS man to Mr. Jones that he should quickly terminate the ceremony, but after he did so, several minutes of time were still available. . . . Next time, I think it might be better to give Mr. Jones a stopwatch and tell him when you wish him to finish his part. . . .

(6) We have no real objection to it, but I doubt that it is proper or correct for

CBS to state that Augusta is the golfing capital of the world. . . . About the only thing in Augusta to support the statement is the Masters tournament.

In conclusion . . . we are wondering if it might be better for both sponsors to devise opening and closing commercials that are a little more of an institutional nature. . . .

Very Sincerely Yours,
CR

Roberts always signed correspondence with his initials. After pontificating on the differences between "mounds" and "humps," and suggesting that Bob Jones carry a stopwatch while on the air, Roberts simply couldn't be bothered by such mundane details as signing his full name. Then there were those pesky sponsors who had the audacity to actually "sell" something in their commercials! Of course, Cliff handpicked Travelers and, later, Cadillac as "official" advertisers, the latter by picking up the phone, dialing the number for Cadillac Motor Division president Don Ahrens, and saying, "You're it." Therefore dictating the content of the commercials was no big deal. His point in bringing it up to MacPhail was, "I caught this; why didn't you?" The letters, like the Oreo cookies and the ass chewings, became a Masters ritual, a rite of spring that MacPhail, Chirkinian, and CBS braced for like a coming plague.

One year, CBS inadvertently showed a soggy piece of paper lying on the ground during a torrential rain. Roberts threatened to pull the contract, writing to MacPhail that "the public at large must have gained the impression that the whole affair was a most untidy event." When CBS provided aerial shots of the golf course from a helicopter in 1964, Roberts went ballistic and claimed that the incident had caused patrons to experience "discomfort and illness in some cases caused by the pine-tree pollen stirred up by the helicopter." Another year, CBS trucks parked in what Roberts deemed "an inappropriate area." Not only were they moved, Roberts insisted they be painted green, a demand even the CBS brass couldn't take. As a compromise, the television trucks were covered with a Masters-green tarp while on the premises.

The old autocrat wielded his power on the peons at CBS with brutal impertinence. The always-happy Bill MacPhail remembers: "Eighteen straight years I went down there and I dreaded it every time. I had to be chewed out at least eleven times in the course of seven days. . . . [Roberts] was hypercritical and calculating—I think it was his intention to have me scared to death for the sake of the Masters. If one of the sportscasters said the wrong thing, I was immediately summoned and told that if he ever said it again, he'd be gone and so would CBS."

Roberts also dictated the "pictures" that would be used by the network and the broadcast innovations that would have their start at the Masters. CBS learned that they would be broadcasting in color in 1966 when Roberts made the announcement after the 1965 event. They learned who the broadcasters would be when Roberts gave Chirkinian the list of "suggested" commentators. CBS executives also had to wait, every year, to see what new wrinkle Mr. Cliff would insist on while either eating his Oreo cookies or staring down at them. In the words of one CBS executive, "You've never known what hell is until Cliff Roberts stared at you through those thick glasses and poked a bony finger into your chest."

FOR ALL THE CRITICISMS OF ROBERTS AND HIS INTERMINABLE BERATING, THE DEMANDS PLACED ON CBS IN THE EARLY YEARS HAVE NOT ONLY RESULTED IN THE MASTERS BEING THE MOST-WATCHED GOLF EVENT ON THE PLANET, THEY HAVE HELPED CBS BECOME THE LEADER IN GOLF COVERAGE.

For all the criticisms of Roberts and his interminable berating, the demands placed on CBS in the early years have not only resulted in the Masters being the most-watched golf event on the planet, they have helped CBS become the leader in golf coverage, a position it rightly attributes to the Masters.

Chirkinian says: "I learned about good golf coverage because of the Masters. The one thing that impressed me about meeting with Bobby Jones was his telling me to 'Show your viewers as many golf shots as you can. That's why they've tuned in.' We [CBS] have mastered that philosophy ever since. You won't see CBS using all those videotaped packages featuring players. At this year's Open carried by NBC, they twice cut away from live golf on Sunday to show six-minute pieces on Jack Nicklaus and on Davis Love III and his father. Between those two interruptions they must have missed something like a hundred shots of live action. That's the equivalent of cutting into five minutes of live action at the Super Bowl to show a videotaped feature. It's insane! Why do that to golf and not to any other sport? You will never see that at Augusta [nor at any other CBS tournament].

"Working with the Masters people, the greencoats, has been awesome. I don't think I've ever run into a display of solidarity like that before. There's a total sense of power that has permeated every move we've made. It's something that we've all learned to live with. There's always been the sense that they know exactly what they want and, by golly, that's the way it's going to be. And that's good. It eliminates confusion. I learned a lesson in all this—democratic rule is not an effective form of government. With autocratic rule, there is no confusion. I became autocratic running the golf coverage. I had to because that's really the only sensible way to do things. Pat Summerall even nicknamed me 'the Ayatollah.' "

While Chirkinian looks back with certain fondness on all those finger-pointing sessions, it's good to remember that a softness has befallen the world's premier golf tournament since Mr. Roberts's passing. Hord Hardin, whom Chirkinian calls "a really nice person," attempted to put velvet Augusta National gloves on Roberts's iron-fisted behavior long after Cliff's death. Hardin said: "Anybody who has any knowledge about TV, and I don't claim to have much [as Hardin would continuously display during his utterly amateurish once-a-year interviews from the Butler Cabin], knows that it's a very sophisticated business. And most of us who are on the outside are really not qualified to judge. But we do know what we like. Now when television started in golf, the golf people, such as Mr. Roberts and, of course, Mr. Jones, knew a heck of a lot more about the game than the TV people did. And to that extent, they gave them a lot of advice [Hardin's sanitized description of Roberts's mandates]. They [TV people] had to learn a lot about golf, and Mr. Roberts and Mr. Jones were especially qualified to give them that kind of help."

Chirkinian and MacPhail would question Hardin's use of the word "help," but even they would admit that as nit-picking and condescending as Roberts was, the Masters and golf broadcasting as a whole are better because of his attention to detail. Today people in more than one hundred countries see some version of the Masters telecast. Even those who don't watch any other golf tournament tune in to see Augusta in the springtime. Chirkinian says: "It's akin to people tuning in to see the Kentucky Derby. That is the one horse race most of them will watch all year. People are very comfortable with Augusta. They can turn it on at any moment and see the action at, say, the fourteenth hole and know immediately that they are seeing the fourteenth hole."

Even though it has always been the most meticulously scrutinized event in golf, the Masters telecast has had its share of gaffes, not the least of which have come from chairman Hardin. He told *Golf* magazine: "[The post-tournament ceremony] is the toughest part of the job. I caught the devil with Bernhard Langer in 1985. I'd said, 'Bernhard, at what point did you think you might have it won?' And he said, 'I came off the fourteenth green and I looked at the leaderboard and said, "Jesus Christ, I can win this!" ' Well, you're not supposed to say that on television. I thought about replying with something like, 'Well, you were certainly leaning on the right guy,' which would have made it worse, so I let it ride."

Hord also became known for his infamous Seve interview after the dashing Spaniard won the Masters in grand style. In the basement of the Butler Cabin, Hardin asked, "Seve, how tall are you?" His defense for these off-the-wall moments was, "If you don't specialize in these interviews, it's very awkward."

In fact the entire Butler Cabin presentation is very awkward and so silly that even those in charge of putting it on television can hardly bear to watch. Chirkinian says: "The worst thing in the world to do is to go into that cabin. We've just finished on this high, and all of a sudden there's this deathly silence because we're down in the catacombs saying, 'Well, it was very nice,' and 'I parred seven, and I hit an eight-iron,' and 'Well, isn't that wonderful. Get up and put on your green jacket.' This presentation has always been so sanitized that you can just hear all the sets clicking off."

Since CBS, at the insistence of the National, has its on-site studio in the basement of the Butler Cabin, the green jacket ceremony—a tradition since 1949 and a television tradition since the Masters first appeared on television—continues to be held "in the catacombs."

The official explanation from the club is: "The Butler Cabin ceremony which started with Bob Jones and Cliff Roberts is unique in golf and perhaps all of television sports. A member is always present because at Augusta National the winner is given honorary membership in the club, and only a member of the club can bestow that honor. The club thinks that the public understands that its members are not professional announcers and accordingly do not hold them to the same standards."

Those standards have varied over the years in spite of Roberts and the greencoats' constant scrutiny. While none of the paid CBS announcers have ever said, "Jesus Christ, he could win this thing," on television, there have been plenty of Masters bloopers throughout the years. Brent Musburger, an obvious golf neophyte brought on to give more "depth" to the broadcast team, referred to 1987 winner Larry Mize as Johnny Mize. The entire 1967 telecast could be summed up as an "oops." That year, CBS technicians were on strike and the entire show was produced by management. During Sunday's coverage, a manager-broadcaster who made Musburger look brilliant said, "And here comes Tommy Walker, a former member of the U.S. Aaron Cup team."

Through it all, the CBS–Augusta National relationship has remained poised, dignified, and professional, but never, ever, too comfortable. Chirkinian says of the process today: "When we have that meeting each year, there's only one greencoat there, and that's the chairman. It's always a cordial meeting. When Hord was the chairman, he'd always

The international appeal and flavor of Augusta and the Masters was evident as far back as the fifties. Golf fans throughout much of the world today get to watch the Masters Tournament thanks to satellite technology. (*Augusta Chronicle* photo)

say, 'Let's first play some golf and then we'll sit down and talk.' The meeting wasn't particularly long at first, but it has gotten progressively longer with additional international considerations. All of a sudden, every year it seems we were adding another vital organ: Japan, Germany, Spain, England, on and on. At one time the only TV compound belonged to CBS. Today it's a metropolis. We didn't have all that when Cliff was there."

Nor did they have such innovations as high definition television (HDTV), direct satellite links, or Internet updates. As Chirkinian fondly recalls: "For the first Masters telecast we had two trucks with a director in each. The B unit televised the fifteenth and sixteenth holes, and the A unit did the seventeenth and eighteenth. In those days, using two separate trucks was a technical necessity because camera cable could not run beyond one thousand feet. Today we have eighteen cameras out of one truck."

Looking forward, Chirkinian continues: "The future plan at Augusta, like it already is at other tournaments CBS covers, is to use wireless—radio frequency—cameras. We just did the PGA Championship with eighteen wireless cameras. With them, you have no cord between camera and truck. Today all eighteen holes at Augusta are already wired, ready to go each year. Cable has been buried there over time to serve that purpose. There will come a day when all that underground cable will just be buried there as a testimonial to television in the 'good ole days.' It will be our underground monument."

CHAPTER 10

SOUTHERN BY THE GRACE OF GOD

I THINK EVERYBODY LOVES HAVING THE MASTERS HERE. THE
WHOLE CITY TAKES ON AN AIR OF HAPPINESS, AND IT'S ALMOST LIKE
A CARNIVAL-TYPE ATMOSPHERE. YOU GET PEOPLE FROM ALL OVER
THE WORLD IN HERE FOR SEVEN DAYS. EVERY TIME I TAKE SOME-
BODY OUT THERE, THEY CAN'T BELIEVE IT'S SUCH A BEAUTIFUL
PLACE. I TOOK SOME PEOPLE OUT THERE LAST YEAR, DURING THE
LAST MASTERS, AND THEY WERE SAYING, "THIS HAS GOT TO BE
HEAVEN FOR A GOLF COURSE." THEY MAKE IT THE VERY BEST IT
CAN BE.

—LARRY SCONYERS
MAYOR OF AUGUSTA

Abandoned trolley tracks still bisect Sixth Avenue in
downtown Augusta, offering a gentle reminder of an era
when ladies and gentlemen rode in open train cars down from
the hilltop Summerville section onto Broad Street and over to
the river. The turn-of-the-century architecture also hints of a
genteel era when people with such names as Maytag, Hutton,

229

and Vanderbilt escaped from the harsh northern winters to this springtime Shangri-la.

Today the buildings sit empty. At the corner of Broad and Sixth, several young black men lean against a wall outside Lucifer's Tavern, one of several less-than-Demi-Moore-like strip clubs that dot the urban landscape of central Augusta. With most of the retail outlets gone, Broad Street is an eclectic mix of abandoned department stores and half-vacant commercial buildings where a few lawyers still hang their shingles (the courthouse is within walking distance) and the biggest tenant is *Augusta Chronicle,* whose offices take up a half block along Broad and Seventh. There are a few quaint antique and craft shops in downtown, along with the charming and seemingly out-of-place White Elephant Cafe, a favorite of many Masters goers. Two blocks away construction continues on the Georgia Golf Hall of Fame, a complex devoted to the great golf names in the state's history and an attraction the chamber of commerce hopes will lure an ever-dwindling visitor population back to the city.

There's the River Walk complex; the sprawling walkway and amphitheater that buffers downtown from the Savannah, and Fort Discovery, a science and education center designed to attract young scientists. There's minor league baseball, with a team appropriately named the Green Jackets. Augusta also has a symphony, a ballet, and an opera. But, for the most part, Augusta remains the city that commentator Paul Harvey described as "the sort of place where people go to the barbershop to watch haircuts."

Nightlife and entertainment, sans the "Girls, Girls, Girls" at Lucifer's and the Discotec, are limited at best. Masters contestant Ken Green remembers being starved for things to do while in Augusta: "One place we used to hang out in Augusta was the Post Office. We'd go to shoot pool and drink. One night I was with a couple of guys at the Post Office with Calc's [Mark Calcavecchia's] father-in-law, shooting some pool. It was getting late and I had to leave, so one of the guys drove me back to the house. When my buddy got back to the Post Office about forty minutes later, Calc's father-in-law was taking his cue stick and poking some guy in the ribs. Then all hell broke loose and it ended up with a bunch of guys pulling each other apart.

"Another thing we did during Masters week [for lack of anything better to do] was what we called Nip Opens. You grab a sand wedge and play alternate shots around the house, picking out holes all over the yard. It could be a mailbox, a car tire, or even a trunk. We would open [the car's trunk] and you had to land a chip in it. The year we had two houses rented we were able to play back and forth between them, even using the Jacuzzi or the pool as a hole. At my last Masters, we would sneak into the neighbors' yards for some holes. One day we looked next door and saw the people had posted a cardboard sign saying, 'O. B.' That was a nice way of telling us to leave them alone."

Those neighbors could have very easily been representative of any one of more than one hundred companies that rent houses during Masters week. They do not necessarily go to the event, since there aren't that many tickets, but they sign sponsorship deals, promote new products, meet, greet, entertain, and, if they're lucky enough, spend a few days on the most magnificent golf course in the world.

As for the native Augustans who live in east Georgia the remaining fifty-one weeks of the year, the memories of a more-vibrant time still linger. Locals take great pride in telling

231

of the time Buffalo Bill came riding through town sporting the freshly cut scalp of Chief Yellow Hand, a Native-American renegade. They will also tell you about the Wright Brothers' flying school that used to be in town, and the fact that the entire U.S. Army Air Corps (all five planes of it) was once headquartered in Augusta. They will tell you about the Bon Air Vanderbilt Hotel and of the time President Taft came to play golf but was turned away from the Palmetto Golf Club in nearby Aiken. It was, after all, a private club.

Perhaps the most befitting irony is that the passersthrough who used to support the local economy, even after Augusta's resort luster began to tarnish, have all been routed around town by the Eisenhower interstate project hatched during the 1950s. Interstate 20 connecting Atlanta and Columbia, South Carolina, funnels traffic past town at speeds that make it impossible to appreciate the subtleties of "the Garden City."

It isn't a garden, but if you get off the interstate and meander through downtown, there is a grassy divider median with park benches, flowers, fountains, and several monuments separating the north- and southbound lanes of Broad Street. As in most southern towns, the tallest monument honors local Civil War veterans. The statue is Augusta's likeness of Berry Benson, Confederate scout and sharpshooter, standing watch atop a marble podium. Berry appears at ease in his uniform, gazing down on the few businesspeople who venture across the street during the lunch hour. But there are other likenesses in the park that don't look quite so at ease. Unlike the main drags in other towns, Augusta's Broad Street sports a bronze statue of Arnold Palmer standing guard in a community that is both aware of its presence and somewhat suspect of its reason for being. Four more statues—of Jack Nicklaus, Raymond Floyd, Bobby Jones, and Ben Hogan—were scheduled to be unveiled in spring 1997, coinciding with the opening of the Georgia Golf Hall of

Fame. Augustans know the statues are there because of one thing—the Masters. And as far as downtown Augusta is concerned, the Masters is both their greatest blessing and, in some regards, their cruelest curse.

The Masters Tournament is the townfolks' biggest claim to fame, and the only reason people around the world know the small southern city even exists. "The Golf Capital of the World" is what the mayor, vendors, and folks at the chamber still insist on calling their town, despite Mr. Roberts's warnings written almost thirty years ago that this was "too much of a claim for us to support." But Augusta National and the city of Augusta are like siblings, bound by genetics and geography but so far apart in personality that outside observers are shocked when they experience the differences for the first time.

"This is the home of the Masters?" they ask.

"Where are all the plantation houses?"

"What is there to do down here?"

"This could be in New Jersey."

Augusta, good and bad, is the home of the Masters, although the men in the green coats strongly object to that reference. To them, the National is as the National does; its location is totally irrelevant, and its many names (Masters, Augusta National, and even just Augusta if it's used in a golf context) are proprietary.

Nowhere is the dichotomy between "Augusta, the Garden City" and "Augusta, the Golf Capital of the World" so exemplified as along Washington Road, where sixty-three years ago Bobby Jones built his dream club. Today, the Piggly Wiggly that sat across the street from the National's main entrance is home to a ministry.

Business along Washington, however, is better at Burger King, McDonalds, Wendy's, Captain D's, Popeye's Fried Chicken, and for the more sophisticated diner, Long Horn Steakhouse and that blossoming bastion of all things

THE AREA THAT HOUSES

GOLF'S GREATEST

WONDERLAND NOW IS A

COMMERCIAL MECCA OF

GAS STATIONS, FAST-FOOD

RESTAURANTS, AND TACKY

NIGHTCLUBS. WHEN

AUGUSTA MAGAZINE RAN A

FEATURE SOLICITING IDEAS

FOR IMPROVING THE

WASHINGTON ROAD AREA,

"BLOW IT UP," WAS THE

MOST POPULAR

SUGGESTION.

good in America, Hooters, where you can get a pitcher of beer and a basket of deep-fried hot wings served by one of Augusta's prettiest young women dressed in skimpy shorts and an even skimpier T-shirt.

The area that houses golf's greatest wonderland now is a commercial mecca of gas stations, fast-food restaurants, and tacky nightclubs. When *Augusta Magazine* ran a feature soliciting ideas for improving the Washington Road area, "Blow it up," was the most popular suggestion. Washington Road merges into the Calhoun Expressway a mile or so south of the National, and, suddenly, the dichotomy becomes even more black and white. The area is known as "the Terry," short for "the Territory." Poor and cluttered, with rows of shanty dwellings, it provided and continues to provide employees for the private 365-acre golf course just up the road. Then, as Frank Deford said in his HBO segment on Augusta, when you enter the gates of the National, you leave the real Augusta and "fall through that magnolia hole into golf wonderland."

Just outside that magnolia hole used to sit the Green Jacket restaurant, a curiously nondescript eatery where a patron could get surf and turf, sweet tea (or "sweetea" as the

234

"The Terry" in Augusta reflects quite the opposite image of the pristine grounds of Augusta National, just a mile away. (Photo courtesy of Heather Fritz)

charmingly southern waitress used to call it), and a toothpick for $12.95. Despite the restaurant's name, the National apparently did little in the way of stimulating business there. Then again, the National has little to do with anything else in town. Says Barry White of the Augusta Convention and Visitors Bureau: "The Masters brought in around $108 million to the Augusta economy last year. There are twelve hundred private rooms rented; forty-nine hundred hotel and motel rooms sold out as far away as Thomson [some one hundred miles to the west] and Columbia, South Carolina [about the same distance to the east]. However, I have to admit, Masters week is an unusual week in Augusta; all the schools are on spring break, the locals take vacation to avoid the crowds, and they rent out their homes; so the local businesses miss out, and the guests in town focus on the tournament. The hospitality business does real well, but the small business owner sees a slowdown. Even in our office, the Welcome Center traffic increases, but the phones in the bureau slow down."

For every resident escaping an Augusta home fast enough to avoid getting hit by a closing-behind-you screen door, there is a group of out-of-towners willing to fork out thousands of dollars to secure the one-week rental of a home during "Masters Hospitality Week." The idea of forsaking a packed hotel or motel for the creature comforts of someone's accommodating house became popular around 1960, when a San Francisco real estate agency inquired about reserving a large house for two clients requesting anonymity. A quick look here and a couple of phone calls there, and Bing Crosby, Phil Harris, and a party of six had for a thousand dollars secured a one-week lease on a home on Walton Way in a section of town known as the Hill.

Not all the locals profit by the annual arrival of the Masters. Robert Gray, owner of Radio Active Music on Eighth Street in downtown, says: "Businesses might as well shut down. People leave town and the businesses in the city are really hurt by [the Masters]. I've been in business eleven years, but it wasn't until the spring of 1996 that I got revenue from the Masters; a guy came in and bought a CD for his son. I made thirteen dollars."

A few Augusta natives—those whose interests rest in things other than chasing after a little white ball—see the National and the Masters as completely out of sync with the surroundings. Augustan Sonny Hill told *Sports Illustrated*: "They take that whole entire thing out there [meaning the National] and pave it over with cement, ain't twenty-nine people in this town gonna miss church on Sunday. The people of Augusta built this thing up from nothing, and I'll tell you quite honestly, folks out there at the National don't give diddly back."

In fact, not giving diddly back is club policy. The club states: "Bob Jones and Cliff Roberts did not start the Masters in order to further charitable purposes. Their single objective, and one which is still adhered to, is to provide a service to the game of golf by putting on the best golf tournament possible." As evidence of this policy, Dennis Williams of the NAACP's Augusta branch says: "Our local branch has solicited support from the National and I received a letter back from them stating that they were not financially able to provide any assistance to our branch, which I thought to be rather funny to put it simply."

Whether the members do anything for the community is a matter of speculation. Certainly, Warren Buffett, Jack Stephens, Ron Allen, and others are heavily tied to charitable organizations, and their philanthropic endeavors are open for all to see, but when it comes to what they do in Augusta, for Augusta, or in the name of Augusta, the magnolia hole slams quickly shut.

In defense, a National member says: "A lot goes on that nobody sees. One time a local golf pro was diagnosed with cancer and some people had an auction to help raise money for him. [The National] sent over some of those prints they have of all the holes to be auctioned off. Nobody knew about it until that night. Nobody makes a big deal out of what they do. If they did, everybody would want something."

Certainly, the donation of prints to an auction for a local cancer victim is noble, but given that PGA Tour events raise millions for charity on a weekly basis, the impression left by the National's total lack of involvement is one of selfishness. Says an *Augusta Chronicle* writer: "A lot of members out there don't agree with the policies. There are two groups out there: the members who are just a bunch of old guys who play golf and mind their own business, and the management who always dictates stuff then goes to the members and says, 'Hey, look what we're doing for you.' "

MANY PUBLIC OFFICIALS,

INCLUDING AUGUSTA'S

MAYOR, WERE SURPRISED

TO LEARN THAT THE NAME

"AUGUSTA" AND THE

GEORGIA MAP WERE

PROPRIETARY PROPERTY OF

A GOLF CLUB.

Vendors who set up shop are advised to beware of what they sell and say. On May 25, 1993, a few specialty vendors—mostly small entrepreneurial operations—received a notice from Augusta National general manager Jim Armstrong: "Any goods imprinted with indicia such as 'Masters' or 'Masters Tournament,' designs of golfers, and reference to 'Augusta' or 'Augusta National' with or without reference to dates, will be considered an intentional infringement of Augusta National Golf Club's proprietary rights. Furthermore, merchandise bearing legends such as "Augusta, Ga. . . . Home of the Masters" with or without golf motifs, United States or Georgia map design motifs or dates, will constitute an infringement of Augusta National Golf Club's proprietary rights."

Many public officials, including Augusta's mayor, were surprised to learn that the name "Augusta" and the Georgia map were proprietary property of a golf club. "I think anyone who lives here for any length of time takes golf and the Masters personally," then-Mayor Charles DeVaney said. "If you have a trademark infringement suit that upsets some people, it makes everyone a bit more concerned."

It made some people downright mad. Said Regis Harrington, owner of Harrington Sporting Goods: "I opened for business in 1978. I've sold shirts since 1980. They say 'Augusta—Home of the Masters.' We've done it for [more than] ten years, and now they say that any golfing shirt or any

These Masters hats are the genuine articles, piled on a counter inside the Augusta National golf shop.

picture of a golfer or any shirt with a golf ball, tee, flag or whatever and the city's name is illegal. I think it's ridiculous. 'Augusta—Home of the Masters' is kind of public domain. The disturbing thing to me is you, as a private citizen, cannot walk into my business and buy a shirt with 'Augusta, Ga.,' and some reference to golf on it. I don't know if it's an over-extension of their greed or their egos, but I know it's intimi-dation. I can't think their legal rights are any different than mine but money talks. We're all running scared. We all have something to lose and simply put, I don't have the bucks."

Another vendor who didn't have the bucks but who refused to buckle under was Kathie Edwards. Operating Kathie's Special T's, a small but successful specialty retail shop in Augusta, Kathie took on the National when, in March of

239

1994, she learned that she had to either turn over her inventory or destroy it. Edwards said: "Since 1985, I've been selling my T-shirts, golf shirts, towels, tote bags, sweaters, mugs, jackets, and the like outside the Augusta National with my own design and slogan, 'Augusta, Ga.—Home of the Masters.' Now, they want my business, too. I support the Masters. I think it's great for Augusta. We probably do between twenty and thirty thousand dollars that [Masters] week. We employ four or five additional people, and other vendors do the same. I guess probably one hundred people will be out of a job because of this. It's typical David versus Goliath and I ain't that good with a slingshot." But off she went to take her best shot at Augusta's mythical giant. "All the attorneys around here were saying, 'She's wasting her money. You can't fight God, and the National is bigger than God," Kathie says. "I had to go to Atlanta and hire an attorney."

That attorney, Ronald Doeve, could not withhold his utter dismay at the National's apparent arrogance: "The Augusta National contends that the name 'Augusta' and golf are one and the same. . . . It seems to be their contention that the City of Augusta is known for only one thing." While the rest of the world might agree with the National on that point, Edwards was the sole defender of her right to use her hometown name with any golf reference, and she found a great deal of support in the media and among the public.

Edwards settled her case with the National and, as part of her deal, she is sworn to silence. But, she definitely won in the battle of public opinion. The *Augusta Chronicle* was flooded with letters of support for Edwards and outrage for the National. In one such letter, a local Augustan wrote: "I just read with disgust the corporate arrogance of the Augusta National filing suit over the use of Augusta with a golf symbol. You might find it interesting to know that the Augusta National is furnished free water from the city of Augusta in return for letting the city run its water

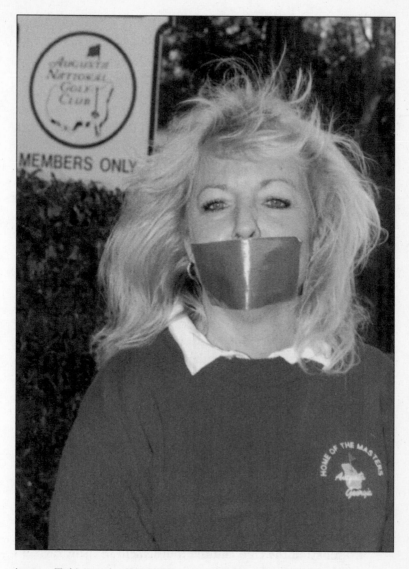

Augusta T-shirt vendor Kathie Edwards stood up to Augusta National's stringent, some might even say strong-handed, application of trademark-infringement policies. Pictured outside the National's front gate, a gagged Edwards symbolizes the conditions of her settlement with Augusta National. (Photo courtesy of Heather Fritz)

lines through the golf property. This is an ancient agreement and anyone else would have had their property condemned and taken by the city.

"If I opened a private business and it clogged up the city and county streets (like the National) I would be closed down. Yet the Augusta National is a private business that takes in millions of dollars in television rights and gives the city back nothing. No one gets a dime from them. Not a dime goes back to Augusta or any public agency or charitable organization in Augusta." Other comments included, "Fight, Kathie, fight!" and a suggestion by one livid reader that vendors file a "class action lawsuit" against the National.

A fair portion of the outrage was due to the fact that Augusta National did not go after Federated Department Stores or Wal-Mart, but the small, independent, mom-and-apple-pie entrepreneurs like Kathie Edwards and Michael Pisanello, a restaurant owner, who have few resources and a great deal to lose. According to one vendor, who has also signed an agreement with the National that requires anonymity, "They go after the little guy, because if they lose, Pandora's box will be opened."

In terms of giving back to the community, the National chooses to pass. Certainly Augusta benefits from the worldwide recognition it receives because of the Masters, and the hospitality industry can show substantial benefits from having the club and the tournament in their town. As for the rest of the city, many angry vendors would seemingly prefer to shut the club down, cancel the Masters, and put cattle back out to graze on the azaleas. Others simply don't care.

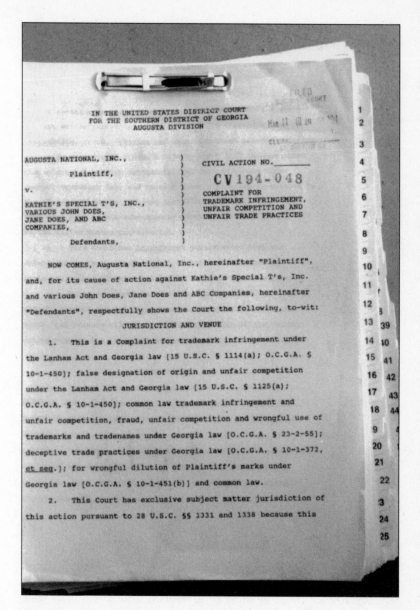

IN THE UNITED STATES DISTRICT COURT
FOR THE SOUTHERN DISTRICT OF GEORGIA
AUGUSTA DIVISION

FILED

Mar 11 10 24 '94

CLERK

AUGUSTA NATIONAL, INC.,

    Plaintiff,

v.

KATHIE'S SPECIAL T'S, INC.,
VARIOUS JOHN DOES,
JANE DOES, AND ABC
COMPANIES,

    Defendants,

CIVIL ACTION NO._____

CV 194-048

COMPLAINT FOR
TRADEMARK INFRINGEMENT,
UNFAIR COMPETITION AND
UNFAIR TRADE PRACTICES

NOW COMES, Augusta National, Inc., hereinafter "Plaintiff",
and, for its cause of action against Kathie's Special T's, Inc.
and various John Does, Jane Does and ABC Companies, hereinafter
"Defendants", respectfully shows the Court the following, to-wit:

JURISDICTION AND VENUE

1. This is a Complaint for trademark infringement under
the Lanham Act and Georgia law [15 U.S.C. § 1114(a); O.C.G.A. §
10-1-450]; false designation of origin and unfair competition
under the Lanham Act and Georgia law [15 U.S.C. § 1125(a);
O.C.G.A. § 10-1-450]; common law trademark infringement and
unfair competition, fraud, unfair competition and wrongful use of
trademarks and tradenames under Georgia law [O.C.G.A. § 23-2-55];
deceptive trade practices under Georgia law [O.C.G.A. § 10-1-372,
et seq.]; for wrongful dilution of Plaintiff's marks under
Georgia law [O.C.G.A. § 10-1-451(b)] and common law.

2. This Court has exclusive subject matter jurisdiction of
this action pursuant to 28 U.S.C. §§ 1331 and 1338 because this

Kathie Edwards's legal battle with Augusta National began with a civil action
filed in the U.S. District Court in Augusta. (Photo courtesy of Heather Fritz)

Outside the doors of what used to be known as the Green Jacket Steakhouse, a local man in a pickup truck unloads a ladder, some tools, and several cans of paint. An affable sort with a broad smile and confident nod, he wears a T-shirt that proclaims its owner to be "American by Birth; Southern by the Grace of God." When asked what he thinks about the Masters, he shrugs. "Don't know much about it."

"Ever been inside the gates?" he is asked.

"Nope, and don't want to go."

"Any idea who Nick Faldo is?"

"I know a Nick Baldo from Lincolnton."

Putting a painter's perspective on the relationship between a city and its most famous landmark, on a town and the traditions of one of its enterprises, and on the one yearly event that has made Augusta in the spring the most famous venue in all of sports, you see that at the end of it all the Augusta National is just a golf course. Granted, it is a nice golf course, with lots of history, lots of traditions, and lots of drama during its once-a-year foray into the public eye. But for all its glory and in spite of all its arrogance, the Augusta National Golf Club should be looked upon for what it is: a great golf course that has produced some of the most dramatic and memorable moments in the history of golf.

Members will come and go, join and die; policies will change; grass will grow; politicians will pontificate and the city will continue to change. If you view Augusta in its proper perspective, as a nice little town that just happens to host the first of golf's four annual major championships, then you can once again look at the Masters with the wondering eyes of a child. You can look out over the rolling hills and onto the greenest grass you've ever seen and know nothing but goodness, while settling for nothing short of greatness. And if golf is in your veins, you will know when you've found perfection: at the Masters.

DO THE RIGHT THING

Millionaire investment banker Jackson Stephens has, throughout his professional life, supported and contributed to Republican causes and candidates. He made an exception in 1992 when fellow Arkansan Bill Clinton, the Democratic nominee for U.S. president, needed some assistance. Then Mr. Stephens, like other Arkansas businessmen, saw the practical benefits of changing party alliance, at least for one election. This proved beyond a shadow of a doubt that Jackson Stephens is, above all else, a pragmatist. Now that he's retired from investment banking, Mr. Stephens can, and hopefully will, bring that same pragmatic approach to the chairmanship at Augusta National and the Masters. For as the National and its one commercial venture, the Masters Tournament, starts toward the end of its seventh decade, the American golf club most steeped in tradition must come to terms with the realities of the 1990s and, speculatively, the new millennium.

Tiger Woods in 1996 reportedly signed sixty million dollars' worth of endorsement contracts right after winning his third consecutive U.S. Amateur title. Will CBS and the Masters allow Woods, with his swoosh-enriched Nike wardrobe, to remain front and center on television, or will the commercially sensitive committeemen deem such blatant yet high-powered marketing to be anathema to the best traditions of the Masters? Stephens already has broadened the scope of Masters television coverage by allowing USA Network, in conjunction with CBS, to broadcast the Thursday and Friday rounds. Hopefully, in the next few years, Stephens and his fellow Augusta members (assuming they have the input) will see the wisdom of allowing live eighteen-hole coverage on Saturday and Sunday. Viewers got a glimpse of this in 1996 with the Sunday coverage of Greg Norman and Nick Faldo's duel, and it is the kind of live-event access that's almost taken for granted by today's discriminating golf spectator.

Perhaps the Augusta folks also will see the worthiness of setting aside a portion of their income for charitable purposes. The tournament is better than the average tour stop because of many of the commercial restrictions it insists on maintaining, although this is one club policy that serves no useful purpose other than to make the Masters and the Augusta National look pretentious and mean. Like it or not, greencoats, your tournament, despite being contested at a private club, has effectively become a public domain with an "ownership" that extends well beyond your 365 acres. Likewise, whether you believe it or not, the city of Augusta exists in part to support your club and tournament, as neither could survive as an island set apart from the rest of mankind. It's a matter of being a part of the community, not apart from it. If advertising rates and ticket prices were raised modestly, even just a tad, to benefit, say, abused children or other worthwhile charities, do you really believe anyone would mind? Bobby Jones surely wouldn't.

Of course, the Masters is never going to be confused with the "Bud World Party," but golf has become so intertwined with charity and charitable causes that it is not only a shame but counterproductive for the first annual major championship contested each year to have no charitable connections. Consider it an opportunity to thank God and country, the former for providing such a rich setting and the latter for

Gate 3, the main entrance onto the grounds of Augusta National, is "the magnolia hole into golf's wonderland." (Photo courtesy of Heather Fritz)

embracing a wonderful tournament that would be nothing if it existed in anonymity. Were Jones and Eisenhower alive today, they would certainly recognize the need for Augusta National and the Masters to reach out and broaden their contributions. Doing things for "the good of the game" rings hollow when a mile from your clubhouse black children don't have shoes and the number-one career goal among teens appears to be hitting the streets to sell dime bags of crack. Golf, in other cities and in other tournaments, knows its place. Augusta would be well served to learn from others in that context. Start by consulting with some of your CEO members familiar with corporate philanthropy. Ask for some honest input. It's amazing to think that some of those rich executives whose businesses make such a public charitable show would allow themselves to be associated with a club so private and self-serving. It reeks of hypocrisy. They can still have their great golf and clubhouse privacy, too.

In defense of privacy, men having their own place at which to mingle with other men, and women having a place to associate with other women, is, to everyone outside of Washington, D.C., and certain ACLU offices, reasonable if those associations "do no harm" to others. If the National wishes to preserve its rights to privacy and freedom of association, it must demonstrate some restraint, some openness, and some reasonableness for its actions. And would it be asking too much for President Clinton to do the civil thing by interceding and nicely asking his benefactor, Stephens, to get his club's membership to enact a spirit of charity and openness that reflects twentieth-century sensibilities, especially with the twenty-first century fast approaching?

When asked why the National is so secretive about all things pertaining to golf course maintenance, such as the speed of the greens, former assistant superintendent Greg Asmond said: "The club is only open a little over five months a year, and it gets very little play even then. They don't want to [announce] the green speed because that would become the standard, and clubs that play thirty-five thousand rounds of golf a year can't maintain those standards no matter how much money they spend. If the National published its green speeds, half the superintendents in the country would lose their jobs inside a year."

That reasoning makes sense, so why not just tell the world why they're not publishing those numbers for the world to hear? Why treat everything from the color of jackets to the name of the town as proprietary? This is a golf course, not a national security installation. (For the record, according to *Golf Digest* research published in 1991, Augusta National's green surface ratings—using USGA standards—add up to an astonishing difficulty of 148, compared to 110 for an average U.S. Open course and a figure of 72 for all

Workmen Cliff Harris and Charles Leverett perform some last-minute trimming of the shrubs outside Augusta National's main entrance before the start of another Masters Tournament. (*Augusta Chronicle* photo)

U.S. courses. Furthermore, Augusta National's 1991 course rating of 76.2 made it one of the ten toughest courses in the United States. However, none of these ratings were sanctioned by the National.)

As for the Masters, as long as the tournament has the beauty and the drama that have defined its existence, there will always be devoted fans, and the tournament itself will always be considered a major. Golfers are, by their very nature, traditionalists. Augusta National has its identity, forever cast by the memories of Bobby Jones, Cliff Roberts, Dwight Eisenhower, Hord Hardin, and others, and forever enshrined in the memories, good and bad, of tournaments and incidents

To a young southern belle visiting Augusta National in the fifties, the sight of (what apparently is an earlier version of) the Masters trophy was something to behold! (*Augusta Chronicle* photo)

250

that have followed the course of history for more than sixty-three years. It also has a future, one not yet written, but one that is bound to continue in the long shadows cast by those who have come before. Someday soon, there will be a black Masters winner and an Asian Masters winner. Perhaps someday a woman will don a green jacket as an Augusta member. What is certain is that change will come. Hopefully, it will be change not just for the good of the game or even for Augusta National, but for the good of all whose eyes gladly look southward in the springtime.

If the men in the green coats respond positively to the future by embracing the world and setting the standards for the game, then they can still defend golf's most ardent traditions. They can still run the greatest golf tournament in the world; and they can continue to socialize and play golf in a private environment where their business is their business. They can also evolve to voluntarily meet the needs of those around them and graciously share their triumphs and profits with others less fortunate. If that is the future of the Augusta National and the Masters, they will then have the blessings and support of most everyone. And somewhere looking down on them, Mr. Jones will be pleased.

The annual Masters Champions Dinner always brings together many of golf's most legendary champions. Pictured here at the 1965 dinner are all past Masters winners (to that point) except for Horton Smith, who had passed away. Front row, left to right: Craig Wood (1941 winner), Doug Ford (1957), Art Wall Jr. (1959), Jack Burke Jr. (1956), Gene Sarazen (1935), Jimmy Demaret (1940, 1947, and 1950), and Henry Picard (1938). Back row, left to right: Ralph Guldahl (1939), Byron Nelson (1937 and 1942), Claude Harmon (1948), Cary Middlecoff (1955), Ben Hogan (1951 and 1953), Herman Keiser (1946), Sam Snead (1949, 1952, and 1954), Jack Nicklaus (1963), Clifford Roberts (tournament chairman), Arnold Palmer (1958, 1960, 1962, and 1964), Robert T. Jones Jr. (president, Augusta National Golf Club), and Gary Player (1961). (© Morgan Fitz Photographers, Globe Photos, Inc. 1997)

BIBLIOGRAPHY

Books

Ambrose, Stephen. *Eisenhower: Soldier, General of the Army, President-Elect, 1890–1952*. New York: Simon and Schuster, 1983.

——*Eisenhower: The President*. New York: Simon and Schuster, 1984.

Beard, Frank, with John Garrity. *Making the Turn: A Year Inside the PGA Tour*. New York: Macmillan, 1992.

Boswell, Thomas. *Strokes of Genius*. Garden City, New York: Doubleday, 1987.

Brendon, Piers. *Ike: His Life and Times*. New York: Harper and Row, 1986.

Broun, Heywood Hale. *Collected Edition of Heywood Broun*. New York: Harcourt, Brace, and Company, 1969.

Childs, Marquis. *Eisenhower: Captive Hero*. New York: Harcourt, Brace, and World, Inc., 1958.

Christian, Frank. *Augusta National and the Masters: A Photographer's Scrapbook*. Chelsea, Michigan: Sleeping Bear Press, 1996.

Cook, Blanche Wiesen. *The Declassified Eisenhower: A Divided Legacy*. Garden City, New York: Doubleday, 1981.

Crowell, Thomas. *The Encyclopedia of American Facts and Dates*. Toronto, Ontario, Canada: Fitzhenry and Whiteside Limited, 1972.

Derr, John. *Uphill Is Easier: A Reporter's Journal*. Pinehurst, North Carolina: Cricket Productions, 1995.

Flaherty, Tom. *The Masters: The Story of Golf's Greatest Tournament*. New York: Holt, Rinehart, and Winston, 1960.

Gutman, Bill. *Tiger Woods: A Biography*. New York: Pocket Books, 1997.

Harris, Joel Chandler. *Uncle Remus: His Songs and Sayings*.

Jacobsen, Peter, with Jack Sheehan. *Buried Lies: True Tales and Tall Stories from the PGA Tour*. New York: G. P. Putnam's Sons, 1993.

Jones, Robert T. *Bobby Jones on Golf*. Garden City, New York: Doubleday and Company, 1966.

——*Down the Fairway*. New York: Minton Balch and Company, 1926.

——*Golf Is My Game*. Garden City, New York: Doubleday and Company, 1960.

Keeler, O. B. *The Bobby Jones Story*. Atlanta: Tupper and Love, 1959.

Lyon, Peter. *Eisenhower: Portrait of the Hero*. Boston: Little, Brown, and Company, 1974.

McCormack, Mark H. *The Wonderful World of Professional Golf.* New York: Atheneum, 1973.

Miller, Dick. *Triumphant Journey: The Saga of Bobby Jones and the Grand Slam of Golf.* New York: Holt, Rinehart, and Winston, 1980.

Murray, Jim. *Jim Murray: The Autobiography of the Pulitzer Prize-Winning Sports Columnist.* New York: Macmillan, 1993.

Nelson, Byron. *How I Played the Game.* Dallas: Taylor Publishing Company, 1993.

Price, Charles. *A Golf Story: Bobby Jones, Augusta National, and the Masters Tournament.* New York: Atheneum, 1986.

Roberts, Clifford. *The Story of the Augusta National Golf Club.* Garden City, New York: Doubleday, 1976.

Rosaforte, Tim. *Tiger Woods: The Making of a Champion.* New York: St. Martin's Press, 1997.

Sampson, Curt. *The Eternal Summer.* Dallas: Taylor Publishing Company, 1992.

———*Hogan.* Nashville, Tennessee: Rutledge Hill Press, 1996.

Schaap, Dick. *The Masters: The Winning of a Golf Classic.* New York: Random House, 1970.

Sifford, Charlie, with James Gullo. *Just Let Me Play.* Albany, New York: Briton American Publishing, 1992.

Snead, Sam, with George Mendoza. *Slammin' Sam.* New York: Donald I. Fine, Inc., 1986.

Strege, John. *Tiger.* New York: Broadway, 1997.

Wade, Don. *And Then Arnie Told Chi Chi.* Chicago: Contemporary Books, 1993.

Articles

Anderson, Dave. "30 Questions the Masters Won't Answer," *Golf Digest,* April 1987, page 77.

Augusta Chronicle, "Windsor in Augusta for Masters Event," 5 April 1952, page 1.

Avery, Brett. "Final Edition: Lawsuit Brings Washington Road Vendors to Their Knees," *Golf World,* April 1994, page 92.

Bamberger, Michael. "Forced to Resign from Augusta National," *Golf Digest,* April 1995, page 54.

Barrett, David. "European Territory," *Golf,* April 1995, page 54.

———"100 Questions about the Masters," *Golf,* April 1991, page 72.

———"Improving the Masters," *Golf,* April 1993, page 88.

———"10 Things about the Masters," *Golf,* April 1994, page 62.

Bartlett, James Y. "The Golf Bag," *Forbes FYI,* 18 March 1991, page 34.

———"The Golf Bag," *Forbes FYI,* 11 March 1996, page 69.

Bisher, Furman. "Big Noise from Augusta," *Golf Digest,* April 1964, page 36.

———"Golf's Teen-age Sensation," *Golf Digest,* April 1965, page 29.

Bryan, Mike. "Talking Golf: A Conversation with Hord Hardin," *Golf,* April 1989, page 34.

Callahan, Tom. "Where Time Stands Still," *Golf Digest,* April 1994, page 82.

Capel, Dave. "Tiger, Inc.," *Business Week,* 28 April 1997, page 32.

Cooke, Alistair. "What Have We Left for Bobby Jones?" *Golf Digest,* April 1996, page 121.

Deacon, James. "Ready to Roar in Augusta," *MacLeans,* April 1997, page 52.

Deford, Frank. "Of God, Golf, and Green Jackets," *Sports Illustrated,* 7 April 1986, page 112.

Diaz, Jaime. "Ron Townsend Joins the Club," *Golf Digest,* April 1991, page 108.

———"The Men the Masters Forgot," *Golf Digest,* April 1993, page 132.

Earl, David. "18 Holes with Hord Hardin," *Golf,* April 1990, page 72.

Edmondson, Jolee. "It's Not All Peachy Keen for CBS in Georgia," *Golf Digest,* April 1984, page 66.

Farnham, Alan. "Augusta: The Course CEO's Love Best," *Fortune,* 18 April 1994, page 163.

———"Teed off in Augusta," *Fortune,* 17 April 1995, page 28.

Feinstein, John. "Master of All He Surveys," *Golf,* June 1997.

Fitzpatrick, John. "Ike Likes Golf . . . and It Booms!" *Golf Digest,* July 1953, page 32.

———"Augusta National Golf Club," *Golf Digest,* April 1954.

Golf Digest, "A Discussion of the Masters Site Produces Strong Opinions Both Pro and Con," April 1978, page 52.

Goodner, Ross. "The Man Who Could Walk on Water," *Golf Digest,* April 1986, page 60.

———"Just How Tough Is Augusta," *Golf Digest,* April 1991, page 82.

Griffith-Roberts, C. "Augusta Returns to the River," *Southern Living,* May 1989, page 101.

Hannigan, Frank. "The Power Broker," *Golf Digest,* April 1996, page 146.

———"The Stars Come Out," *Golf,* April 1989, page 24.

———"Heaven, with Reservations," *Golf Digest,* April 1992, page 108.

———"The Lost Letters of Bobby Jones," *Golf Digest,* April 1994, page 108.

Hatch, Bert H. "Buck Nekkid at Amen Corner," *Golf,* April 1994, page 98.

Hawkins, John. "Against All Odds," *Golf World,* 18 April 1997, page 30.

Jenkins, Dan. "Augusta without the Crowds," *Golf Digest,* April 1991, page 92.

Johnson. Roy. "Tiger!" *Fortune,* 12 May 1997, page 73.

Kindred, Dave. "Is It Heaven? Or Is It Hell? *Golf Digest,* April 1995, page 94.

Kirker, Thomas, "Pen Pals," *Golf,* April 1989, page 80.

McCallum, Jack. "Augusta Fresh Air," *Sports Illustrated,* 29 May 1995, page 16.

McCleery, Peter. "Tickets: If You Don't Have One, You Can't Get One," *Golf Digest,* April 1985, page 81.

———"A Wisecrack Gone Wrong," *Golf Digest,* November 1994, page 143.

Moore, Terrance. "Wake Up, Tiger. This Is America, and You're Black," *Atlanta Journal,* 23 April 1997, page 18.

Murphy, Jack. "Goalby's Ordeal . . . Since Winning the Masters," *Golf Digest,* April 1969, page 46.

Netland, Dwayne. "The Genius Behind Golf's Best TV Show," *Golf Digest,* April 1978, page 58.

Nicklaus, Jack. "My Masters Memories," *Golf,* April 1994, page 81.

Pavey, Rob. "Broker Kills Self After Ticket Deal," *Augusta Chronicle,* 13 April 1997, page 1C.

Pavey, Rob. "Dream Ends with Failed Ticket Venture," *Augusta Chronicle,* 19 April 1997, page 1C.

Reilly, Rick. "Strokes of Genius," *Sports Illustrated,* 21 April 1997, page 35.

Russell, Geoff. "War of the Words," *Golf World,* 2 May 1997, page 12.

Rosaforte, Tim. "Inside the Masters," *Sports Illustrated,* 17 April 1995, page G70.

Schrock, Cliff. "Bobby Jones's Last Major," *Golf Digest,* April 1990.

Searby, Bill. "What It's Really Like to Belong to Augusta National," *Golf Digest,* April 1967, page 36.

Seitz, Nick. "Inside the Masters War Room," *Golf Digest,* April 1971, page 58.

Stachura, Mike. "Savoring the First (and Maybe Last) Ride to Augusta," *Golf Digest,* June 1994, page 276.

Tarde, Jerry. "An Iron Hand Still Rules Augusta," *Golf Digest,* April 1983, page 94.

Tresniowski, Alex. "Eyes on the Tiger," *People,* 28 April 1997, page 89.

Westin, Dave. "The Way They Were: Augusta and the Masters," *Golf Illustrated,* April 1991, page 44.

Whitten, Ron. "Retouching a Masterpiece," *Golf Course Management,* March 1983, page 17.

———"Perfection vs. Reality," *Golf Digest,* April 1994, page 123.

———"The Evolution of a Great Course," *Golf Digest,* April 1995, page 98.

Wolf, Steve, "The Lion and the Tiger," *Time,* 28 April 1997, page 86.

INDEX

257